William A.

MW00716974

THE
SMALL BUSINESS
LEGAL ADVISOR

McGraw-Hill Book Company
*New York St. Louis San Francisco Auckland
Bogotá Singapore London Madrid
Mexico Montreal New Delhi Panama São Paulo
Hamburg Sydney Tokyo Paris Toronto*

Library of Congress Cataloging in Publication Data

Hancock, William A.
  The small business legal advisor.

  Includes index.
  1. Small business — Law and legislation — United States.   I.
Title.
KF1659.H36   346.73'0652   81-12400
ISBN 0-07-025979-8   347.306652   AACR2
ISBN 0-07-025999-2 (pbk.)

234567890   DOCDOC   893210987

ISBN 0-07-025979-8

ISBN 0-07-025999-2 {PBK.}

The editors for this book were William R. Newton and Carolyn Nagy, the designer was Elliot Epstein, and the production supervisor was Paul A. Malchow. It was set in Garamond by Datapage.

Printed and bound by R. R. Donnelley & Sons Company.

THE
SMALL BUSINESS
LEGAL ADVISOR

CONTENTS

Preface   ix

Acknowledgments   xi

1 HOW TO FIND AND USE A GOOD LAWYER   1

*How Do You Find a Lawyer? / How to Use Your Lawyer / How Do You
Know If You Have a Good Lawyer? / What If You Are Not Satisfied with
Your Legal Services? / What About Getting Business Advice from Your
Lawyer? / Should You Get Personal Services from Your Business Counselor?*

2 STARTING YOUR BUSINESS   15

*What Are Your Choices? / Why Should You Form a Corporation? / Corporate
Taxation / Limited Liability / Forming the Corporation / Conclusions / Sample
Incorporation Documents*

3 INVOLVING OTHER PEOPLE IN YOUR BUSINESS   41

*Partnerships / Corporations and Shareholders / Employment Contracts / Sample
Employment Agreement*

4 BUYING A GOING BUSINESS   65

*What Are Your Options? / Compliance with the Bulk Sales Act—and Its
Drawbacks / The Importance of the Legal Audit / What About Buying a
Business Where the Seller Stays On to Help You? / What About the
Employees of the Business—Should They Get Employment Contracts? / Legal
Fees for Buying a Business*

5 FRANCHISING   73

*What Is a Franchise? / Why Do You Need a Lawyer in a Franchise
Deal? / Franchise Example / Franchise Danger Points*

**6   PENSION, PROFIT SHARING, AND DEFERRED COMPENSATION
PLANS**   81

*Why Is This Subject So Complicated? / Employee Retirement Income Security
Act (ERISA) / The Coverage Tests / ERISA Requirements / Simplified
Employee Pension Plans / Individual Retirement Accounts*

7   YOUR PAYROLL   93

*Federal Income Tax / Workers' Compensation / Unemployment
Compensation / Overview of Wage and Hour Laws / Child Labor Laws / The
Portal to Portal Act / Garnishments / Record Keeping / Getting Help from the
Government*

8   EQUAL EMPLOYMENT OPPORTUNITY   115

*Selection Process / Measuring People's Ability / Equal Pay / Treatment of
Pregnant Females / Health Considerations / Your Employment Application
Form / Promotions / Discharges / Age Discrimination / What about
Statistics? / The Economics of Title VII Litigation / State Agencies / Help from
the Government*

9   LABOR LAW   131

*What Are the Implications of Having a Union? / Why Employees
Organize / How to Remain Nonunion / A Fault and Need Analysis / The
importance of Location / The Union Organization Drive / Checklists / Selected
Readings on Unionization*

10   FORMS, WARRANTIES, AND CREDIT   147

*Your Purchase and Sale Order Terms and Conditions / Warranties / Terms and
Conditions of Purchase / Standard Conditions of Sale / Sample Warranties / Fair
Credit Laws*

11   OCCUPATIONAL SAFETY AND HEALTH   173

*Employee Discipline / Records and Reports / OSHA Inspections / Your Rights
during the Inspection / The On-Site Consultation Program / Special Rules for
Small Business / Help from the Government*

12   PRODUCT LIABILITY   185

*What Is the Problem? / Do You Have the Problem? / How Can You Minimize
the Problem? / The Consumer Product Safety Act*

13   INTELLECTUAL PROPERTY   195

*Patents / Copyrights / Trademarks and Trade Names / Trade
Secrets / Summary / Employee Invention and Confidential Information
Agreement / Sample Unsolicited Idea Letter / Form 1. Confidentiality
Agreement Where You Are Granting Another Company Access to Proprietary*

*Information / Form 2. Your Company Is Assuming Confidential
Obligations / Form 3. Both Parties Have Confidential Obligations*

14 YOUR LAWYER AND YOUR INSURANCE   223

**15 MISCELLANEOUS CALAMITIES THAT CAN SEND YOU TO JAIL
     (WHITE COLLAR CRIME)**   229

*Tax / Antitrust / The Securities Laws / Political Contributions / Environmental
Laws / Occupational Safety and Health / Bribery / Ancillary Criminal
Laws / Conclusion*

16 ANOTHER VIEW   239

     Index   253

PREFACE

I wrote this book to provide business people with a convenient and inexpensive way to have a "conversation" with a lawyer about some important legal aspects of starting and running a small business. I intend this to be an informal chat and definitely not a substitute for specific legal advice.

I graduated from law school in 1966 and practiced law with a small Cleveland corporate law firm for the next 4 years. During this time I assisted in providing legal advice to a relatively wide spectrum of small businesses. I left private practice in 1970 to join TRW Inc. (a large multinational conglomerate corporation) and was a member of their legal staff for 10 years. I left TRW in 1980 to devote full time to my writing and publishing activities. The name of my own small company is Business Laws Inc. We publish legal newsletters and reference books for corporate lawyers.

It is from these perspectives that I would like to offer my experiences on how to avoid some of the legal difficulties I have seen others encounter. As a businessman, I am well aware that the last thing you want to spend your time on is legal matters. We would all like to run our businesses free of disputes or interference from the government. On the other hand, we all know that this is impossible.

The basic premise of this book is that, in the long run, you can run your business with less legal hassle if you spend a small amount of time in the beginning to understand the relevant laws, and what you must do, should do, and don't have to do. The theory is much like the tag line of the popular oil filter commercial on television: "You can pay me now, or you can pay me later."

We all know that legal time is expensive. This informal chat is inexpensive —and you won't be subject to any sales pitch from the lawyer. Remember, lawyering is a business just like any other. Most lawyers will give you their honest opinion on what you need, but there are three things you must be aware of:

1. Lawyers must be conservative. If you might need something, they almost have to recommend that you get it. Put yourself in your lawyer's position. You ask if you need good terms and conditions on your purchase order and sales forms, or a review of your employment practices for Equal Employment Opportunity purposes, or any of the other things mentioned in subsequent chapters of this book. Your lawyer, realizing that your risk is small (though there is no such thing as zero risk), and trying to save you money, says no. The next day you get sued. A lawyer just can't run that risk. He or she must recommend the most conservative approach.

2. Lawyers all have a very high opinion of themselves and their abilities. The idea that you might be able to get a fairly good set of terms and conditions from a book is heresy. The concept of asking the government for help is even worse.

3. Lawyers need to earn a living. There is a surplus of lawyers right now, and there is a strong economic temptation for them to do a good job for any clients they have already—which means charging appropriately.

This book is not intended to take the place of your lawyer, but rather to help you get the most value for your dollar from him or her.

There are a number of ways that "the law" can directly save you money. Most of these involve taxes in one way or another. This book is not a tax planning book per se, but I do want to spend some time on that subject because of its overriding importance. I will also spell out the clear things so you can get the benefit of obvious tax advantages. There are some things, however, which are just too complicated for a book like this. For them, I will give you a brief explanation and recommend legal counsel. Pension and profit sharing plans are prime examples.

While I will attempt to touch all the bases that I know about in this book, *The Small Business Legal Advisor* should be supplemented with *The Small Business Tax Advisor, The Small Business Insurance Advisor,* and *The Small Business Financial Advisor.* You must have access to professional help on all these subjects. The very first chapter of this book is "How to Find and Use a Good Lawyer," and the principles I talk about in that chapter would be applicable to other professionals too.

William A. Hancock

ACKNOWLEDGMENTS

Special appreciation is due the following people for their help on this book. Mr. William Newton, senior editor at McGraw-Hill, suggested the basic idea and subject. Ms. Donna Tomawski and Ms. Angela Lattanzio typed the manuscript. Mr. Robert Crump consented to the interview which appears in the final chapter, and provided additional advice and counsel during its preparation. Ms. Janice Rieth and Ms. Kathryn Shen, members of the Ohio Bar, assisted in the preparation of other parts of the manuscript.

ABOUT THE AUTHOR

William A. Hancock holds J.D. and LL.M. degrees from Case Western Reserve University. He graduated first in his class from law school and practiced law as an associate and later as a partner of a small Cleveland law firm. Subsequently he joined the legal staff of TRW Inc. as counsel and then was promoted to senior counsel.

Currently he is running his own firm, Business Laws Inc., which publishes material on all aspects of federal business law, including a newsletter to corporate lawyers, as well as reference sources on the Foreign Corrupt Practices Act, International Boycotts, The Law of Purchasing, Management Liability, and Corporate Political Activity.

The author's other publications include a three-volume reference set, *Federal Business Laws,* and two books published by McGraw-Hill: *Executive's Guide to Business Law* and *Saving Money through Ten-Year Trusts.*

THE
SMALL BUSINESS
LEGAL ADVISOR

1

HOW TO FIND AND USE A GOOD LAWYER

I am devoting the first chapter to finding and using a good lawyer because I want to make it very clear that this book is not intended as a substitute for legal advice. I do not recommend that you attempt to be your own lawyer or to use the advice contained in this book without discussing it with your counsel. I do, however, recommend that you think about these subjects yourself, try to understand them, and use your lawyer as an advisor to help you anticipate and solve your business-legal problems. If you do this, you will be able to handle these matters much better and more cost-effectively. If you do not, one of the following things *will* occur.

1. The subject will cause you a legal problem and you will have to call your lawyer to get you out of it. In that case, the *best* that your lawyer can do is to get you out of the problem without too much liability. At worst, you will have both the liability and the attorneys' fees. Typically, attorneys' fees in problem situations are higher than in planning situations, simply because more time is involved.

2. If you do not think about the subject yourself and do your own homework, but still realize you need legal help, your legal fees will be much larger than necessary because of the time your lawyer spends doing things you could do yourself.

3. Most likely, you will simply drift along without knowing if you have any risk or are missing any opportunities. No one will sue you, and the government will not cause you any problem. This may seem like a fairly good alternative except for that big factor, *The Unknown*. What you do not know *can* hurt you. You can operate your business for years without any product liability suits,

employment discrimination problems, or labor law problems. Perhaps you can even operate indefinitely that way. In my judgment, however, that is gambling. If you want to do it, just be sure you know what you are doing and what your risks are. I think you will find the risks are too serious to justify the small savings in legal fees that ignoring these potential areas of difficulty entails.

HOW DO YOU FIND A LAWYER?

If you have used a lawyer before and have been satisfied with the service, then that attorney would be a prime candidate for providing you legal advice on your new business venture. However, here are a few words of caution. If you used the lawyer to probate an estate, draft a will, handle a real estate transaction, or pursue a workers' compensation or personal injury claim, he or she may *not* be competent to deal in corporate matters. Lawyers, like doctors and other professionals, tend to specialize. Some lawyers conduct a general practice and handle all of these things. I think your chances of getting good, solid business law advice from a general practitioner is remote. Ask your lawyer *if he or she has any other corporate clients* or does any other corporate work. If the answer is a little vague, you may be well-advised to do a little more checking before you enlist that attorney for your business-legal advice.

If you either do not have a suitable lawyer or are disappointed in the service or fees of lawyers you have used before, you have a slightly more difficult problem. The best way to find a lawyer who can handle business problems is to ask business associates. Your accountant, your insurance agent, or your banker may be able to provide you with the name of a lawyer who is able and willing to handle your kind of legal matters. Again, if you get references for lawyers, make sure you understand the basis for the reference. If someone gives you the name of a lawyer who did a good job of handling an estate or personal injury matter, you really do not have sufficient reason to believe that he or she will be good for your business problems. You will have to make a separate investigation.

If you are unable to find a lawyer through business or personal contacts, you may want to try the referral services conducted by most major city bar associations. Generally, the lawyers who participate in these referral services agree to have an initial consultation with clients for a modest fee. Further, the lawyers who sign up for these kinds of programs indicate which areas of law they practice in, so the local bar association can refer you to a lawyer willing to work on the kind of problem you have. Also, the local bar association will usually make the first phone call and ask the lawyer if he or she is available to see you, thus saving you that effort. Generally, this route will not be very productive for business problems. It works fairly well for personal injury problems, probate matters, or other *personal* legal problems, but corporate lawyers may or may not be in the local bar association referral system, and the people at the local bar association may be little if any help. Nevertheless, it is a possibility, and there is so much variation between local bar association referral systems that no generalization is going to be valid.

A recent Supreme Court case has opened the way to legal advertising, and this *may* also give you a way to find a lawyer if you have no other source. Most newspapers and even the yellow pages will contain advertisements for lawyers—generally one- or two-person law firms. Some of these are referred to as "legal clinics." One of the common services lawyers provide to small business people is to form a corporation, and many of these advertisements will contain a statement of the fees for that legal service. For example, at this writing (early 1981) in Cleveland, Ohio, there are many advertisements for lawyers willing to form a corporation for about $200. Lawyers add the filing fees to this, and, in Ohio, that adds about another $75.

Any good legal clinic will be able to form a corporation for you, but small legal clinics with young lawyers may be totally inadequate to advise you on many of the subjects mentioned in this book. They may not know any more than you about these matters. These are business problems, and lawyers who work for individuals or very small one- or two-person corporations just do not have occasion to deal with them.

In an excellent article appearing in *The Wall Street Journal* in mid-1980, a reporter from that newspaper made up a hypothetical set of facts involving the purchase of a house. The deal was slightly complicated because the seller was going to do the financing. The reporter took his "facts" to various legal clinics, and to a large firm in Los Angeles. The results were so widely different that they just pointed up the futility of making generalizations. The reporter had a panel of experts review the legal advice he had received from the various sources, and some of the legal clinics fared better in the grading process than a large, well-known corporate law firm. Some of the legal clinics ranked so low, however, that the experts felt these clinics had bordered on malpractice to even attempt to handle the matter—it should have been referred to an expert.

While there are certainly exceptions, my advice is to stay away from legal clinics for your business work unless you personally know the lawyers involved or have some excellent references of work the legal clinic did for other businesses. Be prepared to pay more than the posted fee. Legal clinics are a bargain if you want something that can be done routinely by a paralegal, such as drafting a will. If you want special legal help, their hourly rates are likely to be the same as any other lawyer's.

In law, as in anything else, you will get essentially what you pay for. I am all for economizing on attorneys' fees—but I strongly recommend against compromising on the quality of the legal advice. My recommendation is to get a good corporate lawyer in the beginning, even though the hourly fees may be higher. Economize on the amount of time you require of the lawyer on any specific project—not on the hourly rates, nor on the number of situations you discuss with your lawyer. The best way to save your lawyer's time and your money is to do some of your homework yourself.

Like businesses, lawyers and law firms (particularly in the field of corporate law) come in all shapes and sizes. For a small businessperson, I recommend getting a lawyer in your own league. This is probably going to be someplace in between the solo practitioner or legal clinic and the gigantic law firm. If a small business which is going to pay lawyers $1,000 to $5,000 a year tries to retain a big law firm that represents companies which pay tens of thousands or perhaps even hundreds of thousands of dollars per year in legal fees, my judgment is that it will get second-class treatment. You should be aware that the members of these large firms *loudly protest to the contrary.* They say that they give *all* their clients good service, even the one-person operation. You can, of course, be assured that you will not get bad advice from one of these big law firms. On the other hand, you may or may not get prompt advice, and you may or may not get a personal interest in your own business. Sometimes this depends on your personal relationship with the lawyer in the firm handling your account. If you are a friend of the attorney or if you have contact in other social organizations, the lawyer may very well give you better legal advice than if you are solely a client. As a general rule, however, the operation of a law firm is just about like the operation of any other business, and if you are a small customer relative to other customers, you are just not going to get the same kind of service.

By the same token, business law is too complex for the sole practitioner who also handles other legal matters. In today's atmosphere, business people should not depend on someone who does not specialize in business law for legal advice. There are many small law firms which specialize in corporate law. These are usually good bets for a small businessperson. A firm with at least five or six lawyers can do a little better job of attending seminars, doing some advance planning for you, giving you some constructive advice, covering for one another when the lawyers are out, and having enough business to make themselves a good living without charging too much to any one client.

In summary, my advice for a small business is to get a small business law firm. That generally means a law firm of somewhere between 5 and 20 lawyers. In the major cities, a firm of as many as 50 lawyers can still give good service to a small business.

For over 100 years, the *Martindale-Hubbell Law Directory* has been the standard reference for finding out about lawyers. It has now grown to about seven volumes, with five full volumes (each about 5 inches thick) devoted to listing lawyers and rating them. A trip to your library to look up the local lawyers in *Martindale-Hubbell* may pay substantial dividends. You will find that there are two sections. One section is an alphabetical listing of all the lawyers in your city. This service is free, a lawyer does not pay anything to be included in this section. The other section of *Martindale-Hubbell* is the so-called cards, on which a lawyer or law firm can have a personal or firm listing giving areas of practice and some representative clients. *I think you should choose a lawyer or law firm which is listed in the card section of Martindale-Hubbell.*

The directory also has a rating system, but I would not place too much emphasis on the ratings. If the firm takes enough pride in its reputation to obtain a card listing and describe its areas of practice, it is probably conscientious about rendering high-quality professional services to business clients.

My recommendation to use a lawyer who has a card in *Martindale-Hubbell* applies only if your business has about 10 employees, does about $1 million in business, or happens to be involved in a legally complex area. If your business is a professional corporation or a small storefront operation where you do most of the work yourself, this criterion probably is not necessary. A caution, though: If you make a lot of money, be sure you get *top-quality tax advice* from someone.

HOW TO USE YOUR LAWYER

Once you find a lawyer, you should be very careful how you use legal services. My advice is to be completely open and make sure that the lawyer understands exactly what you want and that you understand exactly what the lawyer is going to do and how much it will cost. You should not simply treat your lawyer as a scrivener to draw up papers based upon something your friends have done or something that you read in this book. That is much too expensive. Your lawyer gets paid to provide you *advice* and only incidentally to embody it in proper legal documents.

On the other hand, there is no reason to give a lawyer a blank check to go ahead and provide all kinds of legal advice and services which may be beneficial to you but which you may not want. For example, your first visit to your lawyer may generate a lot of conversation about small corporations, estate planning, wills, etc. All of these are tied together. The lawyer who points out the desirability of having a will, of integrating your business with your estate plan, of having arrangements to handle the orderly buy-out of a business partner, and of providing certain retirement and insurance benefits through your corporation is doing a good job for you. In fact, if your lawyer does not do these things, I think you are being shortchanged. However, the decision as to whether you want all these things and if so when you want them is entirely up to you.

Except for rather simple services such as drafting a will or forming a corporation, a lawyer will almost always charge by the hour. Some lawyers prefer a retainer arrangement, by which you pay them a certain amount per month to be available for consultation whether you use them or not. *My advice is to avoid retainer arrangements.* My experience has been that in almost all cases, one or the other party feels cheated. Either you call the lawyer too much and ask for many services which do not really require his or her time, thereby requiring more time than the retainer covers, or you do not have any questons or problems and are paying money needlessly.

An hourly arrangement places a premium on trying to reduce the time the lawyer must spend on routine or nonproductive things, such as calling you to obtain answers to questions which you should have been able to answer in the first place, writing a letter when none is called for, or coming to visit you at your home or office.

The best way to obtain good and economical legal advice is to think about the problem yourself as much as you can, do as much background work as you can, provide your lawyer with as much data as possible, and then use your lawyer for what he or she gets paid for: providing you legal advice and counsel and making sure the relevant documents are clear and legally sound.

The example on structuring purchasing and sales forms for your new company (discussed in Chapter 10) is illustrative. If you simply ask your lawyer to prepare some purchase order and sales agreement forms for you, it is likely to be a rather costly job. Your lawyer must find some samples, spend considerable time thinking about which terms and conditions would be best for your company, discuss the matter with you and your sales and purchasing people, and then go through several drafts before the final product is completed. There is certainly nothing wrong with this approach; it is just going to cost you a lot more money than if you use the advice contained in Chapter 10. *Do your own homework.* Give your lawyer a draft of the purchasing and sales terms and conditions which you think are good for your business. Give him or her samples of other companies' forms which you think are good. Ask your lawyer to put the finishing touches on the product by making sure that the terms and conditions do satisfy your particular needs. This approach will also give you a better product because you are going to be focusing on each of the terms and conditions. You know your business and your problems. Your own involvement in the process will not only help the quality of the end product but also make you more knowledgeable as to how it should be used.

Another rule in using a lawyer is that you should not be afraid to discuss fees. On the other hand, you should realize that a lawyer does not know in advance exactly how long it is going to take to do certain jobs. However, there is no reason why you should not be given an approximation. Also, there is no reason why you should not know the *hourly rate* that your lawyer charges and *how the time is recorded.* There are many ways lawyers use to record hours. I have seen both extremes—even inside a single firm. One extreme was a partner whose theory was that she spent 8 hours a day doing legal work for about half a dozen main corporate clients. Therefore, at the end of the day she simply divided up her 8 hours among the clients, depending on approximately what she had done that day. This approach was inexact, but it saved her a lot of time, and over the long haul, it was basically fair. Another lawyer at this same firm had a chart which divided the total day into *tenths* of an hour. Thus, a short phone call was a minimum of 1/10 of an hour. A half-hour phone call was *precisely* 0.5 hour, etc. Most lawyers fall somewhere in between these two extremes. It should be noted that the end result of these two extremes was approximately the same. The lawyer with the tenths-of-an-hour chart recorded fewer total hours during a year, but was forced to charge a higher per-hour rate. Lawyers, like most other professionals, focus on their annual income, not necessarily the per-hour charge.

This is a matter you should feel free to discuss with your lawyer. If you know there is a minimum 15-minute time-recording procedure, there is no point in using five or six phone calls which perhaps might be reduced to two or three with a little advance planning. By the same token, even at an hourly rate of a $100, a reasonably short and to-the-point conversation with your lawyer is only going to cost you $25—a bargain if you plan the conversation and get some good advice.

Many lawyers will adjust the fees which would be charged by strict use of an hourly rate to reflect what they feel is the reasonable value of their services. This can work both ways. In some cases, a lawyer may increase the fee if the job required only a small amount of time but was very important, or if he or she did it very fast because he or she had considerable experience. For example, if you ask a lawyer to draft a lease for a commercial building, and the lawyer has just drafted one for another client for substantially the same kind of deal, the lawyer may charge you more than an hourly rate— particularly if a lot of money is involved. Conversely, if you ask a lawyer for a commercial lease and it is the first one he or she has ever drafted, the lawyer may spend a lot of time educating himself or herself and charge you less than the number of hours worked times his or her usual hourly rate. As a general rule, these adjustments will work in your favor. If your lawyer is expert on a certain job, you will get a better product at a lower price. If your lawyer is not expert, he or she should cut the fee because some of the time spent is for his or her own education.

For your purposes, however, these special situations don't change the basic ideas in this chapter. You and your lawyer should still have a mutual understanding on fees, and the cornerstone of that understanding should be an agreement that, in most situations and certainly for all telephone calls and meetings, the lawyer will charge you only for the time he or she spends on your work, and only at rates which have been explained to you.

I recommend that all business people keep their own files. There is no reason why your lawyer has to keep documents which are important to your company. Keep your own. In the first place, it is much more convenient to get to them. In the second place, you never know when you will want to change lawyers, and it will be much easier to do this if you do not have to go get your files. There is no reason why your lawyer cannot keep copies of everything that relates to your business, but the originals should be in your possession.

HOW DO YOU KNOW IF YOU HAVE A GOOD LAWYER?

There are many excellent lawyers who do not know anything at all about business law. There are many fine corporate attorneys who would not be good lawyers for a small business. A good lawyer not only is honest, conscientious, smart, and easy to deal with, but also has some experience in the kinds of problems *you* are going to want help with. It is probably going to be just as hard for you to evaluate the quality of the legal work your lawyer does as it would be for you to evaluate the quality of any other professional's work. There are, however, some rather obvious benchmarks which you can use to evaluate your lawyer. The key is to remember that "good" means good for you and your business, not just good in the abstract.

Following are some things you should ask about your lawyer or law firm:

1. *Are there other clients whose circumstances are roughly the same as yours?*
   A lawyer who represents a number of businesses is going to have a much better base to work from and will be able to provide you with much more constructive advice than one who has only a few clients. The law on the subjects covered in this book is developing rapidly. There are many publications to read and seminars to attend. If your lawyer has a good client base over which to spread these professional expenses, he or she is very likely to engage in them. On the other hand, if you are your lawyer's only business client—the rest of the practice being personal injury or probate—you are unlikely to get the benefits of professional updating.

2. *Does your lawyer respond in a timely fashion?*
   Delay is one of the biggest complaints the public has about lawyers. On the other hand, most people feel that lawyers work hard. The complaint is not that lawyers are lazy, but simply that they take unduly long to do anything. To some extent this complaint

is well-founded, but in many cases it just represents a lack of communication. There is no reason why your lawyer cannot give you a fairly good idea of when your job will be completed. If your lawyer does give you a time estimate, he or she should stick by it. The mark of a good lawyer is not necessarily fast work but rather a reasonable estimate of the time required for a response and a sincere commitment to stick to that promise. Therefore, I strongly recommend that you have a clear understanding of your lawyer's fees and the basis on which they're calculated, and that you get a clear estimate of how long each project will take to complete.

3. *Does your lawyer speak your language?*
There is *no reason* why your lawyer cannot prepare documents and write letters that you can understand. To be sure, there may be a few legal terms now and then which should be explained to you. Generally, however, documents you do not understand are bad documents. If you do not understand them, chances are the other party will not either, and that means trouble. One of the lawyer's jobs is to make things clear and to avoid misunderstanding—not to cause it.

4. *Does your lawyer make an occasional suggestion?*
You do not want to get into a situation where the lawyer can call you up with an idea and expect you to automatically give the go-ahead, along with a blank check for large legal fees. However, you also do not want an arrangement where your lawyer speaks only when spoken to. You want something in between—the "golden mean." If your lawyer speaks only when spoken to, you may not be getting the best legal advice and, in the long run, may be running unnecessary legal risks or missing opportunities for tax or estate planning.

5. *Does your lawyer know your business?*
In order to render truly useful advice, your lawyer must know your business. Has your lawyer seen it? Has he or she asked to tour the plant? Does he or she know your products, competitors, etc.? If not, and if your lawyer doesn't show much interest in learning these things, you probably have a less than optimal situation.

6. *Does your law firm provide client seminars?*
A surprising number of large *and small* law firms are starting to offer client seminars. The subjects are usually items of current interest such as wage and price controls, new state Occupational

Safety and Health Administration or environmental laws, or other recent legal developments. Firm clients are invited to a briefing— almost always without charge. Client seminars are a very positive indication of a top-quality law firm. The reverse is not necessarily true: The fact that your firm does not give client seminars does not mean it is not a good one.

7. *Does your law firm have a Washington office or a firm in Washington with which is has a steady relationship?*
The U.S. government is so pervasive in today's business regulations that many problems simply cannot be solved without going to Washington. Further, advance information on key developments is usually easier to obtain in Washington than elsewhere. Having a Washington office is an almost sure indication of a good business firm. Again, the reverse is not true: If your firm does not have a Washington office, that does not mean it cannot do a first-rate job for you.

8. *Does your firm send out client bulletins on recent developments?*
Many small law firms periodically send out client bulletins about matters they know the clients are interested in. These may be printed, but most often are simply typed letters informing the clients of the recent development. Since they are not personalized, and since the same letter is sent to many clients, the cost is relatively small. Most of the time it is simply absorbed in the firm's overhead, though of course, the clients pay the bill for that, too. I think client newsletters or bulletins are a mark of a good firm.

9. *Does your lawyer have a philosophy similar to yours?*
Many legal matters are so closely related to business matters that it is difficult to draw the line. I feel that a good business lawyer must be a good businessperson. Further, there are conservative business people and very aggressive ones. I have a tendency to be very conservative myself (except in the tax planning area), but there is nothing wrong with being aggressive. However, I think you should understand the category into which your lawyer fits. Many matters, including tax and labor law, are *highly subjective.* You are entitled to know if you are getting conservative or aggressive advice, and to participate in the decision as to the levels of risk you are willing to run.

WHAT IF YOU ARE NOT SATISFIED WITH YOUR LEGAL SERVICES?

If you are not satisfied with your legal services for *any* reason, you have a problem which should be addressed. Do not let the matter fester. The first thing to ask yourself is why you are unhappy. Maybe you have decided that you do not like your lawyer. If that is the problem—and it can be a very real one—do not hesitate to change lawyers promptly. After all, this is somewhat of a personal relationship, involving trust and confidence. If you do not have trust and confidence in your lawyer, just try again.

Assuming, however, that you have more objective complaints, I suggest an effort to correct the problem before making a switch. Switching lawyers will be time-consuming and possibly emotional—it is a good thing to avoid if possible.

How do you go about trying to correct a problem? Following are some commonsense methods which I have seen work. (I have also seen them fail.)

- List the problem(s) and openly discuss them with your lawyer.

- Talk with other lawyers. A friend of mine in the executive recruiting business was upset with his lawyer because he charged $125 for a relatively simple employment contract which my friend thought took at most only half an hour's time. When I explained that even simple letter agreements may require at least two drafts, proofreading, telephone calls to the client, etc., and that even though the lawyer may have spent only 1/2 hour actually dictating the first draft, there was much more time involved than that, he was satisfied.

- In many cases, your objection will be fees. Discuss this with your lawyer and get the facts as to how charges are made, for what, etc. Some lawyers send itemized bills, some very general statements. If you have a concern about fees, ask for a detailed bill. If your lawyer refuses to provide it, I say change. There is no reason why a lawyer—like anyone else—should not be prepared to explain fully what he or she is doing for *your money.*

- In some cases, your problem may be personal incompatibility with one member of the firm, but a better feeling about other members of the firm. Many attorney-client relationships have been saved by simply switching the person in the firm with whom the client deals.

- If you feel that your problem is second-class treatment because the firm is busy with other clients, you can certainly discuss that. Sometimes a discussion clears the problem up right away. Other times it clears it up—but only temporarily.

- If your problem is that you think your lawyer is not using any initiative to provide constructive legal advice, try asking other business associates about their lawyers. Maybe you are expecting too much.

I like to use the analogy of attorneys as employees. You will, no doubt, have employees who irritate you, who do not do exactly as you would like in all cases, and who may not be as smart or aggressive as you would like. You do not, however, fire all such employees. You carefully ask yourself many questions aimed at being fair to both sides. Nevertheless, the bottom line is that you keep the person if it is best for your company and you ask him or her to leave if that would be best. The same basic approach is appropriate for your lawyer. Think of your attorney as an employee. If your lawyer is worth holding on to, treat him or her right. If not, make your lawyer shape up or ship out. You are the boss in the attorney-client relationship when it comes to service. You cannot expect your lawyer to do anything unethical—but I rarely find that to be a problem. *Ninety percent of the problems I have seen in attorney-client relationships have been over time and money.* Businesses are concerned primarily with legal fees, and with the fact that lawyers let too much time go by before bringing projects to completion.

WHAT ABOUT GETTING BUSINESS ADVICE FROM YOUR LAWYER?

Over the years, I have seen some attorney-client relationships which were built *almost entirely* on the fact that the attorney had a very high business acumen. One attorney I worked with during the early days of my career actually saved one of his major clients from bankruptcy through his management skills. Needless to say, the attorney had a client for life. I have seen other attorney-client relationships in which more phone calls were placed to the lawyer by the client about purely business questions than about legal questions. If your lawyer has this kind of business acumen, for heaven's sake do not waste it just because he or she also has a law degree.

One word of caution, though: Be sure you understand when your lawyer is talking business and when he or she is talking law. Lawyers have a unique power to say no to proposed transactions. Few prudent business people will go ahead with a deal over a lawyer's strong objection if the lawyer's objection is based on legal considerations. However, if your lawyer's business judgment is different from yours, you have much more latitude in overruling or disregarding it.

Getting sound business advice from your lawyer requires not only good business judgment on the lawyer's part, but a good attorney-client relationship in which you discuss proposed business transactions with your lawyer while they are still in the formative stages.

Somewhat related to business advice is negotiation advice. Many times, your lawyer will be a better negotiator than you. Partly, this is because of training, but more often it is simply because of the fact that he or she is a lawyer, with all the connotations that brings to the bargaining table, and also because he or she always has an out if things start going badly. A lawyer can simply say he or she has no authority to make a certain concession and must check back with you, the client. Having your lawyer negotiate for you can be a big plus. Do not overlook the possibility if the situation is right for it. Proper use of your lawyer in negotiations depends on a joint effort between both of you. Normally, it is economically feasible only in substantial transactions such as the buying or selling of a business.

SHOULD YOU GET PERSONAL SERVICES FROM YOUR BUSINESS COUNSELOR?

Almost all corporate attorneys consider personal services to the principals of their business clients to be an important part of corporate practice. This is because so many personal things are inextricably woven into the corporation. The stock of the corporation may be the individual's principal asset. The asset may be very valuable, but not liquid. Thus, paying estate taxes can be a problem. Many forms of insurance are most economically provided through group policies taken out by the corporation. If the corporation consists of more than one stockholder, it may be appropriate to have restrictions on the transfer of stock, and a requirement that the stock be sold back to the corporation or to the other shareholders upon death or separation from service with the corporation. A very important asset of the principal shareholder or his or her estate may be the pension or profit sharing plan of the corporation. Also, one of the principal reasons for establishing a qualified pension or profit sharing plan might have been to provide substantial benefits for the controlling shareholders.

During my years representing small businesses, a great deal of the work I did for the firm's clients would fall into this category of business-personal planning. After all, while the lawyer may represent the corporate entity, the person who retains the lawyer and who pays the fees is usually the principal shareholder.

All these matters are so interwoven that, in my judgment, it is almost impossible to get efficient and economical legal services unless you have the same law firm responsible for all of them. Of course, it is not impossible. I have seen arrangements where the corporation had a lawyer and where the principal shareholder had a lawyer. Most of these, however, were situations where the principal shareholder was not actually running the corporation. I have never seen a situation where a controlling shareholder who was actively running and managing a business saw fit to use different lawyers for corporate and personal matters of the type mentioned above.

Of course, your corporate lawyer is not going to be much help to you in personal injury, domestic relations, or criminal matters. If you are using a law firm, there may be other attorneys in the same firm who can help you. If not, your corporate counsel will undoubtedly have attorneys to recommend.

2

STARTING YOUR BUSINESS

When you decide to go into business, the first thing you will want to do is to decide what legal form to use. This is very important—and a decision which will be made automatically if you do nothing.

WHAT ARE YOUR CHOICES?

1. Operate as a *sole proprietorship.* You own the business assets in your own name, and all the income is yours. You pay tax on all the income the business makes, and you are personally responsible for all the debts of the business. You can use another *business name* if you want—e.g., Bill Hancock DBA Business Laws Inc (DBA means "doing business as").

2. Form a *partnership* with one or more other people. The partnership will be a business entity, but *not* a tax entity. You and your partners will have to pay tax on all the partnership income whether or not you actually take that income out of the partnership. You and your partners will also be responsible for all the partnership debts. Any member of your partnership can bind the partnership and all the rest of the partners to business transactions. Doctors, lawyers, accountants, and other professionals have traditionally practiced in this form because, until recently, state laws did not allow them to incorporate. Now, however, most state laws do allow professionals to incorporate so they can take advantage of the federal income tax benefits allowed corporations.

3. Form a *corporation*—either yourself or with your business associates. Here there is a big legal difference. You have a separate legal and taxpaying entity, which receives the income from the

business operations and pays taxes on that income. The corporate entity is responsible for the debts of the business. You and fellow shareholders are not responsible for those debts unless you affirmatively guarantee them. You, as owner, are entitled to salary and dividends.

If you do nothing, you will have a proprietorship. Forming a corporation requires formal legal action—you have to send documents to the secretary of state. If you go into business with others and do nothing, you will have a partnership. The terms of your partnership would simply be the state partnership law. That law is fairly uniform among the states and is generally fair to all parties. Of course, if you elect the partnership route you certainly should have a lawyer draft a partnership agreement for you.

WHAT SHOULD YOU DO?

There are many compelling reasons to form a corporation. You can test the water by starting your business as a sole proprietor, but in my judgment, you should limit operations as a sole proprietorship to very small undertakings. I would never recommend going into *any* partnership without a complete partnership agreement. Since it is generally more costly to have a lawyer draft a good partnership agreement than to form a corporation, and for the reasons stated in the remainder of this chapter, it is unlikely that a partnership would be the best form of business for you.

Many business counselors tell me that I am simplifying the picture too much, that incorporation is a decision which is not necessarily best for everyone and that the proper analysis is much more complicated. I agree that *potentially* the analysis can get very complicated. However, in the overwhelming majority of cases, you will find that after you do the analysis the decision is clear—a corporation is best. That raises the obvious question: How much should you pay a lawyer or accountant to do a complicated and detailed analysis and explain all the possible alternatives to you when chances are extremely high that the result will be to simply form a corporation? My answer to that is straightforward: Not very much. I hope that your lawyer does explain the various alternatives to you, but that he or she doesn't try and make too big a deal out of it.

There are two exceptions. The first is where the business is just *so* small that no legal fees or state registration or franchise fees are justified. A hobby-business (e.g., selling some of your photographs or short stories, or an occasional sale of antiques you collect) would be an example of a business which may be just too small to justify any expenses. The second exception is real estate ventures or tax shelters. These kinds of deals almost always depend principally, if not solely, on the tax benefits to be economically feasible. Typically, they generate tax losses, and you must be able to deduct those losses from other income. A partnership or limited partnership is therefore necessary.

WHY SHOULD YOU FORM A CORPORATION?

1. Required decisions will be made early. Forming a corporation is relatively easy, but there are some decisions which must be made. By forming the corporation, you will focus on these problems at the beginning of your business when they are easy to solve. If you let them go, they will only get more complicated. Examples of those decisions are the following.

   a. Who owns the corporation? You personally? You and others? You and family members? Forming a corporation requires you to issue shares, and you will have to issue shares to somebody. It forces the issue as to who you are in business with and who owns what percentage of the business.

   b. What are you putting into the business? When you form a corporation, you have to spell out in the documents what you are putting into the business.

   c. Whom are you going to use as lawyer and accountant? I do not recommend forming your own corporation without a lawyer. That is not because it is hard to form a legal corporation—you can go into any business form store and get the forms, call the secretary of state and find out the fee and where to send the forms, and you have a "corporation." However, there are a number of important long-range decisions which should be made when you incorporate. If you don't do it in the most advantageous way, you will sacrifice many of the benefits incorporation can give. Getting a good lawyer and accountant early is a benefit. A secondary benefit is that you can evaluate your lawyer and accountant early on a relatively easy job. You can see how much they charge and whether they explain enough to you, or waste too much of your time on details and technicalities. In short, you can have sort of a trial marriage before you get into any serious legal or accounting problems, and I think that is a benefit.

2. You will build a good base for the future. Forming a corporation is simply a good, businesslike thing to do if you are going to run a business. You build a solid foundation for making sure that your business operations are kept *separate* from your personal affairs. *This is very important.* Many tax problems small business owners

encounter arise out of their failure, in one way or another, to respect their corporation as a separate and independent entity— and to keep records which substantiate the fact that it is a separate and independent entity. The corporation facilitates this process, and that is a benefit.

3. You get Uncle Sam's bag of tax goodies. Congress in its wisdom has elected to allow certain very advantageous treatment to certain transactions if they involve a corporation. This includes *any* corporation, even one where you are the only shareholder. The following examples are worth noting.
   a. Qualified benefit plans, including pension and profit sharing plans, are more advantageous for a corporation than for proprietorships or partnerships.
   b. Several forms of insurance can be provided much more economically because the corporation can deduct the premium and you don't have to report that amount as income.
   c. Corporate income tax rates are generally lower than personal tax rates, and since the corporation is a separate taxpaying entity, it begins paying tax at the lowest rates.

4. Many future transactions are simplified. When you start your business, you will be tempted to get the paperwork over with in the fastest, cheapest, and easiest way. That is fine, up to a point. However, you should spend some time thinking about possible future developments and, if it can be done easily and cheaply, plan for them. For example, a corporation facilitates estate planning. You can give your children or spouse an interest in your business much more easily by giving them stock than by giving them a share of a partnership or proprietorship. In fact, for practical purposes, it is almost impossible to transfer interests in any business other than a corporation. Theoretically, you can transfer a partnership interest, but as a practical matter, this requires so much legal and accounting effort that it can be a real problem. Also, in a corporation, you insulate the ownership from the management of the business. That, of course, is no big deal when you are both owner and manager. But, what if you get sick or want to do something else and have a new person manage your business? It is much easier to make these arrangements with a corporate entity where you have shares of stock—perhaps both common and preferred—to use.

5. It is cheaper to incorporate before you have a going business. Forming a corporation at the beginning is usually about a $300 deal—give or take a few bucks and not counting any planning that your attorney or accountant does. Forming a corporation into which you are intending to put a going business can be a much more substantial task. It usually requires much more legal and accounting effort—and therefore the fees are higher. When you talk about the benefits of incorporation as against the costs, the costs are relatively small. Delaying incorporation will almost undoubtedly increase the costs.

6. Forming a corporation will *probably* save you taxes—and maybe a lot of taxes. In my experience, clients desiring to begin a business are most concerned about this point. The previous points are interesting, and they are glad to hear about them, but they really make the decision to go ahead with the incorporation on the basis of the tax savings. That is why I would like to spend considerable time making sure that you *understand the fundamentals of corporate taxation*

First, let's acknowledge that you aren't going to be your own tax lawyer or tax accountant. I am not advocating that. What I do advocate is knowing enough about corporate taxation to:
1. Understand the reasons for the recommendations of your tax advisors.
2. Recognize when you might have an opportunity for tax saving if you consulted with your tax advisor.
3. Avoid doing anything unfortunate before you get advice. Sometimes you can do things which simply cannot be undone and which cost you a lot of taxes that could otherwise have been saved.

CORPORATE TAXATION

The theory of corporate taxation is quite simple, at least for our planning purposes. Following are the basic rules—and they are very important.

1. A corporation is a separate taxpayer. The corporation pays taxes on its income, at its rates, in substantially the same way as a private person.

2. A corporation has its own tax rates, which are as follows:

17% on the first $25,000 taxable income
20% on the next $25,000 taxable income

30% on the next $25,000 of taxable income
40% on the next $25,000 of taxable income
46% on everything over $100,000

NOTE: For comparison purposes, the tax table for married persons filing a joint return is as follows:

Married Taxpayers Filing Jointly
and Surviving Spouses

Taxable Income	Tax on Column 1	% on Excess
$ 3,400 or less	$ 0	14
5,500	294	16
7,600	630	18
11,900	1,404	21
16,000	2,265	24
20,200	3,273	28
24,600	4,505	32
29,900	6,201	37
35,200	8,162	43
45,800	12,720	49
60,000	19,678	54
85,600	33,502	59
109,400	47,544	64
162,400	81,464	68
215,400	117,504	70

3. Corporations can deduct from their income 85 percent of any and all dividends they receive. This includes investment dividends from public corporations received by privately held corporations. For example, if a corporation invests $10,000 in a common stock paying a 10 percent dividend, that will give the corporation $1,000 of income. The corporation will also have a deduction of $850, thus having only $150 on which it must pay income tax. If you personally had that $1,000 dividend income, you would have no such deduction and would have to pay a tax on the entire amount. Thus, one of the big advantages of having a corporation is the ability to invest in dividend-paying stocks and avoid any tax on the dividends.

4. Corporations also can deduct salaries—including a salary paid to the sole shareholder—as long as the salaries are reasonable. Thus, the economic effect of a corporation's earning $50,000 and paying $50,000 to a sole shareholder is substantially the same as if the shareholder earned the $50,000 himself or herself. There is no double taxation in this situation.

5. Corporations *cannot deduct dividends.* Thus, if a corporation earns $50,000 and pays the sole shareholder a dividend of $50,000, there will be one tax at the corporate level and another, *second* tax at the individual level. This double tax is the biggest drawback of a corporation. You must avoid it wherever possible.

6. As long as you respect certain formalities, and as long as the transactions are bona fide, you can loan a corporation money and receive interest, and you can lease the corporation property which you own and receive rent. The interest and rent will be deductible by the corporation and taxed to you as ordinary income—but *not* as salary, with all the payroll taxes which salary payments entail.

7. There are provisions in the tax law which allow you to take losses which are incurred by a corporation as deductions against your personal income. Therefore, even if you expect your new venture to incur losses for the first year or two and want to offset your other personal income with those losses, you can still take advantage of the corporate form of doing business. The way this is done is to use a so-called subchapter "S" corporation, which, in essence, eliminates the tax at the corporate level in place of one tax at the individual level. If there is a loss, that loss is available as a deduction to the individual. This is a particularly useful thing for someone with a job who is starting a small business on the side and expects losses to begin with. You can elect subchapter "S" treatment and offset your salary income with the business losses. Another technique is so-called section 1244, or "small business" stock. This kind of stock, which is basically stock in any small business, gives rise to an ordinary loss if your business goes bust. If you are willing to invest $10,000 in a new venture but want to make sure you get an ordinary loss deduction if it fails, section 1244 stock is the route.

Caveat: Section 1244 stock and subchapter "S" are rather technical tax rules. Though I do not recommend forming a corporation completely on your own, you probably could get away with it without any serious tax problem. Subchapter "S" and section 1244 stock are different animals; for them, you need a tax advisor.

Election of subchapter "S" and establishment of your business with 1244 or small business stock is very common. It should not give rise to significant increases in your attorneys' or accountants' fees. They should do this for you as a matter of course if you want it. The use of these techniques is *very simple* —but technical. Form books that lawyers use automatically qualify the small corporation under 1244. There are no disadvantages whatsoever. In the case of subchapter "S" there are a few simple forms to file. Subchapter "S" has its pros and cons; it also requires a little crystal-ball work. You will not know for sure whether your corporation will have a profit or loss, or the extent of the profit or loss, until after the tax year, and you have to make the election before the tax year starts—or when you form the corporation in the case of a new one.

8. There is one overriding tax principle which you must always keep in mind. *Everything you do with your company must be bona fide and must reflect economic reality.* If it doesn't, there are ample tax laws which allow the Internal Revenue Service to not only collect more taxes, but also cause you payment of interest and penalties and consume a lot of your time in arguments. For example:

Salary is deductible by the corporation even if paid to a sole shareholder so long as it is reasonable. But if it is unreasonably high, the IRS will call it a dividend.

Rents and interest are deductible by the corporation so long as they are ordinary and necessary business expenses. If they are a sham, the IRS will disallow the deductions.

Interest must, under the tax law, be computed and paid at a *reasonable rate.* If you try to peg the rate too high or too low, the IRS can impute interest and tax the transaction as though a realistic interest rate had been used.

I know of a professor of law who uses the illustration of a skinny pig and a fat pig to illustrate the concept. If you are a skinny pig you can get fatter, but fat pigs go to market. In tax matters, this translates into an ability to structure your deals with your corporation to minimize taxes *within a reasonable range.* If you do that, you can "get fatter." If you go outside the reasonable range and get too greedy, you will more than likely "go to market." This is one of the big reasons to get a good tax advisor as soon as the corporation generates reasonable profits. Unless you want to do a lot of study and reading yourself, you are probably going to need help to tell when you are within a reasonable range and when you are trying to be too greedy.

With a little thought and planning, you can take your own figures and assumptions and work with these principles to see if incorporation would save you taxes. I think the chances are very good that it will, and that it will save you enough taxes to make all the other considerations secondary.

To help you make your own analysis, here are two examples for you.

Example One—Small Business Started as a Sideline

Let's assume that you have a job and an average amount of interest and dividend income but want to start a small business as a sideline. Your intention may be recreational (you always wanted a restaurant), or it may be that you want to supplement your income (you do repair work, teach, sell handicrafts, etc., on the side), or you may want to start a business with the intention of developing it into a full-time operation.

On these facts, it would be very tempting to forget about incorporating. Typically, there would not be very much income involved. If the thing took off, you could incorporate later. By not incorporating you would:

- Save attorneys' and accountants' fees. While they are modest, even $300 to $500 in this context is substantial.

- Avoid the paperwork involved with a corporation, including federal and state income tax returns which would be eliminated.

- Avoid a few miscellaneous fees, such as a state corporate or franchise tax fee, which would be eliminated. (For example, in Ohio all corporations are subject to a $50 minimum franchise fee. Thus, even if you made only a couple of hundred bucks on the side, you would have to pay this tax if you incorporated.)

Clearly, some businesses are so small that incorporation would be a waste of time and money. However, I think that the cutoff point is very low. Consider, for example, the case of a person with $25,000 of taxable income who wants to start a business which, in his or her best judgment, will make, after business expenses, $10,000. Here is how you would do the analysis:

If you do not form a corporation, the $10,000 this business made would be taxed at approximately a 37 percent effective rate. (Illustrations in this book assume a married person filing a joint return.) You would have approximately $6,300 profit left over after federal income tax. (I am going to eliminate state taxes from these comparisons.)

Let's assume that you form a corporation and pay the entire $10,000 to yourself as salary. There is no difference in tax. The corporation would pay no tax, and the entire $10,000 would be taxable to you at the 37 percent effective rate. Thus, again, there would be an aftertax profit of $6,300.

However, let's assume that you want to build up the business. You don't need the $10,000, so you leave it in the company. *There would, in that case, be no tax to you personally,* but the corporation would have to pay a tax of 17 percent or $1,700. Thus, there would be $8,300 available for future corporate use. Remember that this $8,300 is the corporation's money. Some day you are going to want to take it out, and you will then have to pay a tax.

In the meantime, however, you have the ability to accumulate more money in the corporation at a low tax rate.

Let's assume further that you do not know what you want to do with the $10,000 income, so you just invest it in high-grade utility stocks or preferred stocks. If you did that individually, the annual tax on the income from $10,000 would be taxed at your rate. In our example, that is around a 43 percent tax rate. However, this corporation's effective tax rate on $1,000 of dividend income is only about 1.5 percent, or only about $15. Thus, assuming a 10 percent yield, you have a tax of around $430 versus a tax of about $15 for the corporation on the dividend income.

How do you equalize these calculations to take into account the fact that you may have to pay a tax someday when you get the money out of the corporation? That is a hard question. You may be able to get your money out at capital gains rates. You may have to pay the maximum 70 percent rate, or you may be able to get it out at a very low rate through payments to you at a time when you have losses to offset the income. In short, you have to guess at a "discount," and I offer the figure of 25 percent. If you assume 25 percent tax at the time of withdrawal of the money from the corporation, you will have a fairly good approximation of similar tax treatment—how much money is left in *your* pocket after *all* the taxes.

Returning to our example, you can see that factoring in this second tax changes the picture quite a bit. The picture is now a $1,700 tax paid by the corporation and then an assumed 25 percent tax on the amount left over: 25 percent of $8,300, or $2,075, for a total of $3,775 in *total* taxes. Thus, the double-tax treatment involved in corporations is an important consideration. That second $2,075, however, has been postponed to some indefinite future date and *might* never be paid at all.

Recapitulation

- $10,000 income to business corporation.

- Paid as salary means $10,000 deduction to corporation, so no tax at that level. Also means $10,000 added to your income. At 37 percent assumed rate, that is $3,700 tax.

- Kept in corporation. Tax is 17 percent or $1,700. *Temporary* savings of $2,000 to use to build up the business.

- Assume $1,000 income from the money. If paid to you, taxed at about 43 percent rate or $430 tax. If paid to corporation, only $15 in tax because of dividend credit.

Example Two—A Larger Business

Let's do one more example. Suppose you want to start a business and do not have any other salary. To make the calculations easy, let's assume you have enough other income to offset your deductions and exemptions. That makes the business income equal to taxable income. Let's assume that you think that the business will generate $80,000 annually. You need $30,000 to live. That leaves $50,000 to use in building up the business for future years.

If you pay yourself a salary of that extra $50,000, you would be getting into a fairly high tax bracket. Using round figures, even allowing for the 50 percent maximum tax on earned income, you would be paying tax at the rate of about 45 percent on that added $50,000, or about $22,500. Of course, the money would then be yours to spend, save, or do with what you want. However, if you left the money in the corporation, the corporation would have a tax of only $9,250, or a savings of about $13,250.

Short-term, the corporation would have over $40,000 to invest in dividend-paying securities to generate income at an extremely low effective tax rate.

Applying our 25 percent "discount" factor, you add another $10,000 or so in taxes, but they would not be paid until a later date.

In conclusion, you will usually find that incorporating will be a big benefit in allowing you to keep more aftertax dollars for building up the business. It may or may not, however, save a lot of taxes when you factor in the additional second tax that you will have to pay to get that money out of the corporation. If building up capital is important to the business, incorporating is almost certainly very advisable. If it is not, however, the computations become much more difficult and involve some estimates of future potential tax liability.

The Disadvantages of Incorporating

Besides the slight increase in administrative expenses we discussed before, the biggest disadvantage of incorporation is that troublesome *double tax.* The corporation pays a tax when it makes money, and you pay another tax when the corporation pays it to you. We mentioned that the double-tax problem can usually be avoided. However, returning to our skinny pig–fat pig analogy, there are some serious problems that you can get into if you go too far in avoiding that double tax. The first is the "unreasonable compensation" problem, and the second is the "unreasonable accumulation" problem.

Unreasonable compensation

We said before that a corporation can deduct salary, but not dividends. Thus, there is no double tax problem so long as the corporation pays its income out in salaries. There is only one tax—paid by the employee who receives the salary.

EXAMPLE: Corporation makes $100,000 and pays you a $100,000 salary. Corporation pays no tax because it gets a deduction for the $100,000 and you pay a tax just as if you got a $100,000 salary from un unrelated corporation. Or, corporation makes $100,000, pays you no salary, and then you take the money out later as a dividend. Corporation pays tax when it makes the $100,000, you pay a second tax when you get the dividend, and the corporation gets no deduction for the dividend.

Because of this, owners of closely held corporations will always want to get money from their corporations in the form of salary rather than dividends. Indeed, we saw that this was one of our guiding principles earlier in the chapter. However, there comes a point where this just does not reflect economic reality, where part of the payment you took out of your corporation was not *really* a salary, even if you called it that.

For example, suppose you run a restaurant as your business. You start with a salary of $25,000 per year and the restaurant prospers, so you increase your salary each year until you are making $100,000 a year as a restaurant manager. Of course, you have other responsibilities and this salary *may* be reasonable in light of all the factors—even though you could certainly hire a restaurant manager for much less than that. However, this probably would cause the IRS to say that what you really receive is some lesser amount in salary and the rest in dividends. In other words, the IRS would disallow a certain portion of this high salary because it was not "reasonable." The burden would then be on you to justify the reasonableness of the salary.

The unreasonable-compensation problem can also come up in the context of relatives who may work for you. For example, if you hired your son as a waiter in the restaurant and paid him a dollar an hour above the going rate, there would be no problem. However, if you paid him two or three times more than the going rate, the IRS would say that this was not reasonable compensation and, in reality, you had received a dividend and made a gift to your son. Were this not the rule, you could, for example, have the corporation put your child through college by the ruse of giving the child a job at the higher pay.

Another example is getting older relatives on the payroll. There is certainly nothing wrong with this if they perform services for the corporation, but if they don't, it's just like your receiving a dividend and making a gift, and the IRS will tax the transaction that way.

Unreasonable-accumulation penalty

Because of the relatively low corporate tax rates, and the disadvantages of paying dividends, you may be tempted simply to accumulate money in the corporation rather than paying it out. This will happen almost certainly if your salary gets into the range where an unreasonableness argument could be made. To prevent unwarranted accumulation of money in a corporation for the purpose of avoiding paying additional taxes, the tax law imposes a penalty tax on unreasonable accumulations of money in corporations. However, this tax applies only at fairly high levels.

1. There is a $150,000 exemption. Thus, you can accumulate $150,-000 of cash in your corporation and invest it in dividend-paying stocks without any unreasonable-accumulation problem.

2. The penalty applies only if the accumulation doesn't have any purpose. It is usually fairly easy to justify rather large accumulations.
   a. You may need a building.
   b. You may need to hire more people.
   c. You may need to purchase additional capital equipment.

All you have to do to avoid most accumulation problems is to have a reason for the accumulation and have that reason fairly well documented. For example, you may have some corporate minutes about purchasing a building, or you may have some proposals made to you about capital equipment. Of course, you have to remember the bona fide rule: You have to really intend to do these things. Otherwise, after a number of years of only shuffling paper and never spending your accumulated money, you could run into this problem. However, good tax counsel ought to be able to minimize it for you.

I'm sure you will agree that these are "good" problems. If you make so much money that your salary is unreasonable, or if you accumulate enough cash that the unreasonable argument could be made, you can certainly afford good tax advice.

LIMITED LIABILITY

One of the best-known advantages of incorporation is that it limits the liability of the shareholders to their investment. Shareholders are not personally liable for the debts of the corporation. This seems important indeed. Why, then, do I list it last?

I agree that it is important, but don't forget about the following two factors:

1. Liability for personal injuries of people should be covered by

insurance. Further, many times shareholders of corporations are found to be personally liable for personal injuries in spite of the corporation. It is extremely dangerous to rely on the limited liability aspect of a corporation in the context of product liability or personal injury. There are just too many reasons why a jury could find the shareholders liable—sometimes even pure sympathy would be enough.

2. When you borrow money from a financial institution, it will almost always want personal guarantees from the shareholders.

That leaves trade creditors as the principal debt that is purely corporate and will rarely be imposed on shareholders. If you're in the kind of business where trade creditors constitute a large part of your debt, limited liability is important. However, if you are not, it may be an overstated benefit.

Another problem with the limited liability aspect of corporations is the legal doctrine of "Piercing the Corporate Veil." Under this doctrine, the courts sometimes look through the corporation and hold the individuals actually running the business liable for debts, taxes, or personal injuries. Courts will pierce the corporate veil whenever it appears that the people running the corporation have not respected the corporate entity themselves. For example, if you form a corporation but don't have separate corporate bank accounts, don't keep separate corporate books, comingle the corporation's money with your own, and don't respect the corporate entity by dealing at arm's length with it, courts may well not respect the corporate entity either. It is very important to keep in mind that the corporation is a separate and distinct entity. If you borrow from or loan to it, if you enter into a lease with it, or if you buy from or sell to it, there must be proper documentation and the transaction must be reasonably fair. If you don't respect your own corporation, the courts may not respect it either.

FORMING THE CORPORATION

Sold—I'll take one corporation—how do I get it?

Corporations are creatures of state law. The way you form a corporation depends on your own state laws—but the following is typical. It is a *very easy procedure.* The hard part is not forming the corporation, but figuring out exactly what to contribute to capital, what kind of shares to issue, how much debt the corporation should have, and the other matters mentioned in this book.

The first step is generally to file articles of incorporation with the secretary of state. The articles of incorporation make you a legal corporation. They also keep anyone else in your state from using the name you picked. Conversely, if you happen to have picked a name already registered, the secretary of state will refuse to register your articles until you change the name. The fee is relatively modest—in Ohio it is $75. The articles of incorporation establish the capital structure. They say what classes of shares the corporation can issue and what the voting rights of those shares are. Here is where you authorize preferred and different classes of common stock if you want.

The next step is to prepare documents which show what you are going to put into the corporation. This can be done in a simple letter, but if you are actually transferring automobiles, contracts, or real property, you will have to eventually assign or transfer these items just as you would in any other sale. The incorporators then accept this offer and issue the shares to the persons making the offer. Now you have a corporation and shareholders.

The shareholders then meet to adopt a document which Ohio calls a Code of Regulations and most other states call bylaws. It spells out the relationship between the shareholders, how and when they meet, etc. Essentially, it is a boilerplate document for a small business. The shareholders also elect the directors. Now you have a corporation, shareholders, and directors.

The directors then meet to elect the officers of the corporation. That's just about it. You can do all this in writing—you don't have to actually meet. Almost all states have special statutes which recognize the fact that closely held corporations don't follow the same formalities as large publicly held corporations. Most states allow any action which could be taken at a meeting to be taken by simple written consent.

This practice is so standardized that every lawyer has a set of pre-prepared forms. Legal clinics even advertise the formation of corporations at low fees—typically about $200. Most corporate lawyers charge a little more, but not much. We are talking here about a simple corporation. If it is complicated —perhaps because you are incorporating an existing partnership—the fees will be higher.

This chapter contains some sample incorporation documents. *The intention is to show you how the process works, not to recommend you incorporate yourself without professional help.* Only the key documents are included.

What Kind of Stock Should I Use?

There are two basic kinds of stock available for use by small corporations— but a tremendous number of hybrids which can be used to satisfy special needs. In fact, one of the big advantages of a corporation is the availability of all these different kinds of ownership.

The two basic types of stock are *common* and *preferred.* Typically, the common stock owns the equity of the company and has the right to control it through the election of the board of directors. The preferred, on the other hand, has no right to elect directors and has only a right to the dividend assigned to it. Upon liquidation of the company, the preferred receives "preference" as to assets. The preferred shareholders will get paid before any of the common shareholders. The law requires only that corporations have common stock. Everything else is a matter of individual preference. Within wide latitude, you can create any kind of stock you want. Following are some hybrids which have been used frequently in the past.

Two classes of common stock with different voting rights can sometimes satisfy the requirements of investors with different interests. For example, perhaps one investor wants to have at least 50 percent of the voting power of the company but has only a small fraction of the capital. There could be a class A voting common, and she could be given 50 percent of that. There could then be a class B nonvoting common which would be given to the other investors who invested more capital.

Classes of stock which become voting on specified events, or which are voting for specific purposes, are also used. For example, preferred stock is normally not voting, but it can be given voting rights if the corporation doesn't pay the preferred dividends for 2 years in a row. Preferred stock can be cumulative or noncumulative. Cumulative means that if the corporation does not pay a dividend on the preferred, it would be required to pay all past dividends on the preferred stock before any dividends were paid on the common. A noncumulative preferred would not have this requirement.

Convertible preferred stock can be used to advantage in some cases. This kind of stock starts out to be normal nonvoting preferred stock, but can be converted into voting common at some prescribed rate at the election of the shareholder.

While these hybrids are useful in some instances, the standard preferred stock is still the most often used additional stock for small corporations. One of the nicest things about preferred stock is that its value is fixed. For example, a $100 preferred stock is worth $100. There is no need for any subjectivity in valuation if you want to give it away for estate planning purposes or if you want to redeem it. That value will also stay the same throughout the life of the corporation. Dividends on preferred are paid at the discretion of the board of directors. It is like the common stock in that respect. Thus, you can pass the dividends on the preferred during the early years of the corporation if that is appropriate.

As a typical example of family planning using the corporation and preferred stock, consider the case of the owner of a closely held business with a child going to college. Here are some of the things which could be done—all completely free of any controversial tax problems.

1. You can provide the child a job—so long as you pay the child a fair wage.

2. You can give the child preferred stock which may pay a dividend. True, the dividends are not deductible by the corporation and are taxed as ordinary income to the child, but the child may be in a very low bracket, and you may not be talking about a lot of money where the lack of deduction to the corporation would be a problem.

3. If you give the preferred stock to the child when the child is young and then redeem the child's stock when college time arrives, you *may,* if you issued the preferred stock upon incorporation, be able to have the child treat that money as a *capital gain.*

The last point deserves a little explanation. You *can* issue preferred stock after incorporation and then redeem it. That gets money into the hands of the person you gave the stock to. However, it is an obvious tax loophole which would allow corporations to bail out their assets to the shareholders at capital gains rates. Over the years, Congress has established a number of safeguards to assure this doesn't happen. These safeguards include the following:

1. When you redeem preferred stock, the redemption will be treated as ordinary income, not capital gains, to the recipient *to the extent of the earnings and profits of the corporation at the time of issuance of the preferred stock.* However, at the start of the life of the corporation, there are no earnings and profits. That is why it is sometimes useful to issue preferred stock when a corporation is formed rather than waiting until later.

2. In the case of redemptions of common stock, there are many technical rules which apply to determine whether the redemption price is ordinary income or capital gains. The difference in treatment can be extremely important. If the redemption can qualify for capital gains treatment, it is a good tax planning tool. If not, it can impose a very substantial—and possibly unanticipated—tax liability on the shareholder whose shares are redeemed.

The bottom line on redemptions is simple: *Never* redeem *any* shares of the corporation without thoroughly understanding the consequences— which generally means paying a few bucks to your attorney or accountant for an analysis.

What Should I Put in the Corporation?

By asking this question, you are halfway to the answer. Too many times persons starting out in business just put the business assets in the corporation because they are "business assets." That is a very logical thing to do, and has *economic* merit. Unfortunately, it usually has a rather high tax price tag, and that is why most practitioners do not recommend it.

Instead, the corporation should be "thinned" by putting in only *part* of the assets as a contribution to capital and *loaning* the rest. Of course, this may not be possible. When I started my business, the entire capital contribution was $500 in cash and some office furniture that I had around the house. Obviously, no room for thinning there. You may be in roughly the same position. However, if the circumstances warrant, thinning the capital structure of your corporation initially will usually reduce taxes and get more money in your pocket.

Let's assume that you have $100,000 to put into a business. This can be either $100,000 cash to start a new business or $100,000 to buy an existing business. For this purpose, you would use exactly the same analysis either way.

The first possibility would simply be to form a corporation with $100,000 of capital stock. You put in $100,000 in cash, you get back all the common stock of the corporation, and the corporation then buys the business or uses the money to start the new business. You would have a capital structure of $100,000 capital and no debt. Solvent indeed, but probably not the best thing to do.

Let's thin the capital structure of the corporation by putting in only $50,000 capital and loaning the corporation the other $50,000. The terms of the loan would be 8 to 12 years with an interest rate of 12 percent. Notice that we have not changed the economic deal. The business still has $100,000. However, if you thin the capital structure of the corporation in this way, you will get the following benefits:

1. The debt can be repaid tax-free. Remember that putting money into the capital structure of a corporation is very easy and involves no tax problem. *Getting it out again is an entirely different matter.* In many situations there is simply no way to get your money back out again without *some* tax (at least a capital gains tax), and you may get trapped in a dividend. However, if you loan the money to your corporation, it is just like a loan to anyone else—when you get repaid, there is no tax.

2. You can get interest on the money. That is a plus because there are many additional costs involved in salary payments. Even assuming you are well under the levels where you have to be

concerned with unreasonable-compensation problems, salary payments will necessitate social security contributions for both you and the corporation and a fairly substantial and increasing array of other state and federal payroll taxes. Interest, on the other hand, is deductible to the corporation and taxable to you—but there are no other incidental taxes.

Using the cash example presents the clearest case of thinning the corporate capital structure. However, you can also accomplish the same thing by retaining certain real or personal property and leasing it to the corporation.

Real property is perhaps the most obvious way to get money out of the corporation via rent. As a general rule, you will want to analyze the situation carefully before you contribute real property to a corporation or have a corporation buy real property with its own funds. It is usually a substantial investment, and the opportunity to have the tax benefits involved in real estate ownership available to the individuals directly is almost always appealing.

Personal property can also be leased to the corporation. I am not talking about paper and pencils here; the property should be something substantial, such as a large piece of equipment you were going to buy. In some cases there may be advantages in buying the equipment personally and leasing it to the corporation. This involves some rather complicated calculations, taking investment credit, depreciation, and depreciation recapture into account. The point is that in these kinds of large transactions, it is *sometimes* appropriate to consider alternatives to a traditional purchase by the corporation.

Key rule: Remember that it is easy to put money or property into a corporation tax-free, but very difficult to get it out again without paying taxes. Before you make sizable contributions of money or property to the capital of a corporation, analyze the effects of that contribution because once done, it will be hard to undo.

Tax Reality

I do not want to belabor the point about tax reality, but I think this is another area where some fairly obvious questions will arise and where this discussion is important to you. Remember that the reason for this discussion is to highlight the need for professional tax advice—not to make you your own tax planner.

You may ask, If it is good to put $50,000 in as debt, why don't I just put all, or almost all, of the money in as debt? If a little is good, a lot is better—right? Further, why do I have to lock myself up for 8 to 12 years? What is wrong with using a demand note or one which has a 1-year maturity which I can extend if I want? After all, I'm the sole shareholder. Further, why do

I have to have 12 percent interest? I don't want interest right now from the corporation, and the corporation needs the money more than I. How about an interest-free loan at least for a while?

The IRS is not stupid, and the tax law—mostly—reflects economic reality. When you contribute money to a new corporation in exchange for common stock, the tax treatment is simple.

- There is no tax when you incorporate.

- Your basis in the stock equals the amount you paid for it.

- When you sell the stock in the future, gain will be measured against that basis.

- The corporation cannot "repay" the amount you contributed, because it is not a loan but a contribution to the capital of a corporation.

- Dividends paid on the stock are *taxable to you* and *not deductible* to the corporation.

What if you simply called the capital contribution a loan, though it did not have traditional loan features such as a maturity date and a fair interest rate? If you did have a maturity date, assume you made it 100 years. Alternatively, assume you made it "on demand."

Now, you say, the $100,000 you paid in is debt so that:

1. You can get it out tax-free as a repayment of a loan.

2. The payments to you based on the $100,000 are interest and, therefore, deductible by the corporation.

Do you really think that the IRS is going to believe that the $100,000 is debt and not stock just because you called it debt? Of course not. The IRS is going to say, quite properly, that the money you paid in was a capital contribution, and they are going to disallow the deduction to the corporation of the "interest." If you take your $100,000 back, the IRS is going to say that it is a dividend, taxable to you and not deductible to the corporation. Why? Because that is the economic reality of the transaction. You have tried to be *too* greedy.

Take the other assumption—you set a short maturity date for the "loan." If you repay the loan at the maturity date, that is all right. However, this is a new corporation and its earning power is uncertain. Suppose you set the maturity date at 1 year, and after the year you do not have enough money in the corporation to pay the debt. Are you going to go to a bank and borrow the money at high interest rates just to pay yourself? Of course not. You are going to extend the loan. Okay, so you extend the loan—what is wrong with that? Put yourself in the position of the IRS. If they come in and find that you extended a loan which was supposed to be paid, are they going to believe that you really intended to pay the loan on maturity in the first place? Probably not. They are going to say that this was just a paper sham—you really made a capital contribution and never intended to pay it back in one year, even though you had a paper that said you did. Suppose you extend the payments again a second time. That looks even more suspect.

Suppose you make the contribution payable "on demand." The IRS is going to say no dice—in a closely held corporation where you are both the lender and the lendee, that just isn't kosher. *Again, you got too greedy.* You tried to have your cake and eat it too, and that will almost always cause tax problems. I give advice to *stay out of trouble.* If you are audited and have to spend your time and money for professional fees—you lose even if you "win." Further, your odds of winning cases like those I have described above is poor—at best.

If you want to "get creative" with the suggestions I give you, *see a lawyer or tax accountant first.* Even if you do not want to get creative, it is worth the money to have a good professional handle your incorporation—it may cost you a few dollars, but I think it is worth it.

In summary, then, whenever possible, seriously consider thinning your capital structure and follow the following guidelines:

- Do not contribute more than 50 percent of the money in the form of debt. Try to keep a one-to-one ratio between the equity and the debt. This is very conservative advice, but it is guaranteed to please the IRS and not cause you any problem.

- When you contribute "debt," make it *real.* Generally, this means a maturity of between 8 and 12 years. A shorter period runs the risk of not having the money available and having to extend the maturity. A longer period runs the risk of having the contribution look like capital rather than debt. Either way, the IRS will more than likely challenge the transaction. The 8-to-12 rule is a conservative and safe approach.

- Make the interest rate somewhere between what the IRS charges and the prime rate. Right now, the IRS charges 12 percent on tax deficiencies, so that is certainly a proper rate for you. You can go higher or lower, depending on the circumstances *at the time.* It is only important to have a legitimate interest rate fixed at the time you loan the money—you do not have to change it as interest rates fluctuate.

CONCLUSION

Let's summarize what you've learned from this chapter.

1. When you start your business, you should think carefully about the legal form that you are going to use. I think you will usually find that a corporation is best.

2. However, forming a corporation is only a part of the initial structuring of your business. You have to decide:
   a. What kind of stock the corporation should authorize and issue
   b. What should be contributed to capital and what to debt
   c. Whether the corporation should elect subchapter "S" so that losses are passed through to your own tax return

3. The basic corporate tax structure, with its separate, relatively low rates, represents many opportunities for tax savings. However, there is an extremely adverse double-tax bite when a corporation pays dividends. You therefore should vow to always try to structure things so you could get your money out of your company in some other way besides a dividend.

4. During the course of the discussion you saw—I hope—that incorporation, redemption of stock, issuance of preferred stock, and many other things which go into proper tax planning are rather technical. Forming the corporation was easy, but for the other parts of the deal—those which save the tax money—professional advice is a good investment.

That is basically it. Many lawyers use a preprinted package of material which contains a nice-looking binder and some fancy share certificates. The package sometimes also contains a preprinted copy of a sample code of regulations and a "seal." In Ohio and most states, a seal is not required.

SAMPLE INCORPORATION DOCUMENTS

The following sample incorporation documents are based on Ohio law and procedure. Documents in other states are similar but may differ in some respects.

> CAUTION: These forms are for illustration only—they have not been included with the intention that they would be used in any specific case. They are slightly abbreviated and not necessarily in correct form for actual use. *I do not recommend forming your own corporation without a lawyer.*

Articles of Incorporation

In Ohio, the secretary of state will provide you with a form for articles of incorporation. All you have to do is fill in the blanks. It is that easy if you want a very simple corporation with one class of common shares and no special provisions enlarging or restricting the rights and powers of the shareholders, directors, or the corporation itself. Most articles of incorporation fall into this category. Remember that articles of incorporation can always be amended to add these things later if appropriate.

ARTICLES OF INCORPORATION

of

_____

(Name of Corporation)

The undersigned, a majority of whom are citizens of the United States, desiring to form a corporation, for profit, under Sections 1701.01 et seq. of the Revised Code of Ohio, do hereby certify:

FIRST. The name of said corporation shall be _____
_____ .

SECOND. The place in Ohio where its principal office is to be located is
_____, _____ County.
(City, Village or Township)

THIRD. The purposes for which it is formed are:

To engage in any or all other lawful acts or activities for which corporations may be formed under Sections 1701.01 to 1701.98, inclusive, of the Ohio Revised Code.

FOURTH. The number of shares which is authorized to have outstanding is 750 common shares.

FIFTH. The amount of stated capital with which the corporation shall begin business is five hundred dollars ($500.00).

IN WITNESS WHEREOF, We have hereunto subscribed our names, this
_____ day of
_____, 19_____.

_____

(Name of Corporation)

_____
_____
_____

NOTE: Ohio law also requires a form for appointing a person to accept service of legal process.

Simple Letter Offering Money and a Few Assets to the Corporation

---

Incorporator's name (your own name if you are the incorporator)
Address
Gentlemen:

I hereby offer to give the _____ Corporation the sum of $5,000 in cash and the following described personal property (or the property listed on an attached page) in exchange for your issuance to me of 100 common shares of The _____ Corporation, which shall be all the issued and outstanding shares of the corporation. The transfer shall take place on the date you accept this offer.

(Signed and dated)

Gentlemen:

(The Corporation), an Ohio corporation, does hereby accept the foregoing offer.

(Incorporator [s])

That is really all there is to it. It can, of course, get much more complicated than that. You may have a going business to offer to the company and you may want to thin the corporation by offering the property in exchange for both stock and notes. There may also be leases of real or personal property involved. However, many small companies are formed with documents just this simple.

After you have filed your articles of incorporation and had them approved by the secretary of state, you then have a first meeting of the shareholders. In this case, you are the only shareholder, the offeror of the money/property, and the incorporator. You have executed the Offer and Acceptance as noted above. Since there is no use in having a "meeting," you simply use the state procedures allowing actions to be taken by written consent and execute a document which looks something like this.

ACTION BY SHAREHOLDER BY WRITTEN CONSENT

Pursuant to Section 1701.54 of the Ohio Revised Code, the undersigned, being the sole shareholder of (name of corporation) does hereby take the following action in writing.

1. The action of the incorporators in accepting the offer from _____is hereby ratified.

2. The following people are hereby elected directors of the corporation to serve for a period of one year or until their successors are duly designated or elected. [I recommend at least three directors and possibly four—they can all be family members even if they are not active in the business.]

3. A Code of Regulations for the company is hereby adopted in the form attached hereto. [I have not included a copy—they can be quite long, and they are not very important for a small company.]

Signed _____

Now you have yourself a corporation with directors. You still need officers and you probably need a banking resolution. Your bank will supply you with a copy of the resolution it uses.

ACTION OF DIRECTORS BY WRITTEN CONSENT

Pursuant to Section 1701.54 of the Ohio Revised Code, the undersigned, being all the directors of _____, do hereby take the following action in writing.

1. The following people are hereby elected officers of the company, to serve for one year or until their successors are duly designated or elected.
   [There are very few requirements here. The following is a usual list—sometimes one person holds more than one office, but you should have separate people as president and secretary (or vice president and assistant secretary) because many documents require the signature of both these officers. You may want your lawyer to serve as an assistant secretary.]

   President _____
   Vice President _____
   Secretary _____
   Treasurer _____

2. The company hereby adopts the following banking resolution. [Use the bank's form—they will want a copy attested to by the corporate secretary.]

Directors

Date: _____   _____

_____

_____

_____

3

INVOLVING OTHER PEOPLE IN YOUR BUSINESS

From 15 years of practicing law, I can say without any qualification whatsoever that the single biggest problem—by several orders of magnitude—in operating any business is the relationships with the other key people in that business. This includes your fellow stockholders (or partners) and the key employees in the company who feel that they have some important stake in the success of the enterprise. We all know sorry tales of people who started out with the best intentions but came to unhappy and costly partings of the way because of differing views as to what should be done with the business or how it should be done.

Further, if I had to pick the one area which is the subject of most dispute, it would be the proper dividing of the corporate pie. *Everyone* involved will have a higher view of his or her contribution to the success of the corporation in relation to the contribution of others. Those who supply the money will think that they should get the lion's share of the profits; those who do the work will think the opposite.

On the other hand, except in the very smallest of enterprises, the involvement of other people is going to be key to the success and profitability of that business. We all know that you simply cannot do everything yourself and that it is extremely difficult to hire good people in a small business unless they have some piece of the action.

First, let me state my personal preferences so that you will understand my biases in reading the rest of this chapter. Despite the fact that you cannot do everything yourself and despite the fact that it is difficult to hire good people on a straight salary, I always strongly recommend that this approach be carefully considered and analyzed before you let someone else into the action of your company. Further, when you do have to let somebody in on a piece of the action, I recommend that you try to do it via the employment contract approach, where the person's salary or compensation is based upon increased profits or some other rather easily measurable criterion. If you need additional capital, explore *debt, leasing,* or *preferred stock* before giving up equity for money. I recommend sharing the ownership or the responsibility for managing your corporation with other people only as a last resort. These personal biases are partly the result of my psychological makeup, but they are also the result of 15 years of reading case after case involving all forms of wrangling among business partners.

I would like to devote the rest of this chapter to discussing the *legal* problems involving the use of other people in your business. I think it is useful to divide this discussion into three categories, because virtually all of the cases I have read and the problems I have personally encountered can be grouped into one of these classes.

1. The partnership and the problems of partnership law

2. The problems of having more than one common stockholder in a corporation

3. The problems and opportunities inherent in the employer-employee relationship—specifically employment contracts.

PARTNERSHIPS

A partnership is a form of doing business where two or more people join together to share the profits of an undertaking and do not form a corporation. As was discussed in the preceding chapter, a partnership is a business entity but not a tax entity. The partnership will not save you any taxes, but on the other hand, if there is a loss, it will allow you to deduct your share of the loss from your other income. Partnerships are generally of two types: "general partnership," which is the kind I have been talking about; and "limited partnership."

Limited partnerships are used in real estate syndications and other tax shelter investments where the investor wants the tax advantages of a partnership but not the unlimited liability that typically goes with being a general partner in a general partnership. In a limited partnership there is one or more general partners and then a group of "limited partners" who are only investors. Essentially, these people are much like the shareholders in a corporation. Their liability for business losses extends only to the money they have contributed to the partnership. Thus, if someone sells you a limited partnership interest for $10,000 in a million-dollar real estate venture and the whole thing goes bankrupt, you are subject to losing only your original $10,000 contribution. You will not have to make good on the hundreds of thousands or even millions of dollars of liabilities which can be generated when one of these big deals goes down the drain. Limited partnerships are useful for tax shelters but are not generally used for business deals.

In a business deal, the typical pattern is that two or three people will get together to informally conduct a business and will not bother to incorporate. They will simply shake hands, or perhaps draw up a very sketchy agreement which says that they will all work together for the common good of the company and share the profits on some basis—usually the same basis on which they contributed capital.

Though informal, that kind of arrangement does have legal implications. *The law will infer a partnership.* The fact that you may not have any "partnership agreement" does not matter. The terms of your partnership will be those contained in the Uniform Partnership Act, which provides for the following key rules:

1. Any partner can bind the other partner or partners to business debts.

2. Partners are *individually and personally* liable for partnership debts if those debts exceed the assets of the partnership. (In our real estate deal, if that was a general partnership rather than a limited partnership and you contributed $10,000 to a deal which went bankrupt because it had liabilities of $1 million more than its assets, you would be individually and personally liable for the entire $1 million.)

3. Any partner can terminate the partnership at any time for any reason. If the partner has contracted not to terminate the partnership, there may be a cause of action against the partner for damages, but that does not change the basic fact that a partnership can be terminated at the virtual whim of any partner.

4. The death of any partner automatically terminates the partnership. You can usually work around this problem in a well-drafted partnership agreement, but it is a rather complex and cumbersome problem.

5. The liability of a partner for partnership debts is *joint and several.* This means that *each* partner is liable for *all* the partnership debts. If you are 50-50 partners with someone, you can be stuck with 100 percent of the debts if the other partner turns out to be insolvent or skips town.

6. You cannot change any of this by contract. You can, of course, enter into any kind of partnership agreement you want which establishes the rights *as between partners.* But, when the creditors

are involved, there is simply nothing you can do to change these basic rules about liability. Creditors cannot be cut off from these rights by any private deals you make with your partner.

7. A partnership interest is subject to the normal rules of family law. If your partner gets divorced, you may find yourself in partnership with the spouse or, more likely, the spouse's lawyer. If the court awards the spouse all or a portion of the partnership interest in your partnership, there is simply nothing you can do to prevent it other than terminating the partnership.

8. Essentially, the same thing is true for tort liability. If your partner runs over someone and gets sued for more than the insurance coverage, the injured person can attach the partnership interest and you could end up in a very difficult situation.

These are the kinds of problems which make lawyers very nervous when clients want to enter into a business partnership. Again, investment partnerships and tax shelters are separate animals. We are talking here about an active business venture. Because of these problems, it will almost always be better to join forces with other business associates via the corporate route than through a partnership. Some of these problems are thereby eliminated, and many other problems can be solved by tested and proven techniques which any good business counselor will know.

In summary, then, I would like to give you two cautions. First, if at all possible, try to avoid going into business as a partnership. Second, if there is some reason why this must be done, be sure to have a comprehensive partnership agreement drafted by a good lawyer, and be sure to read and understand that agreement.

CORPORATIONS AND SHAREHOLDERS

I would like next to discuss the legal principles involved in corporations and shareholders in terms of how a corporation is run and who has the power to make major decisions.

A corporation is a creature of state law, but in all states the principles for how a corporation is operated are substantially the same. The corporation is owned by the common shareholders. The common shareholders have one principal right, and that is to elect the directors. *It is very important to note that a shareholder has absolutely no right whatsoever to participate in the management of the corporation.* The shareholders' only right is to elect directors. All states provide that a corporation shall be run and managed by its board of directors; and further, that the board of directors will operate by majority rule. Thus, on a five-person board of directors, any three directors can effectively dictate the course of action of the company.

Further, the officers of the company who are in charge of the day-to-day management of the company, subject to the direction of the board of directors, are all elected by the directors. Again, the majority rule applies. A majority of the directors can elect the officers of the company.

These basic principles seem to effectively preclude participation in the corporate entity by the minority shareholders—and indeed, they do. But in order to protect minority shareholders, the law has given them certain rights and imposed certain obligations on the majority. For example, a corporation must deal "fairly" with the minority shareholders. If the corporation's assets are to be sold, the minority must be given their fair share of the proceeds. Many states have a so-called right of appraisal and buy-out, whereby in certain key transactions, such as the sale of all the corporate assets or the liquidation of the company, the shareholders who disagree with the majority are entitled to have the corporation buy their shares at a fair value. Of course, exactly what is fair in these kinds of situations is always subject to much dispute.

Minority shareholders have other rights, too. The chief one is to bring lawsuits against the company. A minority shareholder is entitled to attend the annual shareholders' meeting; to vote for directors (even though the minority holding may not represent enough votes to elect any directors); and usually, to examine the books and records of the company. In short, minority shareholders do not have any important *substantive* rights to dictate how the company is run, but they have a lot of *procedural* rights which they can use to harass the company and make a general nuisance of themselves. For this purpose, a minority shareholder is anyone who holds even a single share.

If you stop and think about the above general legal principles for a minute, you can see some of the obvious problems.

1. If you give your good associates a few shares of your company, you have not given them anything except the right to cause you a lot of trouble if they get mad at you.

2. If you are going into business with somebody in the form of a corporation, and you end up with 49 percent of the stock and they end up with 51 percent, they control the *entire* company and you have *almost nothing* to say about it. Essentially, your rights are the same as they would be if you had only one share. You can cause a lot of trouble, but you cannot really do anything important.

The right of the majority to run the business, as a practical matter, includes the right to substantially dilute the interest of the minority. Suppose, for example, that you have a company with a net worth of $100,000 and majority shareholders of 51 percent, with you holding the other 49 percent. There is virtually nothing in the law—except for vague concepts of fairness and fraud—which would prevent those 51 percent shareholders from paying themselves salaries sufficient to reduce the assets of the corporation substantially. They could then liquidate it, and while you would be entitled to 49 percent of whatever was left when it was liquidated, that might not be very much.

Suppose you have a 50-50 ownership of your corporation. This will effectively prevent the other party from taking advantage of you because you will have an effective veto power over everything. By the same token, the other party has an effective veto power over anything important that you want to do, and so you have the classic standoff.

Because of these problems, I do not recommend any of these kinds of transactions. I will explain this in more detail later on, but let us look again at some things which don't strike me as being a very good idea.

1. Giving a few shares of stock to employees or friends can cause you nothing but trouble. You haven't really given them anything important (except perhaps psychologically), but you have given them the opportunity to cause you a lot of legal headaches if there is a falling out later on. I recommend you don't do it.

2. A 51–49 percent deal is very good if you have the 51 percent and very bad if you have the 49 percent.

3. A 50-50 deal has a lot of problems, the key one being that there is simply no good way to break a deadlock. While you and the other 50 percent shareholder are wrangling about some problem, the whole business can go down the drain, and there is nothing either of you can do about it unless the other agrees.

The above discussion assumes we are talking only about common stock. Common stock, you will remember, is the voting stock of the corporation, and the common shareholders are those who own the equity interest in the corporation and are entitled to elect the directors. The directors, in turn, manage the company. There are, however, other kinds of stock, and indeed, there are many different kinds of common stock. Because of these other alternatives, you do not have to get involved in the above three kinds of situations which present so many problems. Let us take them in order and see how they can be dealt with.

Instead of giving friends or relatives common shares of your company, you could give them preferred stock or nonvoting common. Depending on what you want to accomplish, it seems to me that some other arrangement besides giving away voting common shares of the company could accomplish the same result. For example, suppose you had two classes of common, class A being entitled to vote for directors and class B being nonvoting. If you wanted to allow other people to participate in the equity growth of the company, there is no reason why you could not create a class B stock and either give some of it to them or let them purchase it. By the same token, if you wanted to give someone income, you could create preferred stock and give him or her that so you could pay dividends on the preferred and provide the income that way. If you wanted to provide someone with a share of the current profits, you would not have to use stock at all; you could simply use a contractual arrangement to pay them a bonus equal to whatever share of the profits you thought appropriate, calculated in any way you think appropriate.

Going to our 51–49 percent deal, it seems to me that the problem here is the fact that the 49 percent shareholder has almost enough stock to control the company, but not quite. It is one thing to get frozen out if you have only one or two shares and quite another to get frozen out if you have 49 percent of the stock—although legally these amount to approximately the same thing. Assuming you want to have an arrangement where one party has the sole and complete right to run the company but the other has a very important share in the profits and income of the company, there are a number of ways you can do this and safeguard the 49 percent shareholder. Again, nonvoting common and preferred stock can be used for this purpose. For example, you can have one person own all of the voting common and another person own all of the nonvoting common. That way you have it spelled out right up front that the person who does not own voting common stock cannot vote for the directors and is subject to the rights of the people with the voting stock to control the company. That strikes me as a lot fairer than a 51 percent-49 percent deal.

The 50-50 deal is much more difficult. It is a classic problem for which lawyers really don't have many good solutions. If you want to have a 50-50 deal, you are simply going to have to live with the deadlock problem. You can minimize it to some extent by trying to reach an agreement as to how you will break a deadlock while you are still friends, rather than waiting until after a problem occurs, when you may not be on the best of terms. You can appoint an arbitrator, who may be your lawyer, an accountant, or a neutral business associate; or, if you think it is necessary, you can go into an elaborate arbitration arrangement pursuant to the rules of the American Arbitration Association. Essentially, these rules provide that each of you picks an arbitrator, those two arbitrators pick a third, and the three arbitrators together resolve any dispute.

In my judgment, the common denominator is that you should get professional help in drafting the documents and issuing the appropriate kinds of stock. I have touched on only a few of the problems and opportunities involved in joint ownership of a corporation. Indeed, there are many books written on the subject, and your flexibility is limited only by your own imagination and that of your lawyer.

One of the key things which would have avoided a lot of the disputes I have seen is simply a meeting of all the parties in question, where corporate counsel explains clearly to each person exactly what his or her rights and obligations are and, correspondingly, what rights he or she does not have. I know that when you are starting a business the last thing you want to do is to get all of your people together for an afternoon in a lawyer's office to discuss this kind of thing. The last thing on any of your minds is that there will ever be any kind of dispute among all you good people who are going to help one another make this business a success. I certainly hope that is true for you, but my experience has shown that it may not be. Getting everything out on the table and all of these problems thrashed out while you are still friends can be done in an afternoon in a lawyer's office. If you wait till a problem comes up, it is going to take many afternoons with many lawyers.

Buying Out Other Shareholders

As a corollary to all of this, after you have decided exactly what kind of working arrangement you are going to have, it is necessary and appropriate for you to decide how the various parties are going to be either bought out or redeemed out should they die, become disabled, or desire to withdraw from the business. Again, the rationale is very simple. These kinds of arrangements are standard and very easy to work out so long as everyone is friends and no one knows who will die or become disabled first. They can be difficult and costly to work out later on, when the interests of the parties become adverse. There are an infinite number of ways to deal with these problems. Many of them involve life insurance. If you are going to buy someone out when he or she dies, life insurance can be used to provide the money to do it with. Even this can become complex, however. Consider the following questions:

1. Should one shareholder take out life insurance policies on the lives of all the rest so when anyone dies, the others have money to buy the deceased shareholders' interest?
   This works for up to about five people (25 life insurance policies in that case), but this relatively simple approach can get terribly complicated if many people are involved.

2. Should the *company* take out the life insurance so that the company redeems the shares of the deceased shareholder? If the compa-

ny takes out the policy, is the money paid on the death of the shareholder to be considered an asset of the company?

For example, suppose you and another person form a company with $50,000 capital each, and agree that if one dies, the company will redeem the deceased person's shares. To provide the money, the company takes out a $50,000 policy on each of you. The other shareholder dies the next day, and $50,000 is paid to the corporation. The assets of the corporation are, at that point, $150,000— $50,000 that you each contributed and $50,000 from the insurance company. When the company redeems the shares of the deceased shareholder, should it pay half of $100,000 or half of $150,000? The answer you choose makes a big difference. There is no "right" or "wrong" approach, but failure to agree on this point when you enter into the redemption agreement is definitely bad and will certainly cause a dispute later.

If you think it is difficult and complex to work out a simple arrangement to redeem or purchase the shares of a shareholder when life insurance can be obtained, try figuring out a way to do it if one or more of the shareholders are uninsurable, or if neither the individuals nor the company can afford enough insurance.

Death is the easiest of all situations to deal with. There is no problem in determining when someone is dead, and in most cases, life insurance can provide all or at least most of the cash necessary to take care of the problem. However, what about disability or a falling out? Those are more difficult problems because there is no easily identifiable event and perhaps no money. They can and should be dealt with, however, while neither party knows who will become disabled first, and while both are friends and neither has reason to blame the other for a falling out. Virtually all corporate lawyers have an arsenal of tools for dealing with these problems. Legal form books are full of sample agreements. Your job is to make sure the problem is dealt with in a planning mode—not in a dispute-settlement situation. If you wait until after a dispute arises, the only winner is likely to be the lawyer.

What to Tell Your Lawyer When You Discuss Buy-Out or Redemption Agreements

The above problems have become so standard that all lawyers have "buzz words" which they use to discuss them—namely, "redemption agreements," which refers to cases where the *corporation* will redeem the shares of a deceased or disabled shareholder; and "cross-purchase agreements," which refers to situations where the individual shareholders purchase the shares of the deceased or disabled shareholder. These documents are not terribly long or complicated, but they require some very important decisions. As always, taxes play a very important role. Therefore, the key thing you have to do is lay all the financial cards on the table and ask your lawyer or accountant to make a recommendation as to which approach is best for you. I recommend against asking an insurance advisor for this advice because of the extremely large number of contracts (and therefore commissions) which can be generated by the cross-purchase arrangement. I have seen insurance agents literally set up for life on one of these deals. While it may be best for you, I think you should have that determination made by a lawyer or accountant who has no particular ax to grind. Redemption and cross-purchase agreements will cost you just about the same in legal and accounting or tax planning fees.

Here is a very brief list of things to think about before you call your lawyer. It will save both of you a lot of time (and should save you money):

1. What contingencies do you want to cover? Death is certainly going to be the first, but what about
   a. disability (How are you going to define disability)?
   b. withdrawal from business or retirement?
   c. business disputes or breakup of the company?

2. How are you going to determine the value of the corporation? This is the most difficult point. Everyone who writes about the subject seems to say that book value is not a good measure. I agree that it *may* not be a proper measure, but I think it is usually a very good measure. It certainly is simple. Perhaps the best way to determine value is to execute a schedule with the agreement saying what the value is, and then reexecute it every year with a revised value. The problem I have seen with this approach is that people forget to do it, and when someone dies there is no recently agreed-upon value and therefore nothing whatsoever on which to base value. That almost always causes a dispute and possibly a lawsuit. Remember that your lawyer is not going to be too much help here. He or she can suggest alternatives, but *you* have to make the judgments. Your accountant is in a slightly better position to help you, but it is still your business, and its value is *always going to be very subjective.*

3. Tell the lawyer about the age and physical health of each party. Remember that insurance is a good way to get money only if it is available and not prohibitively expensive. If one or more of the shareholders is in ill health or old, insurance may not be a viable alternative.

4. Be prepared to share your personal balance sheet (or at least the

important parts of it) with your lawyer. He or she cannot do a good job on this problem without knowing what the individuals involved can reasonably afford to do. If all the parties are independently wealthy, your lawyer is going to have an easy job. If all the parties are young and their principal asset is going to be stock in the business, your lawyer's job is much more difficult.

5. Be prepared to share your views on what to do if someone becomes disabled, and be prepared to talk about what you consider a disability. What if someone has a heart attack and simply has to cut back? What if someone is completely and totally disabled for 1 year (or 2) but can work thereafter? Again, your lawyer cannot make these decisions for you. He or she can ask you questions and provide alternatives, but you have to make the decisions.

6. Be sure to give some thought to the precise mechanics of how the deal is going to work out. What if everyone agrees on a cross-purchase agreement and everyone promises to take out the necessary policies? Upon the death of the first shareholder, you find that someone forgot to do it. Should there be a trustee to physically handle all the insurance policies and make sure the premiums are paid when due? It may not be a bad investment. Then again, it may be wasted money. You have to decide.

Summary of Sharing Ownership

To summarize up to this point: Do not form a partnership unless there is virtually no other way to do business, and do not let things drag out before forming a corporation because, if you do, the courts will impose a legal partnership in the interim. Instead, use the corporation and all the flexibility that it provides to solve the problems inherent in doing business with others. Learn from experience—which has shown ownership-sharing arrangements to be the single most frequent cause of disputes and litigation between business people. Use your corporate counsel and get your full measure of value from him or her by asking for his or her legal judgments and expertise on how to spell out almost everything beforehand while those involved are all still friends. Remember the oil filter commercial, and pay your lawyer a small amount for an "oil filter" now rather than a large amount for an "engine overhaul" later.

EMPLOYMENT CONTRACTS

In order to avoid the difficulties of equity arrangements wherever possible, I recommend the use of employment arrangements as an alternative. If you want to recruit a hotshot sales representative, manager, or engineer and motivate that person to join your company and do a good job, the way to do it is usually money. You do not have to give stock and cause all the problems discussed previously. An employment arrangement which provides that the person gets a salary plus a certain share of the profits ought to be sufficient. This, however, creates its own set of problems—albeit less serious ones than those mentioned above—so I would like to discuss employment contracts in the remainder of this chapter. The reason I have separated the two is that I think that it is impractical to expect a businessperson to deal with the tax and corporate problems inherent in shared ownership arrangements as discussed above. On the other hand, any businessperson can prepare a good draft of an employment contract with the help of this chapter. If you do your homework, your lawyer and accountant should be able to review your work and provide useful comments for minimal fees. In contrast, I should warn you that the legal fees for establishing corporations with different classes of stock, drafting redemption or cross-purchase agreements, or effecting arbitration agreements to break a deadlock will be rather substantial if the lawyer does a good job for you. These are *complicated* and *time-consuming* jobs.

I do not generally favor employment contracts. I think businesses, both large and small, are generally better served by having employment relationships simply be employment at will. However, there may be some circumstances which call for a contract.

An employment contract may be necessary when you want to recruit people who have a good bargaining position and who want to have their rights spelled out in a contract. Also, if you are going to recruit someone based upon a sharing of the profits or some other formalized kind of incentive compensation, you will probably need a contract to spell out exactly how much money the person is entitled to.

An employment contract is not necessary when all you want is to assure that the employee respects the confidentiality of private information or that you will get the benefit of any inventions the employee makes on company time. In these cases, a simple employee confidentiality agreement or an agreement requiring the assignment of inventions will accomplish the desired objective. A sample of such an agreement is contained in the chapter on intellectual property (Chapter 13). However, if the main purpose of the agreement is to keep the employee from going into competition or working for a competitor after he or she leaves, the better approach is the execution of an employment contract.

What Kind of Employment Agreement Do You Need?

Assuming that a contract is necessary, the next question is what kind? Basically, there are three types.

1. The first type is the so-called letter agreement, which is a very short form frequently used by many companies, both large and small. It seems to serve quite satisfactorily despite the fact that it does not cover very many contingencies. Generally, a letter form can be used when it is thought difficult or inappropriate to negotiate with the prospective employee on all of the incidental terms which would be included in a more formal contract, but either the employee wants the assurance of continued employment at a stated salary or the company has one or two very specific requirements which it feels could be set forth in a letter agreement.

2. The second form is what might be termed the "general form." While there is no actual form by this name, there is a basic contract which is frequently used in an attempt to compromise between the very short, informal letter agreement and the extremely elaborate "full form" employment agreement which is used when one or the other parties feels that virtually every contingency must be provided for. This basic contract, which is simply called the general form for lack of any better designation, is the one which is discussed herein and is set forth as an example.

3. The third type is the full-form employment agreement, where the parties attempt to cover every conceivable contingency. While this kind of contract may be necessary on some limited occasions, it is very difficult to negotiate because the parties must focus on and bargain for virtually every single term.

Considerations in Employment Contracts

Following are some of the important considerations which must be decided in drafting an employment contract.

The essentials of the deal

This, of course, is the most important part of the contract and should include the following:

1. A clear identification of the parties.

2. A statement of the length of employment and what happens at the

end of the term, if anything (e.g., is the contract renewable at someone's option).

3. A description of the basic duties of the employee and to whom the employee reports. You should consider the question of moonlighting and whether or not the employee is going to be required to devote his or her full time to the company. A popular approach is to require the employees to devote "substantially" all of their time to the company, except for reasonable vacation periods. The word "substantially" clearly allows the employee to continue to participate in a limited number of outside deals related to passive investments such as managing a stock portfolio or participating as an investor in real estate or other syndications, but would not include a second job or a part-time business.

4. The pay is, of course, one of the most important terms of the agreement. While there naturally can be no form for this, it usually breaks down into the following four parts:
   a. The basic salary.
   b. A bonus, an incentive compensation, or deferred compensation of some type.
   c. The fringe benefits, which, rather than being explained in detail, are usually stated to be simply the same fringe benefits that everybody else in the company gets.
   d. A catchall provision including such other items of compensation as may be agreed upon. These could include the use of a company car and possibly a different vacation period than would normally be allowed an employee with comparable years of service.

If the new employee is to be granted stock options or other rights to invest in the company, it is essential that this provision be drafted by a lawyer. The employment contract is not intended to be used for that purpose.

A troublesome problem in contracts which base the compensation of the employee on the profits of the company is the definition of the term "profits." Following are some considerations:

1. It should be clear whether the profits are to be computed before or after taxes. Also, the effect of the employee compensation should be made clear, as this naturally has an effect on the profits of the company. For example, if the employee is to be paid $10,-000 if the profits of the company are $100,000, it should be made clear whether the profits of the company have to be $100,000 before or after the payments to the employee. Obviously, if the company made $100,000 and was then called upon to pay $10,-

000 to the employee, its profits would, at that point, be only $90,000.

2. Tax considerations are also important. If the company desires to take into account the payment to the employee in the year in question, there will be a very complex set of calculations because the payment will reduce taxable income, which reduces taxes, etc. This can be worked out, but it is difficult. The best approach is usually to base the payment to the employee on profit *before* taxes.

As you can see, then, a seemingly simple employment contract can generate complex legal and accounting problems. I always recommend that any employment contract which includes a formula for paying the employee be reviewed by the company's accountant to make sure that the accountant can actually make the computations which are necessary, and that all parties are in agreement as to how those computations should be made. Lawyers live in fear of deals in which each party is depending on the good faith of the other rather than a clear legal document. Remember that if either party goes to see his or her lawyer about the proper interpretation of an employment contract, all is not well. At that point, amicable agreements are exceedingly difficult to achieve.

The restrictive covenant

Perhaps second in importance to the essentials of the deal is the restrictive covenant. Restrictive covenants are important because in the absence of such a provision, there is no legal rule prohibiting an employee from competing with his or her former employer unless trade secrets or some kind of fraudulent or unfair methods are involved. The provision contained in the sample form has been constructed to attempt to work around a number of legal problems which will be obvious from a reading of the provision. In any restrictive covenant, it is important to include limitations as to time and area.

The restrictions must be reasonable, or the courts will not enforce them. What is reasonable will vary from case to case. Your lawyer can help you make this determination; it is a combination legal-business judgment. However, even with your lawyer's help, there may be no clear answer. My view is that it is better to have a shorter period in a smaller geographical area which is clearly enforceable than to have something the company clearly feels protects itself but which is of doubtful enforceability. Another aspect of the reasonableness question is the extent of the trade secret or confidential information which may be involved. For example, in a case involving Orkin Exterminating Company and one of their employees, the Arkansas Supreme

Court held that an otherwise reasonable noncompetition agreement was not enforceable because there were no trade secrets or confidential information involved. The court said that the basic flaw in the noncompetition covenant of the agreement was that it was directed not against unfair competition but against competition of any kind on the part of the former employees. A reading of the majority and dissenting opinions in this case points out the essential problem.

The majority said that it would have sustained the restriction if trade secrets, special training, or confidential information or access to lists of customers were involved. However, it said that the pesticides used by Orkin were commercially available; that the training was available in numerous colleges; and that although Orkin did train its employees, it did so only as a matter of self-interest, to make them proficient in their jobs. The court said further that:*

> "If Orkin's position is sound, then any employer in any business devoted to selling—whether the sales be of insurance, real estate, clothing, groceries, hardware, or anything else—can validly prohibit its former salesmen from engaging in that business within the vicinity for as long as two years after the termination of employment. Needless to say, the law does not provide any such protection from ordinary competition.

The following quotation from the dissent, however, suggests that there were, in fact, a considerable number of facts which supported the argument that a valid trade secret existed and that some of the information in question was confidential.

> Admittedly, Orkin's confidential technical manuals told its sales and service personnel how to service its customers. An Orkin employee taught Weaver procedures. Confidential technical bulletins prepared by Orkin's research and development section disseminated among its employees, disclosed the latest ideas and recommendations of the employer in treating procedures and on chemicals that can or cannot be used in particular areas. The chemicals are not specifically found on the market, but since Federal law requires that the ingredients be shown on the label, an employee can learn which chemicals to buy on the open market in order to provide service to a customer. Orkin has patent rights, not on the chemicals, but on the mixtures. One can buy the chemicals that go into Orkin's mixtures but not the mixtures.
>
> To operate successfully in the pest control business, one must have a working knowledge of the problems that could be encountered in a particular business being served, of the various insects that might be anticipated, how

---

*Orkin Exterminating Co. v. Weaver, 521 S.W. 2d 69, 1975.

they multiply, where and how they hibernate, the areas to be searched, the particular chemical to be used to treat the specific infestations found, the strength to be achieved by mixing chemicals, and the types of areas in which applications should or should not be made. All these techniques, chemicals and application procedures are kept confidential. Weaver did have access to all Orkin's mixtures of chemicals, methods of applications and techniques, all of which were confidential.

The last portion of the restrictive covenant form that I have included has been carefully drafted to assure maximum enforceability, even though some court in some jurisdiction may determine that some part of it is unenforceable. However, this provision should not be used to justify a basic restriction in terms of time or area which otherwise may be unjustified. In other words, the first line of defense should be that the provisions are reasonable.

So long as a company continues to pay an employee's salary, it can restrict that employee from any kind of competition anyplace in the world. The problem comes when the company stops paying the salary and then attempts to prohibit the employee from earning a living. Courts react against this and closely examine restrictive covenants and, in many cases, hold them unenforceable. The lesson to be learned from this is that if the employee could really severely damage the company by going into competition, then the basic term of employment should be for what the company feels is a long enough period to protect itself. This way, the maximum risk it runs is simply having to pay the salary of the employee at a time when he or she is not performing any service for the company.

This is also a technique I used in order to determine from clients and management just how important the noncompetition agreement was. When the client would first mention the subject, I would be told that it was very important, and that if this employee were not restricted from doing anything even vaguely related to the present job anywhere in the world, disastrous consequences would result. Therefore, I was asked to draft the most restrictive clause I could possibly create. When I agreed to do this but said that the company would have to agree to continue to pay the employee's salary after termination to make it enforceable, the matter was viewed in a different perspective. I suggest you take the same approach. Ask yourself what restrictions you *really* need, and be able to articulate precisely why you need them to your lawyer.

Confidential information and inventions

Perhaps the third most important subject to be dealt with in the employment relationship is confidential information and inventions. As mentioned before, however, I recommend that this be handled in a separate document.

This document can simply be incorporated with the form employment contract I have suggested (see Chapter 13 for a sample).

Other considerations

Following are some other considerations which can arise in drafting an employment contract and which could be extremely important in certain circumstances.

1. *What do you do about the sale or discontinuance of the business?*
   Unless there is something in the contract covering this point, the sale of your business does not, in and of itself, give you the right to terminate a contract of employment if that contract is for a fixed term which extends past the sale date.

2. *What do you do if the employee fails to perform as anticipated?*
   Despite the best of intentions, it may be that that person is not productive for you. The general law on this is rather unfavorable to the employer. Unless you have something fairly clear on which to base your action, you cannot discharge an employee who has a contract. Of course, if there is a deliberate and willful failure to perform, or if the employee embezzles money, becomes an alcoholic, or simply does not show up for work for an extended period of time, you would have the right to cancel the contract. If, however, the problem is simply a dispute as to the value of the employee's services—a question of whether or not the employee is earning his or her keep—it is extremely unlikely that you will be able to discharge someone who has an employment contract. At the first sign of trouble, the best thing to do is to start building a record and to try to establish some objective criteria for measuring the employee's performance. Even this, however, is extremely difficult. Talk to your lawyer *early* if you have a problem like this.

3. *What about changes of duties?*
   A few cases have illustrated the need for the contract to stipulate that the employee's duties may be changed by the employer. Absent such a provision, it has sometimes been successfully asserted by an employee that a change of his or her duties by the employer amounted to a breach of contract.

4. *State laws.*
   As alluded to above, an employment contract is going to be governed under state laws, and these are not uniform. Some states will simply not enforce restrictive covenants at all.

5. *What if the employee already has an employment contract with somebody else?*

If you intentionally induce an employee to leave the employment of someone else, you may be guilty of interference with a contractual agreement and subject to damages by the other employer. The general rule is that unless you have *actual knowledge* of the prospective employee's other contractual relationship, you cannot be guilty of inducing a breach of it. However, when you have actual knowledge and when you do not is subject to what the judge or jury believes when they hear all the evidence. You might want to ask the employee if he or she is subject to any other contract. This rule can operate in your favor if someone with whom you have a contract is negotiating with someone else. If you have an idea that this might be happening, you can enhance your legal position by informing the other company of the employment contract the employee has with you.

6. *Employment contracts for sales representatives.*

If a sales representative is given an employment contract and if his or her compensation is based on commissions, some additional considerations become appropriate.

a. The method of calculating the commissions should be made extremely clear. This issue causes many disputes. Some things which should be considered are the following:

(1) Are the commissions paid on all orders forwarded by the sales representative or only on those accepted by the company?

(2) Does the company have the right to reject orders? (The company should have the right to reject any order either because of the lack of credit of the customer or for any reason deemed appropriate by the company.)

(3) Is the commission on the total sale, or are such things as returns, freight allowances and discounts, and bad debts or other similar items subtracted from the base?

(4) When are the commissions payable—when the sales representative sends in the order, when the merchandise is shipped, when it is received by the customer, or when it is actually paid for by the customer?

(5) Will the sales representative receive a drawing account or some other type of advance on future commissions?

b. What about expenses? Must the sales representative defray all of his or her traveling and other expenses, or will the company pay for a portion or all of them?

    c. What kind of paperwork in terms of reports to the sales representative, etc., should be undertaken by the company? Generally, the company should furnish some kind of report to the sales representative, perhaps on a monthly basis, showing all information necessary to calculate the commissions payable.

SAMPLE EMPLOYMENT AGREEMENT

This Agreement is made and entered into this_____day of
_____, 19_____, but effective as of
_____ ("Effective Date") by and between
_____ a corporation with offices located at
_____ (The Company) and
_____ of _____
(Employee)

WHEREAS, The Employee has certain valuable experience in the business conducted by The Company, and

WHEREAS, both the Employee and the Company feel it would be beneficial to enter into an employment arrangement and both desire to have the terms of such arrangement set forth in an Agreement, and

NOW THEREFORE, in consideration of the mutual agreements herein set forth, the parties agree as follows:

  1. Duties

Upon the effective date, the Company shall employ and the Employee agrees to be employed by The Company to perform the following duties:

Herein specify the *general* duties to be performed by the employee—but do not be too specific. Also, be sure to include the clauses set forth below to specify that the duties may be changed, and state to whom the employee is to report.

The Employee shall also perform such additional or different or other duties related to the business as may from time to time be delegated to him or her by The Company. The Employee shall devote substantially all of his or her time to such duties except for reasonable vacation periods, and shall observe and abide by the reasonable company policies and decisions of the Company in all business matters and shall be responsible to and report to the Chief Executive Officer of the Company.

  2. Term

The Employee's employment shall continue for a period of _____ years, beginning on the effective date of this Agreement and ending on
_____.

  3. Compensation

The Company shall pay and the Employee shall accept as full consideration for the services to be rendered hereunder compensation consisting of the following:

a. [Salary.]
b. [Any other bonus, etc., which might be paid.]
c. The Employee shall also receive such other benefits as may be made available from time to time to other management employees of The Company with similar age and years of service as Employee.
d. Such other items of compensation as may be agreed upon by Employee and The Company from time to time, including but not limited to, reasonable vacation periods, expense accounts, and the use of company automobiles.

4. Illness, Incapacity or Death

If at any time during the term of this Agreement the Employee becomes disabled or is unable for any reason, substantially, to perform his or her duties hereunder and he or she has not breached any of the provisions of this Agreement, compensation shall continue to be paid to him or her as provided in paragraph 3 but only as to the first six-month period, during which he or she shall be so disabled. The Company may, at its sole option, continue payment of Employee's salary until he or she is able to return to work or for such period greater than six months as The Company elects, or may terminate this Agreement. If Employee should die during the term of this Agreement, Employee's employment and The Company's obligations hereunder shall terminate as of the end of the month in which his or her death occurs.

5. Restrictive Covenant [Must be reasonable as to time and territory.]

The Employee and The Company agree that The Company's business depends, to a considerable extent, on the individual efforts both in sales and design of Employee. Accordingly, Employee covenants and agrees that he or she will not, for the period of his or her employment hereunder and for one year from the date of expiration of this Agreement (but in no event for less than four years from the date hereof in the event of earlier termination of his or her employment hereunder for whatever cause) engage directly or indirectly (either as principal, agent or consultant or through any corporation, firm or organization in which he or she may be an officer, director, employee, substantial shareholder, partner, member or be otherwise affiliated) in any activity anywhere in the United States competitive with the business being conducted by The Company at the time of termination of his or her employment hereunder, including without limitation [specify general nature of business].

6. Confidential Information and Inventions

Employee shall execute and abide by an "employee invention and confidential information agreement," in the form attached hereto as Exhibit A and incorporated herein by reference.

The covenants of Employee contained in paragraphs 5 and 6 hereof shall each be construed as an Agreement independent of any other provision in this Agreement, and the existence of any claim or cause of action of Employee against The Company, whether predicated on this Agreement or otherwise, shall not constitute a defense to the enforcement by The Company of either covenant. Both parties hereby expressly agree and contract that it is not the intention of either party to violate any public policy, statutory or common law, and that if any sentence, paragraph, clause or combination of the same of paragraphs 5 or 6 (including the provisions incorporated by reference) is in violation of the law of any state where applicable, such sentence, paragraph, clause or combination of the same shall be void in the jurisdictions where it is unlawful, and the remainder of such paragraph and this Agreement shall remain binding on the parties hereto. It is the intention of both parties to make the covenants of paragraphs 5 and 6 binding only to the extent that it may be lawfully done under existing applicable laws. In the event that any part of any covenant of paragraph 5 or 6 is determined by a court of law to be overly broad thereby making the covenant unenforceable, the parties hereto agree and it is their desire that such court shall substitute a reasonable judicially enforceable limitation in place of the offensive part of the covenant, and that as so modified the covenant shall be as fully enforceable as set forth herein by the parties themselves in the modified form.

7. Miscellaneous

a. Governing Law.

The validity, construction, interpretation and enforceability of this Agreement and the capacity of the parties shall be determined and governed by the laws of the State of _____.

b. Assignment.

This agreement is personal to each of the parties hereto, and neither party may assign or delegate any of the rights or obligations hereunder without first obtaining a written consent of the other party.

c. Rights and Remedies.

Both parties recognize that the services to be rendered under this Agreement by Employee are special, unique and of extraordinary character. Either party may, at its option, terminate this Agreement or elect to institute and prosecute proceedings in any court of competent jurisdiction, either in law or equity, to obtain damages to enforce specific performance of the Agreement to enjoin the other party as appropriate and to recover reasonable attorneys' fees and costs of prosecuting such action in the event of the occurrence of any of the following:

i. If there is a substantial breach by either party of any of their terms and conditions of this Agreement (other than those set forth in paragraphs 5 and 6 herein), and such breach remains uncured after the expiration of sixty days from the date of receipt of written notice by other party, or

ii. If there is a breach by Employee of any of the covenants of paragraphs 5 and 6 of Agreement.

Termination for any cause shall not constitute a waiver of The Company's rights under paragraphs 5 and 6, nor a release of Employee from his or her obligation hereunder.

The rights and remedies provided each of the parties herein shall be cumulative and in addition to any other rights and remedies provided by law or otherwise. Any failure in the exercise by either party of its rights to terminate this Agreement or to enforce any provision of this Agreement for default or violation by the other party shall not prejudice such party's right of termination or enforcement for any further or other default or violation.

d. Collateral Agreements.

This Agreement constitutes the entire Agreement between the parties respecting the employment of Employee, and there are no representations, warranties or commitments, except as set forth herein. This Agreement may be amended only by an instrument in writing executed by the parties hereto.

e. Notices.

Any notice, request, demand or other communication hereunder shall be in writing and shall be deemed to be duly given when personally delivered to an officer of The Company or to Employee, as the case may be, or when delivered by mail at the following addresses:

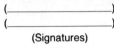

(Signatures)

4

BUYING A GOING BUSINESS

In my judgment, it would be a mistake to attempt to buy any going business without a good corporate lawyer's being thoroughly involved in the transaction, including the drafting of a complete purchase agreement. I will, therefore, devote only a little space to this subject.

WHAT ARE YOUR OPTIONS?

There are two basic ways to buy a going business. First, I will discuss the major alternatives, and then I will give you my personal preferences. To have a concrete illustration to work with, let us assume you want to buy a "home improvement center." It is now conducted in corporate form by a person you know. That person desires to retire, and no family members or employees are in a position to take over the business, so it is "for sale."

One way to buy the business is to *buy the stock* of the corporation. If you choose this route, you could accomplish the transaction by simply giving the seller a check for the purchase price in exchange for his or her shares of stock. Of course, you would want your lawyer to have analyzed the company first to make certain that there were no other shareholders, that the stock was not subject to any restrictions, and that, in general, there were no legal problems in the transaction. Your lawyer's job, however, would be relatively easy.

The other option is to *buy all the assets* of the company. Here, you would have to literally count all the pieces of lumber, hardware, etc., and make a *complete* inventory. Then you would have to assign a value to each item and total it up. Further, in the case of trucks or real estate, you would have to get the appropriate titles reissued in the name of your new corporation.

All other options you have for buying a going business are really variations on these two basic methods. You can pay the seller in *installments,* which may have attractive tax consequences. So long as the seller gets less than 30

65

percent of the sale price in the year of sale, the seller will only report the gain as it is received. Suppose you agree on an installment payment of 20 percent each year for 5 years. The seller reports only 20 percent of the gain in each year. That spreads the income and usually results in a lower tax. From your point of view, it is a method of financing and may have attractive cash flow benefits. The documents are important and complex—I definitely recommend having them drawn by a lawyer. There are many other variations, and a good corporate lawyer will discuss them with you. Remember, however, that it is your money and your business. *You* are entitled to a full explanation of all the alternatives. and *you* must make the decision as to which is best for you.

Which Option Is Best?

My general preference is to buy the assets of the corporation and not the stock. Here is why.

If you buy the stock of the corporation, you get the whole thing—whether you want it or not. Here are some of the things which you get.

1. Past federal income tax deficiencies.

2. Unasserted liability claims (product liability claims are an example —suppose someone was injured by a product purchased at the center but has not made a claim yet).

3. Unasserted claims involving employment discrimination, OSHA violations, environmental protection violations, and wage and hour violations.

4. A union contract which you might not want.

5. Unasserted claims for breach of contract.

To some extent, you can protect yourself from these things by having your lawyer do a good job in the legal audit, and by getting appropriate warranties from the seller. However, your protection is less than 100 percent.

Furthermore, if you buy the stock, you do not have any arm's length negotiations between you and the seller about the value of the assets used in the business and of the inventory. Therefore, the values are subjective. Your gain or profit or depreciation on those things is therefore subject to IRS examination and possible disagreement. The reason there is no arm's length negotiation is that the seller simply does not care how you allocate the purchase price; he or she gets the agreed-upon price for his or her *stock*. If the seller were selling assets, he or she would care about the allocation because *his or her* profit or gain would be based on that allocation.

EXAMPLE: Suppose you agree on a price of $100,000 for your home improvement center. If you have a stock deal, there is no need to have any allocations in the contract as to exactly what the $100,000 is for. The seller will have a profit—usually at capital gains rates—on the difference between the $100,-000 and his or her basis in the *stock*. You will have to allocate the purchase price among the various assets. Typically, the assets will include inventory, tangible property used in the business (e.g., trucks, machinery, etc.), and "goodwill." The seller does not care how you allocate the purchase price, so you would allocate a lot to inventory and the tangible property because this will reduce your future taxes. In the case of the inventory, it will reduce your "profit" when you sell it, and in the case of the assets, it will increase your depreciation. Goodwill is not depreciable, so you would allocate little if anything to that.

In an asset deal, however, the contract will call for the sale of each asset at a certain price. The seller's interest is adverse to yours. He or she will want a lower price for inventory and tangible assets. Because your interests are adverse, there will be bargaining, and in this kind of a situation, the IRS will almost always respect whatever values you finally agree to.

You may ask why in the world I would suggest you sit down with the seller and bargain about an allocation when you could simply avoid the problem by buying stock and making your own allocations.

The reasons are twofold. First, I think it is better to understand completely what you are buying and how much you are paying for it—item by item. Second, if you think the IRS is going to sit still for an unreasonable allocation, you are mistaken. Thus, your choice is not whether to bargain but whom you are going to bargain with—the seller or the IRS. I would choose the seller.

Another important factor is that in the asset deal, you list the assets you want, and they are what you get. You get assets, not a corporation. You form your own new corporation without any old tax deficiencies, unknown or unasserted liabilities, or other problems.

When Might It Be Better to Buy the Stock of a Company?

Sometimes it is better to buy the stock of the company rather than the assets. This will be the case when there are favorable corporate contracts which cannot be assigned. For example, suppose your home improvement center had a valuable distributorship contract for a popular line of hardware. Suppose further that the contract was not assignable and that when you went to the hardware maker to get a distributorship contract yourself, you were turned down. Your lawyer could probably structure the deal so that you would simply buy the stock of the corporation, and there would be no change whatsoever in the relationship between the center and the hardware maker.

A similar situation might be where the home improvement center had a very favorable long-term lease.

COMPLIANCE WITH THE BULK SALES ACT—AND ITS DRAWBACKS

In order for the asset deal to achieve the desired objective of insulating you from unknown liabilities, you must comply with the state *Bulk Sales Act.* These laws say that if you buy all the assets of a going business, you must tell the creditors about it. The creditors need to know because the minute you give the seller that check, all the business assets are liquid and the seller could skip town without paying the creditors. If that happens, and if you did not comply with the Bulk Sales Act, the law will allow those creditors to go after the assets even though you are the new owner.

On the other hand, telling all the creditors and suppliers about a change in the ownership of the business may not be a desirable thing. They might all cancel your credit lines or refuse to continue selling you the products you need. You have to carefully take this into consideration.

In summary, then, one cannot say that it is *always* best to buy assets rather than stock. One can say, however, that *buying assets is generally preferable* unless there is some clear reason not to. The lawyer will have to do a little more work in an asset deal because there are more documents. There must be a bill of sale, assignments of motor vehicles, rather elaborate schedules of the property transferred, and other mechanical details. However, this extra work is a good investment.

THE IMPORTANCE OF THE LEGAL AUDIT

Whatever form you use to buy an existing business, it is essential to have a thorough "legal audit" (of course, a financial audit is important, too). If you structure the transaction as an asset deal, you will minimize many problems, but you will not eliminate them. Some liabilities will "follow" the assets even if you have complied with the Bulk Sales Act. For example, some courts hold that the successor to a business is responsible for personal injuries caused by products made before the new owner took over. Sometimes taxing authorities can follow assets into the hands of a new owner. If there is a union contract in the picture, sometimes that cannot be left behind with the old owners. A thorough legal audit includes an examination of virtually all the important documents relating to a company and its business, and will point out all such potential problems. And, as a general rule, if you know about problems in advance, you and your lawyer can work around them. All potential problems should be taken into account when you are deciding how much to pay for the business.

WHAT ABOUT BUYING A BUSINESS WHERE THE SELLER STAYS ON TO HELP YOU?

One of the best ways to learn a business is to have the person who built it up show you. If it can be arranged, I like this kind of deals—*with some cautions.* Of course, the facts may not allow it. The reason the seller wants to sell may be because of ill health or another business venture which will take all his or her time. However, one possibility which is definitely worth your consideration is to ask the seller to stay for at least a limited time to help you. This has at least the following advantages:

1. Obviously, the seller knows more than you about all aspects of the business.

2. If the seller is going to be staying on, he or she is more likely to be candid and forthright in the negotiations than if he or she is going to take the certified check to the Caribbean the evening of the closing.

3. If problems come up, the seller's advice and counsel can be worth its weight in gold to you.

My only caution here is to *make sure* you spell out *exactly* what you expect of the seller and what the seller is committing to do. You need a contract of some type. It can be an employment contract, as discussed in Chapter 3, or a consulting agreement. Experience has shown that while this is a common and desirable arrangement, it can also produce a lot of conflict. That is why I recommend the carefully negotiated and discussed agreement. I think you should negotiate it yourself, if at all possible. Your lawyer may also be able to negotiate the deal. Perhaps your lawyer could even negotiate a better deal than you could. However, keep in mind that your lawyer is not going to have to work with and rely on this person during the crucial initial stages of the business. After you negotiate everything you can think of and are as clear as possible in your own mind about *exactly* what your relationship with the former owner is going to be, then have your lawyer draft the appropriate documents. Remember that this business may be almost like a blood relative to the former owner. The transition is likely to be traumatic. Someone else is now going to be coming into his or her business and calling all the shots. That is the biggest reason why you *need* a carefully drafted agreement to avoid trouble.

Making the salary or fees you pay to the former owner depend on the performance of the business gets mixed reviews from most counselors. On balance, I think a *fixed fee or salary* is best. The contrary argument is that a formula based on sales or profits gives the former owner an incentive to do a good job and give you good advice. If you do have some kind of formula agreement, however, what I said above about lawyers and the need for a full

and comprehensive agreement is doubled—and you should get the accountants in on the act too.

The former owner might offer to help you informally, with the value of
his or her services included in the cost of the company. This is because the
money he or she gets for the business will be taxed at capital gains rates,
whereas any consulting agreement or employment contract will give rise to
ordinary income. The only response you can give is no. In addition to the
obvious problems, there are *serious tax problems* for *you* in that kind of
arrangement. If some of the money you are paying the former owner is really
salary and you do not treat it as such, serious penalties can be assessed against
you.

WHAT ABOUT THE EMPLOYEES OF THE BUSINESS—SHOULD THEY GET EMPLOYMENT CONTRACTS?

This is a difficult question to answer in the abstract. My general preference
is *not* to have employment contracts unless there is a rather clear reason for
them. In the case of a former owner, there is a clear reason. In the case of
other key employees, there may also be compelling reasons. In fact, it may
turn out that one of the principal assets of the business is its people. In that
event, you will want to carefully consider employment contracts with the key
employees—as well as noncompetition agreements.

In summary, then, before you buy a going business be absolutely sure that
you have done all your homework. You are going to be spending a lot of
money all at once. There are many advantages to buying a going business,
but there are also a few disadvantages, and the large initial capital outlay is
one of them. All those little problems that come up one at a time when you
start a business from scratch may be presented to you all at once if you buy
a business that is already established. If you get a good corporate lawyer who
approaches the purchase of the business in a systematic way and who drafts
a comprehensive purchase agreement, not only will you be assured of a
relatively hassle-free transaction on the purchase itself but, more importantly,
you will have a sound base to continue that business in the future. Remember, also, that all the considerations we talked about at the beginning of the
book apply here. You still have to form the corporation and decide on the
capital structure, what kinds of stock you will have, and whether you elect
subchapter "S."

LEGAL FEES FOR BUYING A BUSINESS

Start out with the assumption that you are going to need the same legal help
to form the corporation and evaluate your alternatives as if you were starting
a business from scratch. That is a minimum of $300 for the smallest and

simplest deal and a maximum of $2,000 or so for one which is larger and a little more complicated. (Of course, I am talking here in very general terms and concentrating on *small* business.) Therefore, you have to remember that these fees are a baseline that you must work from. *Everything the lawyer does to help you in the actual purchase agreement is going to cost extra.* These transactions are too individual for me to provide a general cost estimate in this book. However, in a specific case, your lawyer should be able to give you an estimate.

I recommend against any percentage fees. Some lawyers like to charge a certain percentage of the sales price when they represent a buyer or seller of a business. I do not like those arrangements. Make your lawyer tell you exactly what he or she is going to do, how long it is going to take, and approximately what it is likely to cost. Drafting a purchase agreement can be either a big or a little job, depending on how you use your lawyer. If you are a poor negotiator and your lawyer is a good one, you want to use your lawyer for more than just legal help. I find this to be the case in many situations. On the other hand, if you feel that you are the best person to negotiate the deal, do not waste time and money by dragging the lawyer around to all the meetings. Do, however, make sure you get legal advice on important points before you start negotiating. Keep our example in mind. If you are going to negotiate the prices of the goodwill, assets, and inventory, you have to know which direction to push for. It is usually more complex than the simple example we are using, so I recommend careful discussions with your professional advisors before you start negotiating.

Do not try to save legal fees by not having a *complete* purchase agreement. Remember that your interests and those of the seller are different. The seller is going to get a certified check at the closing and has little use for any agreement. He or she takes his or her money and can disappear if he or she wants to. You have to live with the business and all its problems. *You are the one who needs the agreement.* The seller is likely to want to push for the simplest, quickest deal possible. *Slow down.* Do not let the seller talk you into buying the stock on a handshake. Buying a business is likely to be one of the most important investments you ever make, and it is foolish to try to save a few dollars of attorneys' fees here. The same is true for the legal audit. Let your lawyer do a good job for you.

5

FRANCHISING

If you want to start your own business, you have essentially three ways to do it: Start your own from scratch, buy one that is already established, or enter into a franchise agreement. There are a wide variety of franchise arrangements, and it is probably safe to say that just about any kind of usual business which you could either start yourself or buy is available in a franchise format from somebody. Of course, we all know about the typical examples—McDonald's, Howard Johnson's, Holiday Inn, Midas Muffler, all the gas stations, bookstores, and last but not least, print shops.

In 1980 there was a very important development in the law regarding franchising. The Federal Trade Commission announced a rule which said, in effect, that franchisors had to provide each franchisee with a booklet which explained all the important aspects of the franchise in plain English and gave the net worth and background of the franchisor. This ruling came about in response to widespread dissatisfaction among franchisees, who often felt they did not get what they bargained for from the franchisor. It was the old story of salespeoples' puffing. Franchises can be extremely lucrative things for the franchisor and are sold by sales representatives who are usually on commission. In the past, that situation made for some high pressure and a bit of abuse. Of course, the major companies such as McDonald's did a good job. On the other hand, there were a number of less reputable companies that did not do a very good job of telling the franchisees what they were going to get for their money. Many times, when the franchisees found out, they were extremely disappointed.

Now, however, by federal law, the franchisor must give you a document explaining all of the important things about the franchise. Federal law does not, however, require that you read it. You will also be given a copy of the franchise agreement. Likewise, federal law requires the franchisor to deliver a copy of it to you but does not require you to read it. Should you so desire, you are well within all your legal rights in simply believing everything the sales representative tells you, looking at the nice, pretty pictures he or she will give you and writing out your check without ever reading any of these documents or consulting your attorney. Obviously, I do not think this is a particularly desirable course of action, but history shows that it happens all the time.

WHAT IS A FRANCHISE?

As discussed in this chapter, a franchise is simply a license to use the trademark of the franchisor. In most cases, we are talking about a package deal, where the franchisor allows you to use its trademark, tells you how to set up and run the business, and gives you certain prescribed assistance, such as site selection and a model bookkeeping procedure you can follow. The franchisor sometimes also undertakes certain continuing obligations, such as advertising, training, quality control, and free business advice. Normally, the price for all this is a fixed fee *plus* a certain percentage of sales. I should add at this point, however, that there are many, many different types of franchise arrangements. We are only talking about the most typical format.

The franchisor usually retains some rights as to quality control and advertising (e.g., McDonald's food has to meet certain standards, and the Golden Arches trademark must be used at the location). However, you run the business. Typically, the franchisor is the helper and counselor, but you are the businessperson. The franchisor helps you reduce the risk of starting out in business yourself by providing you a tested and proven package. *However, a franchise does not guarantee success.*

WHY DO YOU NEED A LAWYER IN A FRANCHISE DEAL?

You need a lawyer in a franchise deal for two reasons. The first reason is that you probably ought to form a corporation for your franchise just as you would if you were developing the business yourself or buying a going concern. Everything we said about forming a corporation is equally applicable to going into business via the franchise route. The franchise arrangement typically will not say anything about the form in which you do business. That is up to you. You can use a sole proprietorship or partnership if you want to. The franchisor may advise you to form a corporation or to at least discuss the possibility with your lawyer, but the decision to do so and, of course, the actual mechanics and cost of accomplishing that are up to you. Further, such matters as thinning the corporation, electing subchapter "S," and providing buy-out arrangements if you have more than one shareholder are all your responsibility. The franchise arrangement deals with the business aspects of the deal (how to run that print shop, hotel, restaurant, etc.), not with general business-legal rules such as those involved in forming and operating any corporation.

The second reason why you need a lawyer in a franchise deal is that your first major transaction is going to be the execution of the rather elaborate and very important franchise agreement. The explanatory document the Federal Trade Commission requires is supposed to be written in plain English. It usually will be. You should not have any trouble understanding it if you take the trouble to read it. The actual franchise agreement, however, is another story. It is likely to be many pages of fine print together with a lot of legalese. Your lawyer can make sure that you understand exactly what the agreement says and does not say. You can match your lawyer's interpretation of the franchise agreement with the things the sales representative told you and make sure they square with one another. *You can also negotiate the franchise agreement.* Obviously, your flexibility in negotiating depends on the franchisor. In most situations you do have at least some bargaining position. If a clause in the franchise agreement is particularly burdensome to you or gives you some special problem, it is usually subject to negotiation. Your lawyer can both point out the problems and help you in the negotiation.

Keep in mind that the explanatory booklet required by the Federal Trade Commission is *only a disclosure document.* It only requires the franchisor to disclose the facts to you—it does not require that they be "solid" facts. If the franchisor is bankrupt or close to it, all it has to do is state its net worth in the disclosure statement. It is up to you to read that statement and understand what it means. Your lawyer can help you. Also, remember that our definition of a franchise included many undertakings on the part of the franchisor. It is up to you and your lawyer to make sure that you completely understand what the franchisor will and will not do, that your understanding is accurately set forth in the franchise agreement, and that you have some reasonable basis to believe that the franchisor will be around in the future to carry out its part of the bargain. The government will not help you on any of this—except to require the disclosure statement, which makes your job a bit easier.

FRANCHISE EXAMPLE

Let me give you a brief example of starting into the instant printing business by the franchise route.

Instant printing is usually started at one location—a typical storefront operation consisting of around 1,000 square feet of space and around $35,-000 worth of equipment. Most of the equipment consists of a printing press and a camera for making the offset plates which are used on the printing press. The typical franchise fee for this kind of instant print shop is about $50,000 and a percentage of your sales. For this, the franchisor will find a location for you, select all the equipment and install it, and train you in how to use it. The franchisor will also give you some training on how to keep an elementary set of books, how to advertise, who your customers might be, etc. In addition, you will get a trademark license to display the franchisor's name at your store. In short, the franchisor will assume that you know absolutely nothing about the instant printing business, nothing about how to operate the equipment, and nothing about how to keep books.

If you wanted to start a print shop without using a franchise, you would have to select the location, buy all of the equipment, and learn how to use it. Without counting the value of your time, we have already said that this would cost you about $35,000. Essentially, you can buy the equipment for just about the same price as the franchisor, and you can also finance it at just about the same rates as the franchisor. Indeed, the companies that sell the equipment will usually be happy to lease it to you and to give you some training on how to run it. When you are done, you have spent a lot of time, but you have saved about $15,000, and you do not owe any franchise royalties. However, you also do not have the right to display a franchisor's name, and you do not have anybody to call for help or advice for free.

The decision as to whether to go into business via a franchise or by yourself depends on how much you value what you get from the franchisor and how much the trademark is worth. Pursuing our print shop example, I am afraid that the trademark is not usually worth too much. Do you seek out a particular franchisee when you want instant printing? That leaves you with the other items. *Taken as a whole,* I think it is fair to say that they are worth the $15,000 and the percentage of sales. However, what if you already know how to operate printing equipment and where to buy it, and you know or can easily figure out how to keep books? Perhaps you have even worked in a print shop and know how and where to advertise. Then you start taking away from the benefits *to you* of the franchise, but you still keep that $15,000-plus-royalties price tag.

The decision of whether to start a business through the franchise route or go it alone is largely a personal one. The function of your lawyer should be to make sure you completely understand exactly what you will be getting so that you can make that personal decision based on your own needs and desires. His or her other function is to make sure that the documents you sign obligate the franchisor to do what is required.

In summary, then, make sure you take advantage of the federal laws which require you to receive a booklet describing the franchise in plain English. Study that book carefully, comparing it with the actual franchise agreement and discussing both of these documents with your lawyer to make sure you understand exactly what you are going to get for your money. Involving a lawyer in your franchise should not cost you a lot of money. Once you do all the homework by assembling these documents and explaining to your lawyer exactly what you want to do, he or she can review them rather quickly.

It should not take your lawyer more than a few hours to read these documents and make sure that you understand them completely. That is money well spent in a deal this size.

FRANCHISE DANGER POINTS

Remember that no lawyer can make a bad deal into a good one. Nor can a lawyer make a franchisor live up to the promises contained in a franchise agreement. Your lawyer can, of course, help you sue the franchisor if that becomes necessary, but that is not what you went into business for. In my experience, the biggest danger points in franchise deals are the following—most of which are only marginally "legal."

1. Franchisor either cannot or will not live up to the promise made during the sales pitch. There are two things you should do to minimize this problem:
   a. Read carefully the portion of the franchise disclosure statement which describes the net worth and experience of the franchisor. It may be that the people selling you the franchise have a net worth which is less than the market value of your home, and their experience in the business in question is extremely limited.
   b. Consult with other franchisees. Get their personal experiences as to how this franchisor has performed.

2. You don't make as much money as the franchisor said you would. Franchisors will almost always give you projections as to how much money you will make. They will state clearly that these are not guarantees and you may not make this much money. They will also state that you could make more. However, you will often fail to hear or understand these "qualifications," and when you do not strike it rich, you may tend to blame the franchisor. Of course, there are two sides to every story. I tend to think most of this problem is caused by false expectations which basically already exist in most people's minds and which the sales representative for the franchisor certainly does nothing to diminish. In short, make sure your expectations are reasonable. When someone comes to me with a proposed franchise deal and shows me projections, I carefully cross-examine that person as to their reasonableness. After we scrub these projections down, *I cut them in half.* The net effect of doing this is that it takes the franchisee twice as long as he or she projected to reach an "acceptable" level of profitability. That, in turn, raises the need for working capital and perhaps even living capital. While this is certainly not a "legal"

matter, I feel that making the client focus on this possibility and being certain that the client can make a go of the operation even on these reduced assumptions is a positive thing. If the client does not have enough working or living capital to succeed on the basis of my arbitrary halving of the assumptions, I counsel extreme caution.

3. You underestimate the amount of money you will have to spend to start the business. Typically, a franchise agreement will contain a listing of "all" the things you need to start your business. Hopefully, this list will clearly state exactly what the franchisor supplies as part of the franchise fee, and what you have to buy yourself—perhaps with the franchisor's assistance. This listing will, in most cases, be relatively complete and may make you feel that it is absolutely complete. When something additional comes along, you may feel that the franchisor has misled you. Again, this is a two-sided question. Any person who makes a list of "everything" needed to start a business thinking that the list will be 100 percent complete is just not being realistic. There are too many incidental or indirect items. You simply must realize this and make sure you have sufficient capital to take care of this common problem. However, you should also do everything possible to make the franchisor spell out everything you will need in the agreement. Just because you cannot be 100 percent accurate does not mean you should not come as close as you can. If you use my arbitrary halving technique mentioned above, this problem will not be too significant, because you will have allotted sufficient working or living capital to handle these unforeseen, and perhaps unforeseeable, items.

4. The fourth item, really a variation on the above, is that the franchisor does not do what the agreement provides *in the time provided.* This is another reason for my halving approach. However, it is *absolutely necessary* to make sure that your franchise agreement spells out not only exactly what the franchisor will do, but also when these things will be done and what your remedy will be if they are not done on time. This is a sensitive point. The franchisor will say, in essence, "Trust me." I would not do it. I have just seen too many problems resulting from such faith. Make the franchisor write up a timetable, and provide remedies for you if the franchisor does not make the deadlines. If you fail to do this, even my halving approach will not be sufficient. Things could drag out so long that a greater cushion would be necessary.

As you can see from this discussion, almost all of the franchise danger points involve a breach or possible breach of contract by the franchisor. If you have the agreement drafted and at least partially negotiated by your lawyer so that the franchisor knows you are represented by counsel, I think you can minimize these potential problems. If the franchisor is stretched for time and money—as many franchisors are—the franchisor will delay progress for you unless you are represented by a lawyer who knows your contractual rights and is prepared to insist on them.

I would like to conclude this chapter with a word about "pyramid schemes," because sometimes the purveyors of these schemes call them "franchises." They are not franchises. A pyramid scheme is a deal where your job is principally to get others involved. In its simplest form, it may give you the rights to sell a certain product in a certain territory and to franchise others to sell the product in that same territory. For example, you may have the rights to sell a certain kind of cosmetic in New York City and the rights to authorize others in that city. Typically, you will get a piece of the action in each franchise. Thus, if you are the first one on the pyramid, you can authorize some others, they can authorize others, etc. You get a fee for each one authorized and a percentage of everything he or she sells.

What makes this arrangement different from a reputable franchise system, such as Avon, is that you must depend on your revenues from the other franchises to make a profit. In a normal deal, you would make your profit from the sale of the product itself. Pyramid schemes are illegal in many states. How do you tell when you have an illegal and perhaps fraudulent pyramid scheme instead of a real franchise? You must investigate. The documents look very similar. A key danger signal is the representation that the right to sell other franchises in your territory is valuable. That is usually a sign of trouble.

Why are pyramid schemes illegal and fraudulent? It is simple arithmetic. Suppose you are the first franchise in New York City. In order to get your investment back, you have to sell two other franchises. They, in turn, must each sell two to get their money back, etc. Here is a brief progression of the number of franchises involved.

First layer (you)	1
Second Layer (your franchises)	2
Third layer	4
Fourth layer	16
Fifth layer	256
Sixth layer	65,536
Seventh layer	428,343,296

As you can see, even in New York City, the people in the fifth layer of the pyramid have a problem, and the people in the sixth layer must sell over two franchises to every man, woman, and child in the United States. Now you can say that this is their problem. However, we have made this a good deal for you by putting you on top of the pyramid. What if you are a few layers down?

The moral of this illustration is to be sure to read the federally required franchise statement. If there is none, pass the deal up.

6

PENSION, PROFIT SHARING, AND DEFERRED COMPENSATION PLANS

One of the truly great opportunities for tax saving through your corporation is the ability to establish a qualified pension and profit sharing plan. Here are the key benefits:

1. Your company can deduct the money it pays into the plan in the year in which the contribution is made.

2. The employees do not have to pay any tax on this money until they actually receive it—usually during retirement.

3. All the earnings from money while it is being held in the pension or profit sharing trust are tax-free.

Let us look at a simplified example to see how this works.

Suppose your company establishes a qualified profit sharing plan into which it contributes 10 percent of its aftertax profits every year. The percentage share which is attributable to each employee depends upon the employee's compensation. To make our case simple, let us assume you have four employees including yourself. You earn $60,000 and the others each earn $20,000. Suppose further that the contribution to the plan turns out to be $10,000 a year. When the company contributed the $10,000, it would have a tax deduction. Thus, its income tax would be reduced for that year. Assuming the company was in the 46 percent tax bracket, that is a saving of $4,600 for that year. Each employee's share depends upon his or her compensation, and since your compensation is half the total, 50 percent of that contribution belongs to you. The other 50 percent would be divided three ways among the other three employees. However, none of you have to pay any income tax on this amount, even assuming it is "fully vested," which means that employees are entitled to it even if they quit the company. Further, that

$10,000 contribution is going to be invested in some income-producing securities, and since the trust is tax-free, you can invest in high-income securities without worrying about paying tax. Thus, for example, you can invest in corporate bonds, which are currently paying in excess of 12 percent interest. That money can be compounded tax-free during the life of the trust without any income tax.

When an employee receives a distribution from the profit sharing plan (because the employee either quits or retires), a tax will be payable. However, if the distribution is on account of retirement, the employee may be in a lower tax bracket. If the distribution is in a lump sum, a special income-averaging rule is applicable so the tax bite is not as bad as it might otherwise be.

The ability to establish the so-called qualified plans is perhaps the single most important benefit of a corporation. You can form these kinds of plans even if you are the only employee.

There is, however, a very important problem. This highly beneficial income tax treatment is not given to you for nothing. There is a trade-off. It is a social as well as an economic one. Congress has decided that these kinds of benefits must be available to the employees as a whole, not just to yourself and the highly paid executives. Thus, in order to achieve these tax benefits, you must have a plan which satisfies numerous technical requirements designed to assure that substantially all the employees participate in the tax bonanza. Taking our example above, you could not have a plan that covered you as the $60,000 employee but eliminated the three $20,000 workers. That is the biggest problem in establishing one of these qualified plans. You have to decide whom you must cover and whom you want to cover, and then you have to see what kind of benefits are going to be available to you after you provide the necessary benefits to everybody else.

Obviously, the clear cases are easy to analyze. If you have a one-person corporation, there is nobody with whom you have to share the wealth, and you are absolutely foolish not to have one of these qualified plans. On the other hand, suppose that you run a business where you are really the only "majordomo" and you have 50 other employees. If you establish a qualified plan under these facts, you are going to have to provide benefits to a lot of people, and the percentage of the benefits directly attributable to you may be relatively small. Of course, there are two sides to the question: One is the actual economics and the other is the employee benefits side. You may need a profit sharing plan or a pension plan simply to recruit and keep good employees. The tax benefits may be secondary. However, my personal experience in the case of small businesses is that this is not the case. The owners of the business (and perhaps a rather close group of highly paid officers and family members) desire to have the major benefits. They are willing to share the benefits with the other employees only if it does not dilute their own benefits too much.

This is an exceedingly complicated subject, and I cannot deal with it adequately in this book other than to explain the very basic rules to you and to strongly suggest that you discuss this matter with your lawyer. I can say without much doubt that there will be some kind of plan which will provide you significant tax savings—even if it is only the individual retirement account which you establish personally.

WHY IS THIS SUBJECT SO COMPLICATED?

Here is a very brief and abbreviated review of the factors which make this such a complex area.

1. The social security system has grown to such an extent that your corporate and individual retirement plans—and even your disability and death benefits—*must* be coordinated with social security benefits. Those benefits, however, are difficult to determine unless you are close to retirement age. Further, social security is a politically sensitive issue. It would be foolish to assume that the entire system is going to go broke, but it would be equally foolish to assume that the system will be the same 20 years from now as it is today. Certainly, there will be changes of some sort, and they are out of your control.

   Most pension and profit sharing plans today must, as a matter of sound economics, be integrated with social security. This means that in some way, the wages covered by social security ($29,700 in 1980) give less benefits in the plan than wages over that amount. Thus, employees who make under this amount obtain limited benefits under the plan, and the more highly paid workers get larger benefits. Integration of the plan with social security means that you can usually design a qualified pension or profit sharing plan which provides a substantial portion of its benefits to you and your highly paid executives even though the plan may technically cover all your employees.

2. The number of "experts" in this field is astonishing. I went to a seminar on the subject sponsored by our local chamber of commerce and heard presentations from lawyers, accountants, actuaries, people from savings and loans, banks, insurance companies, brokerage houses, and consultants ranging from those who specialized in the entire area of retirement planning to those who limited themselves to one aspect, such as investment of the plan

assets. Each of them had some kind of ax to grind. They also, of course, had their personal preferences and biases. It is going to be very difficult for you to obtain a complete, unbiased, and accurate explanation of all your alternatives.

3. Whatever you do, it is likely to cost you quite a bit of money. Even a standard off-the-shelf or "prototype" defined benefit pension plan offered by a financial institution is likely to cost you $2,500 in fees by the time you get it instituted and about $1,000 a year in fees and costs to keep it going after that.

4. There is a bewildering array of different types of arrangements. I will list the basic ones for you, but you must keep in mind that there are *very many* variations.

The Profit Sharing Plan

A profit sharing plan is a system whereby a company puts in a certain amount of its *profits* into a trust. The employees as a whole share in the trust—usually in direct proportion to their salary. The example I gave above is typical, but there are a number of ways to divide the pot in a profit sharing plan. The key things which distinguishes a profit sharing plan from most other arrangements are the following:

1. Money must be contributed out of profits. If you do not make any profit, you cannot make any contribution.

2. You do not have to make contributions every year. You have much more flexibility in a profit sharing plan than in most other arrangements. If you make it big in one year, you can make a relatively large contribution, and correspondingly, if you have a bad year, there is no problem in skipping a contribution. Most plans provide for almost complete discretion in the amount of the contribution so long as it comes out of company profit.

Pension Plans

There are many different types of pension plans. In fact, the range of possible pension plans extends from only a slight variation on a profit sharing plan to something which is akin to a private social security benefit. Following are some of the major types of plans which I have seen used by small business.

1. *A money purchase plan.* In a money purchase plan, the company makes a defined contribution which, for example, can be a certain percentage of pay. The money then goes into a trust which is invested, just as in the profit sharing plan we talked about. While

there are no separate individual accounts, there is a separate individual accounting *system* whereby each individual is entitled to a certain amount. That amount, however, depends on the balance in the employee's account, which, in turn, is a function of the company contributions and the earnings of the money while it was in the trust. When an employee retires, he or she gets a benefit of whatever that amount will buy—hence, the name "money purchase." This kind of system is usually used in conjunction with an insurance company. The company pays its contribution to the insurance company, and when employees retire, they get an annuity based upon whatever their account will buy.

2. *A defined benefit pension plan.* The most typical pension plan in large companies—and the one which many smaller companies also use—is a so-called defined benefit plan. There are many ways to define the benefit, but the usual one is to define it as a certain percentage of the employee's salary. For example, an employee may have a benefit equal to 60 percent of his or her average salary for the highest 5 years. In order to provide enough money to pay the employee this benefit, you have to get an actuary to make numerous computations. The company then makes contributions into the pension plan which, according to the actuary's estimate, will assure that the plan has sufficient money when the employee retires to pay the benefits.

While there are many more types of plans available, my experience has been that a small business which operates in corporate form and which warrants a specifically tailored plan uses either the profit sharing plan, the money purchase pension plan, or the defined benefit pension plan. Special cases, however, dictate special plans, and that is why I strongly suggest you find and use a good consultant.

Prototype Plans

Many financial institutions, including banks, savings and loans, and brokerage houses, have already drafted a standard or prototype plan. All you do is fill in the blanks. Obviously, this saves a lot of money. To some extent, it decreases your flexibility, because the prototype plan only offers certain options. Nevertheless, for many small businesses, the prototype plan is the way to go. There is simply not enough money involved to justify having a team of lawyers and actuaries and accountants specifically design a plan for you. As a very gross generalization, I would say that if you have 50 employees or less, a prototype plan is best for you. On the other hand, if you have 50 employees or more, I would say that it would be worth your while to at least carefully consider a specifically designed plan which takes into account your particular circumstances—including most importantly the number of employees that you have, the salaries that they all make, and the kinds of benefits that you want.

EMPLOYEE RETIREMENT INCOME SECURITY ACT (ERISA)

In the mid 1970s, Congress became concerned about a number of abuses in private pension plans. Perhaps their most important concern was vesting. Some pension plans had very long and arbitrary vesting requirements. Vesting refers to the point in time at which the employee's interest in the plan belongs to the employee, even if he or she quits the company. If, for example, a company or union had a 30-year vesting plan and you worked 29 years and 9 months, you got nothing. This appeared to Congress to be extremely unfair. Accordingly, one of the important things Congress did in the pension reform legislation was to require that qualified plans had to have certain minimal vesting requirements so that this kind of thing did not happen.

These vesting requirements are important, because they present both problems and opportunities. While you must allow employees to have a vested interest in your plan at some relatively early date, there is still quite a bit of flexibility. For example, one of the vesting options for a pension plan is simply to have a full vesting after 10 years. This means that if most of your employees do not stick around for 10 years, they are never going to get any benefits from your plan. Similarly, you can have graduated vesting schedules, which can serve to increase your share of the pension and profit sharing pot. Keep in mind the distinction between pensions and profit sharing. In a profit sharing plan, if you have a lot of forfeitures—people who quit before they get a vested interest—you get a larger dollar distribution.

Returning to our first example, suppose that the three employees who made $20,000 a year did not stick around long enough to get a vested interest. In that case, you would obtain virtually 100 percent of all the contributions to the plan. In a pension plan, forfeitures operate to decrease the required contribution of the company. Thus, you do not get any more money yourself, but your company has to pay less money to fund your benefits. Because these vesting requirements are so important, I would like to spend a little time discussing them. Essentially, there are four different ways you can satisfy the vesting requirements.

1. The first test is the so-called 10-year vesting. Employees have a nonforfeitable interest in 100 percent of their benefits after 10 years of service.

2. The next test is the 5- to 15-year vesting. Employees have a

nonforfeitable interest in a percentage of their benefits no less than those provided below:

Years of Service	Percent of Benefits
5	25
6	30
7	35
8	40
9	45
10	50
11	60
12	70
13	80
14	90
15	100

3. Rule of 45. There are two parts to this requirement. The first part provides that a participant with 5 years' service must be vested in the following percentages as soon as the sum of the employee's age and years of service equals or exceeds 45:

Years of Service	Combined Age and Service	Percentage
5	45	50
6	47	60
7	49	70
8	51	80
9	53	90
10	55	100

In addition, any participant with 10 years of service must be vested as follows:

Years of Service	Percentage
10	50
11	60
12	70
13	80
14	90
15	100

4. Class year vesting. This is available for profit sharing and money purchase plans. The contribution for any given year must vest 100 percent no later than the end of the fifth plan year following the year of contribution. For purposes of vesting, a year of services consists of 1,000 hours of service during a 12-month consecutive period.

While there is a certain amount of flexibility in these vesting requirements, you must keep in mind the overriding philosophy on which they are based. The IRS is simply not going to allow you to gerrymander a plan so that you will wind up with all the money and the employees get nothing. Thus, it is important to use the above discussion only as a guide and to be sure to discuss vesting with your lawyer. In some situations, the IRS may insist upon a different and more stringent rule of vesting if that would be necessary in order to achieve what they believe to be the social objectives of these kinds of qualified plans. However, except in the case of the Simplified Employee Pension Plan noted below, you can always arrange some kind of vesting schedule which assures that only your relatively long-term employees will get substantial benefits, and which provides that forfeitures of the short-term employees go back into your pocket or your company's pocket one way or the other.

THE COVERAGE TESTS

I mentioned above that in order to obtain the benefits of a qualified plan, you had to cover all of your employees. This is an oversimplification, and I would like to discuss the rules so that you can discuss them with your counsel to make sure that you give appropriate attention to defining the exact group of people that you want to cover and what is permissible under the law.

There are two coverage tests, one objective and the other subjective. The objective test provides that a plan will cover enough people to be qualified if 70 percent or more of all employees are plan participants or if 70 percent or more of all employees are eligible to be participants and 80 percent of those eligible are actually participants. If you have only two people and both of them are covered, you have met any kind of test the IRS could possibly throw at you. You have 100 percent of your employees eligible, and 100 percent participate. Conversely, however, this objective test is very difficult to meet the minute you exclude anyone at all. Suppose, for example, that you have three employees and want to exclude one. There is simply no way you are going to meet this objective test.

In recognition of the fact that many companies simply will not be able to satisfy this objective criterion, the law contains a subjective test. This simply says that any plan that does not discriminate in favor of employees who are officers, shareholders, or highly compensated personnel will be acceptable. For example, if you have 100 employees, and 90 of them are members of the union and are covered by a union collective bargaining agreement containing a pension plan, you can almost certainly cover the remaining 10 in a pension plan even though that is only 10 percent of the employees. Similarly, a plan which covers only "salaried" people may be acceptable so long as it does not turn out that the only salaried people are shareholders or are highly compensated. The "salaried plan" is sometimes difficult to justify for small businesses. Keep in mind, however, that there is no harm in asking. If you can put together a reasonable story about whether your plan is qualified or not, you simply prepare a submission and file it with the IRS. If they say that your plan is qualified and issue a letter to that affect, that is all you need. Conversely, if you do not get the letter, you simply do not institute the plan. Qualified pension and profit sharing plans are areas where you should run *absolutely no risk.* No matter what kind of plan you have, you must file it with the IRS and obtain their letter of agreement that your plan is qualified. If you do not, you are asking for trouble, while if you do, your chances of running into any serious tax problems are almost entirely eliminated.

ERISA REQUIREMENTS

I mentioned above that ERISA (or the pension reform law) imposed an important substantive requirement for vesting. In addition, however, it imposed an extremely elaborate and burdensome set of other requirements which impose many financial and administrative obligations. For one thing, ERISA makes a company liable up to 30 percent of its assets for the payment of the pensions. Thus, for example, if you promise to pay certain pensions and then run into financial difficulty, your company (not just the pension trust and its assets) can be sued for up to 30 percent of the company's total assets to make good on those pensions. Further, there is substantial administrative work required by this law.

ERISA pension requirements apply most severely to the defined benefit plan. That is where the law wanted to step in, because sometimes employees would work for many years and obtain a vested interest in the pension plan only to find that the pension plan did not have any money to pay the benefits. Some published studies show that fewer companies are establishing defined benefit pension plans since the pension reform law was enacted. On the other hand, my interview with Mr. Robert Crump contained in Chapter 16 shows that, at least in his practice, the pension reform law has not curtailed qualified benefit plans. I think that this means there are still *many situations* where a good benefit plan lawyer or consultant can structure good plans. However, it is not quite as easy as it used to be, and it does require expert help. Also, I strongly recommend that you be sure to understand exactly what your requirements will be under ERISA if you decide to undertake one of these arrangements. Make sure your lawyer explains them fully, including the costs, headaches, and liabilities. In some cases, you may find that ERISA considerations tip the scales toward a profit sharing plan and away from a defined benefit pension plan.

ERISA also raises the specter of *personal liability* for mismanagement of plan assets and makes it extremely difficult to insulate yourself from that possibility. In my own judgment, this problem is overblown by many commentators. If a small business selects a qualified trustee (i.e., a bank or insurance company), I think it is unrealistic to assume that beneficiaries of the profit sharing plan would be successful in a suit against the plan administrators (the company or its employees) based upon an allegation that the investment performance of the profit sharing trust was not what it should have been. So long as you are willing to run your business and let the management of the pension plan assets be done by a reputable financial institution, I do not think this is a real problem, but if you should want to dabble in the investments yourself, you *must* obtain thorough legal advice beforehand.

SIMPLIFIED EMPLOYEE PENSION PLANS

After Congress enacted ERISA, there was a hue and cry from small businesses to the effect that the law had simply put them out of the pension plan business. There was simply too much paperwork, headache, and increased potential liability for a small business to justify a pension plan.

In response to this criticism, a so-called simplified employee pension plan was developed. A very brief discussion of a simplified employee pension plan makes it sound like just the thing for small business. However, when I tell you what the rules are, I think you will agree with me that it may not be as useful as it sounds.

Establishing a simplified employee pension for your employees would be extremely simple. In fact, most banks can do it for you in a few minutes. In essence, it is a "group/individual retirement account." Each employee has his or her own account, and the advantage over an individual retirement account (discussed below) is that the maximum contribution that the employer can make to this account is $7,500 or 15 percent of the employee's compensation. (In contrast, the maximum amount employees can contribute to their own individual retirement account is only $1,500 or 15 percent of compensation.) Thus, for example, if you wanted to establish a pension plan for your employees and you did not want to go through all the hassle and paperwork involved in ERISA, you could establish a simplified employee pension plan and contribute 15 percent of each employee's contribution into the plan (up to the $7,500 maximum) and thereby eliminate almost all the problems that ERISA would impose upon you if you established a "normal" pension plan with the same 15 percent contribution. Further, you would get all the tax benefits. You could deduct the contribution in the year you made it. The employees would not have any tax obligation until money was withdrawn. In the meanwhile, all earnings on the money would be tax-free. Following, however, are some limitations on this plan which, in my judgment, make it potentially undesirable.

First of all, the employee's contribution vests immediately. Thus, for example, someone who works for you for only 3 years has a 100 percent vested interest in all the contributions you made to this plan. Pension plans should not operate this way. Pension plans should provide benefits for people who have worked for the company for some respectable period of time. I certainly agree with the ERISA vesting requirements described above. I think you will also agree that employees who work a relatively long time are entitled to at least some benefit. On the other hand, to say that an employee who works for you 18 months is entitled to 100 percent vesting in his or her pension contribution is, I think, unreasonable.

The frosting on the cake comes, however, in the requirement that *all* employees must agree to have these accounts. If only one employee does not go along with the program, the whole thing is sabotaged for the rest of the group. Even in the closest of closely held corporations, this is an unacceptable risk.

INDIVIDUAL RETIREMENT ACCOUNTS

Individual retirement accounts are an extremely good idea. An individual retirement account is, as the name implies, an individual deal. The company has nothing to do with it. The employees (assuming they are not covered by a company pension plan of any type) simply establish *their own* account into which they contribute a maximum of 15 percent of pay up to $1,500 per year. The *employee gets a deduction for this amount.* Moreover, the deduction is "above the line," so even if the employee does not itemize deductions, his or her taxes are still reduced. Furthermore, interest or income on this money is tax-free until it is withdrawn. There is no requirement that all employees have such an account—it is *entirely* an individual's decision.

IRAs are extremely simple. You can walk into any large brokerage house or bank and set one up in half an hour. You can tell your employees about it so that they can have their own pension plans themselves. There are no administrative costs. There is, of course, one very important drawback, and that is the ridiculously low $1,500 maximum. So long as the employee is young, it is possible to accumulate quite a bit of money. Furthermore, in the situation of a married couple with both people working, you can double this amount to $3,000 per year so long as the spouse earns enough to justify the contribution. $3,000 per year compounded for 25 years at 10 percent interest is about $325,000, and that does provide a good supplement to retirement. On the other hand, if you are older and do not have that long a time to build up the money, an individual retirement account may not be the most appropriate thing for you. One possibility is to start out using individual retirement accounts during the early days of your business when you do not have enough money to justify large contributions and do not have that high a salary where the $1,500 limitation would be a problem. Later, you can simply shift to a qualified pension or profit sharing plan.

To conclude this chapter, I would like to repeat the observation that pension and profit sharing plans are perhaps the most desirable benefits you get from incorporating your business. The only problem is that they are so complex that it is difficult to know how to take advantage of them in an economical and an efficient way. Also, there are so many pitfalls that if you do not do it right, you can be saddled with expensive and burdensome programs. I therefore strongly recommend that you do take advantage of the laws relating to qualified pension and profit sharing plans in some way, but that you also go slowly and obtain good-quality advice along the way.

As a lawyer, I am probably biased, but I believe that you will get good advice from your lawyer. Remember, lawyers do not really have any *products* to sell. Banks, insurance companies, brokerage houses, and savings and loans do have "products," and they will undoubtedly be pushing them, at least to some extent. On the other hand, those people who do have a "product" are not going to charge you for their time. I therefore recommend that you start with the companies that have the "product" and get all the information you can from them. At that point, after you have gotten all the free information you can, you should consult your lawyer to refine that information and see which, if any, of it would be useful to you.

As a final note, remember that one of the biggest advantages of pension and profit sharing programs is the tax-free accumulation of money over a period of years. These years slip away. There is a premium on doing something soon. The key is not to let your haste lock you into a program which is not right for you.

7

YOUR PAYROLL

One of the first things you will have to do when you start your business is to set up a payroll. Any corporation must do this even if it has only one employee. This can appear to be a formidable task at first, but it is really rather easy because most of it is mechanical. However, your payroll does have some important legal implications, which will be discussed in this chapter.

If you have an accountant, many of the processes described in this chapter will be taken care of in the accountant's normal procedures. Accountants are just as good and efficient at setting up a payroll as lawyers are about forming corporations. It is an easy and routine job. The accountants will usually be of less help, however, on ensuring compliance with the wage and hour laws. It is not difficult and there is a lot of good help available from the various government agencies. Very briefly, here are the things you have to do to set up a payroll.

1. Get the federal income tax package of materials which explains about *withholding* and payment of *social security* and *federal unemployment* taxes.

2. Get applicable *state* or *local* income tax forms which explain about withholding for those taxes.

3. Make sure each employee is covered by *workers' compensation* insurance.

4. Make sure you have filed appropriate forms for *state unemployment compensation*.

5. Make sure you understand and abide by the *wage and hour* laws.

FEDERAL INCOME TAX

You have an obligation to withhold federal income tax from employees' wages according to prescribed charts. These provide exact amounts that you have to withhold according to the number of dependents the person claims and the amount of money he or she makes. All the charts and tables will be included in the package that the IRS gives you, and they are not hard to understand. You also have to withhold from each employee's wages a proper amount for social security (FICA), and you have to match that amount yourself. In addition, you have to withhold from the employee's wages an amount equal to 3.4 percent of the first $6,000 of compensation for federal unemployment tax. This amount, however, can be affected by state unemployment taxes. If there is a state unemployment compensation tax, it will be deducted from the federal unemployment tax. Payroll taxes present two potential legal difficulties which I would like to discuss.

The first problem is the withholding—and the fact that you are holding the government's money. The tax procedure requires you to deposit taxes you withhold from your employees fairly promptly. The exact times depend on how much money is involved—usually you must fork over the money within three banking days. This is a sensitive point with the IRS. Payroll taxes are not the place to delay payments. The IRS will assess penalties. Further, if you "borrow" some of this money for your own use, the IRS will get very mad and is likely to attach your bank accounts.

The second problem is that you and your employees will be tempted to try to find ways around these payroll taxes. There is certainly nothing wrong with doing this so long as the ways you select are legitimate. If they are not, however, you are asking for trouble. Here are some of the many ways *not* to try to avoid payroll taxes.

1. Paying people in cash instead of by check.

2. Paying wages to someone else besides the person working—such as an elderly relative or child—so as to avoid reporting taxable income for that person.

3. Trying to treat an employee as an "independent contractor" without any justification, thereby avoiding all withholding.

Both you and the employee have a common interest—reducing taxes. However, this does not mean you have a common interest in fraud—and that is what some of these things amount to. Be careful to avoid going too far in minimizing payroll taxes.

On the other hand, payroll taxes are something to be concerned about, and they can be avoided or minimized by a little planning. Secretarial work is a good example with which to illustrate the problems and opportunities. Let us assume you need a secretary for about 20 hours a week. You have at least the following options:

1. Use a temporary help service. They will provide you with the secretary and you will pay them. They will take care of all the payroll taxes, withholding, workers' compensation, and other requirements, but you will, of course, have to pay a higher rate for the secretary. The temporary help service will want to make a profit, so you will be paying not only the cost of the employee and these miscellaneous payroll costs, but a profit to the temporary help service as well. Generally, temporary help services are worth the money for unusual situations (peak workloads, etc.), but for an ongoing arrangement they may be less than optimal.

2. You can hire someone and put him or her on your payroll. You then pay his or her wages, take care of all the payroll matters mentioned in this chapter, and give that person a W-2 form at the end of the year reflecting his or her wages. The disadvantages to this are at least the following:
   a. The incidental payroll costs are relatively substantial.
   b. Having the person technically on your payroll may cause you other expenses in terms of hospitalization, life insurance, pension, or profit sharing, etc. This depends on your company and how you have drawn up these benefit plans—or indeed whether you have any of them.

3. If your secretarial requirements permit having the work done off your premises, you could hire a secretary as an independent contractor and pay him or her an agreed-upon rate—hourly, weekly, based on quantity of work done, or any other formula—without any withholding. This *could* be beneficial to both of you. The secretary would, of course, have to pay a self-employment tax, but that is slightly less than the combined total of the employee and employer contributions under the normal social security tax. The secretary would also have to pay the same federal and state income taxes, but that would not be your obligation. Also, if the secretary was working, for example, in an office at home specifically devoted to income-producing activity, he or she would be able to claim significant additional income tax deductions which are not available to regular employees.

It is important to note that the net payroll tax savings in the above arrangement are rather small. The only way you and the secretary can save a lot of money is for the secretary not to report the income. That is fraud, and that is what you must stay away from. This brings us to the following methods, which are definitely illegal and which have the potential for causing you serious problems if the IRS finds out about them.

1. You have the secretary work on your premises, under your direction and control, but call him or her an independent contractor. That is not right. It is not even a close case, and the IRS will assess *you* penalties.

2. You have the secretary work off premises—perhaps even while working for other employers—but you pay the secretary with cash and simply put the item under "Miscellaneous" on your books. That is close to fraud. The IRS could very well say you were involved in a conspiracy with the secretary to avoid federal income taxes, and that is a serious matter.

3. You pay the secretary with a check, but fail to report the payments to the IRS on the appropriate form 1099, pursuant to an agreement with the secretary that you will not report the matter. That is fraud, too—it will make the IRS very mad if they find out.

Without wanting to belabor the point, I think you can see that you are risking *big trouble* for a relatively *small benefit*. If you want to treat people who are working for you as independent contractors, make sure the arrangement is at least arguably legitimate, and above all, make sure you pay the person with a check and report the payments on form 1099.

WORKERS' COMPENSATION

I have included workers' compensation under the payroll chapter simply because, as a mechanical matter, the way you pay workers' compensation premiums is usually to calculate your payroll, apply the percentages given by the state workers' compensation authority for the occupations in question, and send that money to the appropriate place.

Workers' compensation laws are *state* laws, and they differ rather widely among the states. In some states there is only one official state workers' compensation bureau, and you have to deal with it for all matters including payment of premiums. In many other states there is more flexibility. The program is still a "legal" one with a lot of legal implications, but private insurance carriers are allowed to actually handle the insurance portion. In some cases, you can even self-insure, but that is usually an option only for large companies.

There are, however, some common denominators to workers' compensation matters, and they involve legal risks which will be described here in some detail. I will be discussing Ohio laws, but the problems and advice would be essentially the same in most other states. For specific advice, you should touch base with your lawyer.

Workers' compensation was probably the first "no-fault" insurance program. It removes fault as a criterion for an award. Injured workers are entitled to medical care and replacement of a portion of their lost wages for any work-related injury without regard to any negligence either of the employee, the employer, or any fellow worker. *Conversely—if you are not protected by workers' compensation insurance, you enjoy no such immunity.* That, then, is the biggest problem. Make *absolutely sure* that all the workers in your facility are covered so that if they are injured on the job, they cannot sue you and recover those large personal injury awards. Here is a brief rundown of the most troublesome areas.

- "Normal" employees should not present any problem so long as you file the appropriate forms and keep the appropriate records as called for by your state system.

- Employees of other people working on your facility can present a problem—e.g., a painter who is painting the outside of your building. You obviously do not cover them because they are not on your payroll. What if their own employer does not cover them either? You *could* have *serious exposure.* Ohio law imposes responsibility for workers' compensation not only on the employer but on anyone contracting with an employer who does not comply. Thus, if the painter did not have workers' compensation insurance, and he or she fell off a ladder and was injured on your job, *you* could be sued. *Moral:* Make sure *everyone* working on your premises is covered, not just your own employees. The usual way to do this is to make sure you include in your contract with painters, repair people, etc., a provision which requires that they have coverage. If they are small operations with doubtful financial resources, you probably should go further and require them to actually *furnish evidence of coverage to you.*

- People who may come in to your plant informally to help out with a project are also a source of difficulty. If you actually get the person's name on the payroll—even if he or she only works one day—that is all right. However, putting someone on the payroll for a single day is cumbersome, so you may want to have some other arrangement. For example, suppose one of your employees is assigned to do a large project over a weekend and wants to have a friend come in to help. The friend would not be put on the payroll; the employee would simply turn in twice as many hours as really worked and turn over half the pay to the friend. You may find this attractive for a number of reasons, the simplicity and lack of paperwork being the most important. However, I recommend against it because of the workers' compensation problem. You have someone working in your facility who is not going to be covered. If he or she is injured, you may become involved in a very large lawsuit. Instead, use a temporary help service. They will take care of all the paperwork and make sure everyone is covered by the necessary insurance. They will even let you pick the person. You will be charged a percentage (about 25 percent) of the person's salary. It may cost you a few dollars more, but I think it is well worth it.

- What about other insurance? Won't your normal liability insurance cover this kind of thing just as if the person were a visitor? *Maybe not.* In Ohio, for example, if someone *should* be covered by insurance and is *not,* no other insurance can be called upon to pay the claim. That is because Ohio has a state system, and no private insurance coverage can be used to pay claims which should be dealt with by the system. Your state may have similar rules; consult your insurance advisor to make sure. It depends on two factors—the state law and your particular insurance coverage.

Workers' compensation is big business. There are many lawyers who specialize in representing injured workers before the relevant authorities to get the maximum amount possible out of the system. As in any other insurance program—especially one involving something as subjective as disability —there are gray cases. There is also fraud. When I worked for a large multinational corporation, our payroll people told me that they were able to save *millions* of dollars by hiring expert firms and consultants to monitor workers' compensation claims in various states to make sure that only proper and legitimate claims were paid—and then only in proper and legitimate amounts. As a small company you will not have this big a problem, but the theory must be kept in mind: *Workers' compensation is no free lunch.*

Most states use a system where all companies are *experience-rated.* The state fund computes your premium by multiplying your total payroll for a given job classification by a factor which represents the general or industry-wide rate of hazard *and* a special factor for your own company which represents *your own claim experience.* The possible premium range is large. If you assume, for example, that a given job represents a certain *general* hazard and would generate $1 of premiums without experience rating, experience rating can affect your premium by a factor of 85 percent either way. That means the premium could be reduced to 15 cents or increased to $1.85. It is easy to see how a good safety program to reduce accidents and a good program to monitor your workers' compensation could pay handsome dividends.

UNEMPLOYMENT COMPENSATION

Unemployment insurance is also a creature of state law. Generally, it is mandatory and provides that if someone gets laid off for lack of work or fired without just cause, he or she can get unemployment benefits in the amount provided by state law. In Ohio, that is roughly half of what the worker earned, with a maximum benefit payable of about $175 a week for someone with three or more dependents. The benefits can last as long as 26 weeks. This too is somewhat experience-rated. Employers who fire people more often, or have layoffs more often, pay a higher percentage of payroll as the premium. The same cautions are appropriate here as for workers' compensation. You have to keep in mind that it is not a free lunch, and if you try to be too nice, it is probably going to cost you money.

Unemployment compensation problems usually deal with whether a person is entitled to a benefit. If someone is fired for proper cause, or quits without proper cause, he or she is not entitled to unemployment benefits. Exactly what is "proper cause" is subjective, and that is where the problem is. As you might expect, the law is heavily weighted in favor of the worker. Ohio, for example, even pays unemployment to people out on strike! Nevertheless, when someone applies for unemployment, the employer will be notified and given the opportunity to contest payments. This is a rather minor problem. Unlike workers' compensation, there is no possibility for huge awards against you. It is only a matter of a few dollars more or less on your premium, and for a small company it usually is not worth hiring a lawyer to contest a claim. You might simply write to the relevant state authority yourself and tell your side of the story. If that does not work, you may just have to forget about it.

OVERVIEW OF WAGE AND HOUR LAWS

This section will discuss the basic requirements of the federal wage and hour laws. This is a very simplified discussion because the laws themselves are lengthy, technical, and complicated. However, in most cases, the actual requirements you have to comply with are relatively straightforward.

One of the difficulties in summarizing the wage and hour laws is that there are two parallel—but somewhat different—sets of rules: one for businesses which are engaged in selling products or services to the government and one for all other businesses. Essentially, the differences are in overtime pay and minimum wage requirements. In private industry The Fair Labor Standards Act requires overtime pay only for hours worked in excess of *40 hours in one week.* For government contractors, the Walsh-Healey Act requires overtime pay for hours worked in excess of *8 hours per day.* The Fair Labor Standards Act establishes fixed minimum wages for all workers, and the Walsh-Healey Act establishes minimum wages which are fixed periodically by regulation and which depend on comparable pay in private industry in similar jobs and similar locations.

The following are the important requirements of the wage and hour laws which small businesses should keep in mind.

1. The law requires certain *minimum wages* to be paid to all covered workers.

2. The law requires overtime to be paid for hours worked in excess of 40 hours per week—or 8 hours per day in the case of government contracts.

3. The law provides rules on when employees must be paid for commuting or other travel time, as well as when compensable work time starts and stops.

4. The law imposes restrictions on the employment of minors and people doing work for the company in their own homes.

5. The law imposes restrictions on the amounts of wages which may be garnished.

The first thing you should do as a business owner is to determine if the wage and hour rules apply to you. Therefore, the first thing I will discuss is the exemptions. After that, I will very briefly discuss each of these requirements.

Exemptions from Minimum Wage Requirements

Perhaps the most important exemption from the wage and hour rules is for businesses whose total annual sales are less than $250,000. There is an additional requirement that the business be engaged in interstate commerce, but almost any kind of activity has been held to satisfy this requirement. The only portion of the exemption you can use for planning purposes is the $250,000 test. If you are in the business of operating a retail or service establishment, the limits are higher: $325,000 beginning July 1, 1980; and $362,500 beginning January 1, 1982. If you are engaged in the laundry or dry cleaning business or the construction business, there is no dollar minimum. You will be covered by the wage and hour laws if you are engaged in interstate commerce, and that includes just about everyone. There are special rules for tipped employees. Essentially, these provide that if an employee receives more than $30 a month in tips, up to 40 percent of the tips can be counted against the minimum wage requirement.

Whenever you want to rely on an exemption from this or any other law, I think you should take some extra steps besides just reading a summary of the law yourself and deciding that you are exempt. Those extra steps include, at a minimum, getting a complete copy of the law and regulations, carefully reading them, contacting the local office of the government agency in charge of enforcing the law, and discussing your exemption with the people there and being sure they agree. Remember that these federal statutes have serious penalty provisions. If you make a legitimate mistake, and if you can show you were reasonable in your actions (such as by a discussion with someone in the government agency or your lawyer) your penalties will likely be very small. Conversely, if the government thinks you deliberately did not comply with the wage and hour law—or any other law—the penalties will be much more severe. Also, remember that if you choose the route of going to the government agency yourself, you have to be completely honest and disclose all the relevant facts. You must also make a careful record of what you said, what the person you talked with said, whom you talked with, and what information you provided him or her.

In addition to the general exemptions from the wage and hour laws, there are several specific exemptions *from the minimum wage rules only* which apply to certain special cases. However, these exemptions require specific permits or approvals from the government. You cannot just assume that they apply even if you meet all the criteria listed below, and even if you have discussed the exemption with the government or your counsel. These exemptions are:

1. *Learners* can be paid less than the minimum wage if the Department of Labor approves the program. Many industries have learners' programs. The requirements and the amounts that have to be paid differ. Office and clerical jobs *do not* qualify.

2. *Apprentices* can be paid less than the minimum wage. There are special regulations. Apprentices differ from learners in that apprentices are in a training program for a skilled job.

3. *Handicapped* people can be paid less than the minimum wage under certain rather formal and approved arrangements.

4. *Full-time Students* may be employed at less than the minimum wage in retail or service establishments, and in colleges if the Department of Labor finds that employment at the lower wage is

necessary in order to prevent curtailment of opportunities for employment.

The key thing to remember if you think one of these exemptions might apply to you is that you need specific advice and approval from the Department of Labor—Wage and Hour Division. First, get their publications describing the general rules, and then go and talk with them to see what specific rules might apply to your situation. Your lawyer can do this for you, but there is generally no reason why you cannot do it yourself.

Minimum Wages

The minimum wage requirements are fairly straightforward. They provide that, with the exceptions noted above, you must pay a minimum wage to all your employees—currently $3.35 per hour.

The minimum wage requirements for government contractors are not so straightforward. First of all, you must decide which statute is applicable. This will usually depend on the kind of work being done. The applicable statutes include the following:

1. The most widely applicable statute is the Walsh-Healey Act. The requirements of this statute will be covered in this chapter.

2. The Davis-Bacon Act covers minimum wages paid to workers engaged in public works contracts. This act is usually applicable in the construction industry.

3. The Service Contract Act covers workers employed by government contractors and subcontractors who provide services to the United States.

Unfortunately, the technical requirements of each of these laws differ, and space does not permit a complete listing of all the requirements of each act. However, the general thrust of the minimum wage laws for government contractors is that there are no set minimum figures in the statute. Instead, the minimum wages are fixed periodically by the administrative agency and published in the Federal Register. Further, the minimum wages are different in many cases, depending on the industry and the geographic location. The following section of the Walsh-Healey Act states the general principle:

All persons employed by the contractor . . . will be paid . . . not less than the minimum wages as determined by the Secretary of Labor to be the prevailing minimum wages for persons employed on similar work or in the particular or similar industries . . . currently operating in the locality.

Overtime

The general rule regarding overtime is that a company must pay workers one and one-half times their regular rate for hours worked in excess of 40 hours per week (or 8 hours per day in the case of government contracts). The trouble comes in defining "regular rate."

"Regular rate" is *not* necessarily the normal hourly rate at which people are paid, nor even their hourly rate computed by dividing their weekly salaries by the number of hours actually worked. In most cases, either of the above would be approximately right but not necessarily absolutely correct. While the Fair Labor Standards Act speaks in terms of hourly rate, it is not necessary to pay workers on an hourly basis; they can be paid weekly, daily, twice a month, monthly, or at whatever other period suits the employer. However, for purposes of computing their regular rate, the whole thing must be factored down to an hourly figure.

Another problem in the overtime area is deciding exactly who is covered. The Fair Labor Standards Act and the Walsh-Healey Act contain the concept of "exempt" and "nonexempt" employees, and it is only the nonexempt group which must be paid overtime. Exempt people include the administrative, executive, and professional employees; nonexempt people include the hourly employees and the salaried people who do not meet the requirements of being exempt. It is easy to get into considerable legal difficulty by failing to pay overtime to people whom the company thinks are exempt but who are later termed nonexempt after analysis of their duties. Typically, the problem will arise when someone who has been classified as exempt either becomes disenchanted or gets fired and sues for back pay. The court or the Department of Labor will then conduct an elaborate analysis of the person's duties to ascertain whether he or she was in fact exempt. If the conclusion is no, the company will have to make up for any lack of overtime pay. In larger cases involving many employees, the Department of Labor may itself institute suit. The concepts of regular rate and exempt versus nonexempt employees deserve further elaboration because these are the cornerstones of the wage and hour laws.

Regular rate

The employee's regular rate is the basis for computation of overtime pay and is, therefore, very important. The trouble usually comes in nonstandard payments. Beginning with simple examples, an employee who is paid a certain amount per hour for a normal work week and receives no other form of compensation would have a regular rate equal to this hourly rate. Similarly, a salaried secretary who works 40 hours a week would have as a regular rate the weekly pay divided by 40 hours.

The trouble will come when some nonstandard payment is made either in the form of cash or otherwise. The regular rate includes *all* of the employee's compensation, not just the base compensation. Thus, if the employees are paid a bonus in addition to the weekly or hourly rates, this bonus would have to be factored into the employee's regular rate. For example, suppose that a company decided to institute an incentive program and pay all the workers a bonus of $25 per week if the company made certain sales or profit levels for that week. In that case, the $25 bonus would have to be cranked into the regular rate, and if an employee worked overtime, his or her overtime pay would have to be based upon the regular rate which was augmented by that bonus. Thus, the employer would be in a position of having paid what it thought was a legitimate bonus, only to find out that it must recompute every nonexempt employee's wage and make an additional payment to those who might have worked overtime during the relevant period.

Fortunately, there are a number of statutory exclusions which minimize this problem. Bonuses seem to present a frequent problem. In order for a bonus to be excluded, it must be either *truly discretionary* or part of a standard profit sharing plan. The typical incentive bonuses, which are based on profits, production, etc., do not qualify under either exclusion. However, it should be observed that even if the bonus is not exempt, if it is computed as a *percentage of pay* rather than a per capita amount or a fixed amount based on some other factors, the overtime problem will automatically take care of itself because, in essence, the pay on which it is based will already have had the overtime pay included so the bonus will be increased by the proper amount. Thus, in the case of a bonus, if it is based on a percentage of pay, there will generally be no problem, but if it is not, either it must fall into one of the exemptions or overtime pay must be recomputed.

A *purely discretionary* bonus is not included in the employee's "regular rate," but the Department of Labor takes a rather restrictive view of what is purely discretionary. Christmas gifts or Christmas bonuses which are not based on hours worked are also not included in the employee's regular rate.

In summary, then, the red flag here ought to be a bonus of any type. If it is a *purely* discretionary bonus or simply a modest Christmas gift, there is no problem. On the other hand, if you try to gear the bonus to the employee's production or the company's output, you must make sure either that the bonus is calculated as a percentage of pay or that you have taken this overtime problem into account. If you do not, your exposure could be quite high, because a worker or the Department of Labor could cause you to recompute all your calculations for the last 2 years and make up any differences. In cases where your operation has been running on a substantial overtime basis, this can generate a lot of money.

Informal arrangements for time off

Another danger point in The Fair Labor Standards Act is informal arrangements for time off. A small business, for example, may have a policy that an employee who wants a day off can simply take it and make up the day some other time. One well-publicized case reported in *The Wall Street Journal* involved a small store in New England where the proprietor allowed employees to take time off during the summer and during hunting seasons on the informal understanding that they would make up the days some other time. The employees were simply paid a weekly salary and there was no deduction for the time they took off, nor any addition to their pay for the weeks in which they worked an extra day. The Department of Labor, quite correctly under the law, said that this was improper. The employer was under no duty to dock the workers when they missed a day, but when they made up that day the employer was under a duty to pay time and a half. Therefore, during the weeks the employees worked an extra day, they should have been paid time and a half for that extra day.

The aspect of this case which made it so bizarre, and the point which you should keep in mind, is that the Department of Labor took this position in spite of the fact that virtually all the employees of this company told the Department of Labor they did not want to do it that way. They wanted to have the informal arrangement where they could negotiate with the boss to take a day off and make up the time later. They did not want to be docked during the week they took the day off, and they did not want time and a half when they made the time up.

All this, however, was to no avail. *The Department of Labor says that employees cannot waive their rights under the Fair Labor Standards Act.* If this were not the rule, employers might pressure the employees to sign waivers of their rights, and this would frustrate the objectives of the law. This case, like so many others, was triggered when one of the employees got mad for some reason and filed a complaint with the Department of Labor.

The moral of this story, of course, is that you want to be careful about being too nice when it comes to granting employees time off which will be made up later. This will almost always result in their working less than 40 hours during one week and more than 40 hours during another. If the pay is kept constant, you will have a technical wage and hour violation. Frankly, I believe that most employers simply ignore this technical problem. I think this is probably a very practical solution, so long as it is not a pattern or practice which can give rise to substantial liability over a long term. If you do it once in a while, there ought not to be any problem. But, if virtually all your employees took advantage of this opportunity on a significant scale, the potential liability over a 2-year period could be large.

EXAMPLE: Suppose that you are operating a retail store which does not do very much business in the summer. You have 10 employees, and you make an informal agreement with them that they will work 4 days during the summer and 6 days in the winter. The employees are happy because it gives them an extra day in the summer when they can use it for personal reasons without costing them any money. You may find the arrangement desirable because it gives you more work force when you need it. Technically, however, the fact that the employees gave up the day during the summer does not entitle you to get it back in the winter without paying time and a half. Pursuing the example, suppose 10 weeks are involved. That means 10 days extra in the winter, times 10 employees, times 8 hours per day. Thus, the number of hours worked for which time and a half should have been paid but was not is 800. The statute of limitations is 2 years for a maximum exposure of 1,600 hours. If the average hourly rate of these workers is $6 per hour, half of that is $3 per hour. Three dollars per hour times 1,600 hours is $4,800 maximum exposure.

Contrary to popular belief, there is nothing in the Fair Labor Standards Act about double time for weekends, triple time for holidays, etc. All of those things have been developed over the years through collective bargaining agreements, and they may be common practice in some industries. The law, however, has a very simple requirement: time and a half for hours worked in any 1 week over 40 hours. It does not matter whether the hours are on Saturday or Sunday or nighttime, or whether there is any holiday involved. Further, there is no requirement that these 40 hours be worked in 8-hour days. Under the Fair Labor Standards Act, there is absolutely no reason why you cannot go to a 4-day, 40-hour week without any overtime problem if you should so desire. However, this would create some problems under government contract rules, which are explained below.

Government contracts

The overtime requirements for persons working on government contracts are essentially the same as those discussed above, *except* that:

1. The workers must be paid time and a half for work in excess of 8 hours a day or 40 hours a week—*whichever gives them the most money; and,*

2. This rule applies only to those workers who are actually working on a government contract subject to the Walsh-Healey Act. Employees who are "exempt" (under the same definition as in the Fair Labor Standards Act) and those who do not work on the government contract are not covered. On the other hand, there

is a presumption that everyone in the plant which has the contract is covered unless separate records are kept.

The important difference between the 8-hour day base and the 40-hour week base will be the situations where employers want to go to a 4-day, 40-hour week or some similar arrangement which calls on the employees to work more than 8 hours a day but not more than 40 hours per week. At the present time, the government will not require time and a half for the extra 2 hours if you go to the 4-day, 40-hour work week, provided certain conditions are met. Also, this is merely an enforcement posture of the government —there is no statutory basis for it. Accordingly, I would recommend that if you have government contracts and you want to go to a 4-day, 40-hour week, you present your situation to the Department of Labor and ask them what they think. In most cases, they will give you a letter stating that, with certain relatively minor restrictions, you can do this without causing yourself potential liability for time and a half on the extra 2 hours.

Exempt Employees

Another important concept in the Fair Labor Standards Act is that of the exempt employee. The general rule is that executive, administrative, and professional employees are exempt from the minimum wage and overtime provisions of the Fair Labor Standards Act. The appropriate definitions are as follows.

- An executive is one whose primary duty (generally agreed to be 50 percent or more of his or her time) is in managing an enterprise or department or subdivision thereof. He or she must customarily and regularly direct work of two or more other employees and must be able to hire and fire or suggest changes in status of other employees. An executive must customarily and regularly exercise discretionary powers.

- An administrative employee is one whose primary duty (generally agreed to be 50 percent or more of his or her time) is in performing office or nonmanual work relating to the management policies or general business operations of the company. An administrative employee is one who regularly and directly assists a proprietor or executive or another administrative employee or who works only under general supervision along specialized or technical lines requiring special training, experience, or knowledge and who executes only under general supervision special assignments and tasks.

An administrative employee must customarily and regularly exercise discretion and independent judgment.

- A professional employee is one whose primary duty (generally 50 percent or more of his or her time) is in performing work requiring scientific or specialized study as distinguished from apprentice training and training for routine work, or in performing regular and creative work in a recognized artistic endeavor depending primarily on the invention, imagination, or talent of the employee.

The act contains certain presumptions about compensation. If an executive, administrative, or professional employee's compensation is above a certain base level, the employee is presumed to satisfy the requirement. Currently that base level is $250 per week. This will take care of most of the clear situations. It should be noted that there are also minimum rates below which it will be presumed that the person is not an executive, administrative, or professional employee. At the present time, the figures are as follows:

- Executives must make $155 per week and are presumed executive if they make $250 per week or more.

- Administrative employees must make $155 per week and are presumed administrative if they make $250 per week or more.

- Professional employees must make $170 per week and are presumed to be professional if they make $250 per week or more.

It should be noted, of course, that these are only presumptions, and the mere fact that someone makes over the maximum amount stated above does not automatically qualify him or her as an executive, administrative, or professional employee—he or she must still satisfy the substantive requirements.

Obviously, the determination of who is exempt and who is not exempt is very important, because you do not have to pay exempt people time and a half for overtime.

Again, the problem is going to come up when you are trying to be too nice. You may have a loyal secretary whom you want to give a promotion to, but you really do not have a job which qualifies as executive, administrative, or professional. You, therefore make one up, give the secretary a new title and a raise (perhaps a substantial one), and call the employee exempt. The employee works hard for a number of years (including spending evenings and weekends on the job), and then there is a falling out. At that point the employee says that he or she should have been paid time and a half for all those evenings and weekends, and there you have the problem.

The practical solution seems to be this: If there just is no way to classify the employee properly as administrative, executive, or professional, either make sure he or she does not work substantial amounts of overtime and keep records to show this or else simply pay overtime where it is due. On the other hand, if you are in the gray area and if you feel that there is substantial value to your business in giving this employee an exempt status even if it may be a close case, there really is not too much of a risk so long as you are not talking about a lot of people.

If you make a *practice* of doing this, and you have a *considerable number of people* on your staff who are not being paid overtime because you consider them to be executives or administrative people but you probably cannot justify that, it would seem that you have a potential exposure. You ought to try to bring the situation more in line with the law.

This area of the wage and hour laws is one where business people and lawyers sometimes get into rather heated arguments. Usually the business-person says to the lawyer words to this effect: "I hear what you are saying, but good old Millie just would never do that to me." The lawyer tells the businessperson that he or she does not know Millie but does have a lot of books which are full of cases where people just like good old Millie did do it to somebody. My own view is that to a certain degree, the businessperson's judgment is more appropriate in this area. Exposures are rather low, there are no criminal penalties, class actions are unlikely so long as the number of employees are small, and the government regulatory efforts are extremely light. This is not at all like Title VII of the Civil Rights Act of 1964 or the antitrust laws, where even good-faith mistakes can cost you an awful lot of money. If you enjoy the personal satisfaction of telling your lawyer that you know he or she is right and you appreciate his or her advice, but you are not going to pay any attention, this is a relatively low-risk place to do so.

This assumes, however, that you really are talking about good-faith judgments and that you do maintain the proper records. As in all areas of the law which are governed by a federal statute, the enforcement authorities do have great power to give you a lot of trouble if they feel you are in bad faith. If you deliberately destroy records or do not keep any in the first place so that the Department of Labor cannot possibly audit whether you are paying time and a half or not, they may very well get mad enough to use some of that power.

CHILD LABOR LAWS

The child labor laws are part of the Fair Labor Standards Act. Penalties for violation of the child labor laws are, in general, extremely weak or nonexistent. Of course, as always, this presumes good-faith violations rather than a deliberate flouting of the act.

On the other hand, there is hardly anything that will cause you to have to sit by yourself in church on Sunday morning quicker than a newspaper story that your company has violated the child labor laws. I do recommend some caution here. Not because you are going to go bankrupt or go to jail if you do not; but because it is just the right thing to do.

Essentially, the child labor laws say that employment of minors (those under 18 years of age) is subject to certain restrictions. The restrictions depend on the age of the minor. Subject to extensive explanation contained in the Department of Labor Regulations, employment of minors between ages 16 and 18 is restricted (but not totally prohibited) in certain high-risk areas, such as manufacture or storage of explosives, motor vehicle driving, coal mine operations, logging occupations, woodworking occupations, roofing, excavating, and operating power-driven machinery. Thus, in the case of minors between 16 and 18 you can employ them unless there is some specific rule that says you cannot.

In the case of minors between 14 and 16, the thrust of the regulation changes—you can employ a minor only in certain areas set forth as being permissible. These include such jobs as office and clerical work, cashiering, selling, modeling, artwork, price marking, assembling orders, packing and shelving, bagging and carrying out customers' orders, errand and delivery work, clean-up work, etc.

The law also contains the concept of an age certificate. If you get the proper age certificate from a minor, you will be protected against an inadvertent violation of the law, even assuming the minor lied about his or her age. If you do not get such a certificate and the minor lied, you will still be liable for a violation.

Child labor laws present both a problem and an opportunity. Employment of minors is obviously highly desirable in many situations, both for the company and for the minor. However, if you want to do this on a substantial scale, I recommend that you talk with the Department of Labor, get their appropriate publications, and read them first. (They are listed in this chapter.)

THE PORTAL TO PORTAL ACT

The Portal to Portal Act is a portion of the wage and hour laws which has to do with the calculation of the number of hours employees work. Essentially, the law says that workers need not be paid for transportation from their home to their place of work. Thus, in a normal case, one computes hours worked from the time the worker actually starts work until the time he or she actually stops, and the time spent going to and from home or washing or walking from the plant door to the work station is not counted. Of course, this general rule can be altered by custom or contract.

If you send a nonexempt employee out of town, I simply recommend the commonsense approach. For example, if you send a nonexempt employee to a training class or seminar, the only additional payments I would make are those which are rather clear. If you ask the employee to work an 8-hour day and then travel to the other city at night, that travel time ought to be compensated. On the other hand, if the employee spends 3 days in another city going to a seminar, I do not view it as necessary to compensate the employee for 72 hours. I would simply pay for a normal 8-hour day unless, of course, the actual training periods are longer. The law on this sort of thing is not as clear as it might be, but I think that common sense should prevail.

GARNISHMENTS

Garnishments are a point of annoyance. The Fair Labor Standards Act restricts the *amount of wages* which can be garnished. Accordingly, the payroll people must be informed of these rules and must be instructed to comply with legitimate garnishment orders only up to the maximum extent required by law.

The federal garnishment law limits the amount of wages subject to garnishment to 25 percent of a worker's "disposable earnings," which are generally defined as the earnings remaining after withholding for taxes and other amounts required by law, or the amount by which the weekly disposable earnings exceed by 30 times the Fair Labor Standards Act minimum wage, whichever is less.

In my experience, the garnishment forms used by most courts explain this fairly well, and there is not much of a problem. If you do have a question, I would suggest calling the court or the local Department of Labor Office—if you call your lawyer, that is what he or she would probably do.

Also, the federal garnishment law *prohibits the discharge* of an employee because that employee's earnings have been garnished for "any one indebtedness." The meaning of "any one indebtedness" is not entirely clear, but it should be noted that it is definitely different than any single garnishment. Accordingly, the mere fact that an employee has had his or her wages garnished more than once does not mean that he or she can be discharged. In addition, a policy of discharging employees with excessive garnishments can be considered to violate equal employment opportunity laws if the policy operates discriminatorily—and, statistically speaking, one is very likely to find this to be the result. Before you discharge someone because of frequent garnishments, you want to be sure of at least two things:

1. The garnishments involve more than one single indebtedness and

2. You are not using the garnishment policy discriminatorily so that blacks, women, Hispanics, or persons of Asian origin are discharged more frequently than white males.

RECORD KEEPING

Employers subject to the Fair Labor Standards Act are required to keep fairly detailed records concerning their employees. Records must be kept for both exempt and nonexempt employees, although the records for nonexempt employees are more detailed. The reason for the records on the exempt employees is to allow the government to make a reasonable audit to see that they were, in fact, exempt. The reason for the records on the nonexempt employees is to allow for checks on whether or not the provisions of the act have been complied with. The company does not have to keep these records in any specific format, so long as they can be audited.

GETTING HELP FROM THE GOVERNMENT

The place to go for help on wage and hour problems is the local office of the U.S. Department of Labor, Employment Standards Administration, Wage and Hour Division. They publish *a lot* of material and usually have capable and conscientious people available to answer your questions. Like government publications in general, many of them are difficult to use. They either simply reprint the entire language of the statute or regulation, in which case they are lengthy, technical, and difficult to understand, or they abbreviate the rules so much that they do not tell you what you need to know. Nevertheless, there are some good publications which you should have. If you get them from the Department of Labor, there will not be any cost.

Overtime Compensation   WH Publication 1262
>An interpretative bulletin stating the official position of the Department of Labor regarding computation of overtime compensation.

Overtime Compensation   WH Publication 1325
>A publication for general information; not to be considered official position. Provides basic information in relatively simple and useful language.

Restriction on Garnishment   WH Publication 1333
>Provides regulations on a section-by-section basis for the relevant laws.

Important Notice—Federal Wage Garnishment Law   WH Publication 1436
Provides a shorter, more easily understood statement on the maximum wage limits for garnishment purposes.

Records to Be Kept by Employers   WH Publication 1261
Provides the regulations on a section-by-section basis on the record-keeping requirements of the Fair Labor Standards Act.

Child Labor Requirements in Nonagricultural Occupations   WH Publication 1330
A very well prepared booklet, summarizing the relevant rules and reprinting the relevant regulations.

Handy Reference Guide to the Fair Labor Standards Act   WH Publication 1282
An excellent general overview of the law. Written in plain English.

Executive, Administrative, Professional and Outside Sales Exemptions Under the Fair Labor Standards Act   WH Publication 1363
A useful, 10-page explanation of these exemptions from the overtime requirements.

Regulations, Part 541: Defining the Terms Executive, Administrative, Professional, and Outside Salesman   WH Publication 1281
Complete copy of all the relevant regulations. Rather lengthy and technical, but complete and accurate.

SUMMARY

In conclusion, we have seen that setting up a payroll can involve considerable paper shuffling, but that adequate help is available from the relevant state or federal authorities. If you take advantage of that free help, there is no reason why you cannot do everything yourself. There are several legal cautions:

- Do not get too greedy in trying to arrange things to avoid payroll taxes or withholding.

- Do not let anyone work on your premises without workers' compensation coverage—even if he or she is working for an independent contractor. Make sure the contractor has coverage and obtain evidence of it if necessary.

- Workers' compensation and unemployment compensation are items of expense which are affected by your experience. Keep this in mind as you conduct your business operations.

- Keep the wage and hour rules in mind as you set wages and schedule work. Do not avoid paying time and a half on the basis of an informal agreement unless you clearly understand the risk involved and are willing to assume it.

8

EQUAL EMPLOYMENT OPPORTUNITY

In the legal guide that I wrote for executives of larger companies, the chapter on discrimination in employment is 64 pages long—which makes it by far the longest chapter in that book. Even so, it only scratches the surface of the relevant laws. Equal employment opportunity has been one of the biggest growth industries in the legal profession. In fact, it has become so much a part of the daily life of business people that the relevant laws and legal considerations have been digested and reduced to standard practices and procedures, so that personnel people now understand the legal requirements as well as many lawyers. There are many seminars which teach personnel people about the basic EEO ground rules and help them understand how to steer their company through the complicated maze of regulations. Having nonlawyers handle many EEO matters is a good idea. Whenever you have a problem this big, you just cannot have lawyers handling it on a continuing basis—it is too expensive.

However, many of the EEO considerations are peculiar to a large company. For a small company, the problems can be quite a bit simpler, and the risks are quite a bit smaller.

EEO laws can usefully be divided into two categories. The first category is the so-called antidiscrimination laws. These are the social laws of the mid-1960s—principally, Title VII of the Civil Rights Act of 1964. The basic concept of these laws is that it is illegal for a company to discriminate in any employment matter on the basis of *race, sex, national origin,* or *religion.* It is very important to note that these laws are *prohibitions.* Unless you have already discriminated against these protected groups and need to adopt a plan to fix that problem, there is no need to have an affirmative action plan to hire and promote minorities.

The federal equal employment opportunity law covers all employers with 15 or more employees. However, almost all states except the southern states have equivalent state laws which cover smaller companies. In Ohio, for example, the antidiscrimination law covers any company with three or more employees. Thus, even the smallest of companies is going to be covered by EEO laws.

The other category of equal employment opportunity laws is the laws imposed upon government contractors. These are the so-called affirmative action plans. They require that if you are a government contractor, you *must* have a *written* affirmative action plan which follows numerous detailed requirements to spell out exactly what positive steps you are going to take to bring more minorities into your company and to promote the minorities you already have into positions of increased pay and responsibility.

By far, the bulk of the administrative work is in the second category. You can easily see why. It applies to any company with government contracts, no matter how good its employment practices have been in the past and no matter how many females or minorities work in the company. Because we are talking about small businesses, I am going to eliminate this second category to simplify the discussion. If you do have government contracts, you must have an affirmative action plan, and you are probably going to need some expert help to draft it so that it passes muster with the government-compliance people.

Another aspect of the EEO laws which can be simplified for small businesses is the requirement to take affirmative action to hire and promote handicapped people and veterans. There are special rules for government contractors which require them to have separate written affirmative action plans for these additional protected groups. Again, however, there is no comparable requirement if you do not have any government contracts. There are some state laws which prohibit *discrimination* against handicapped people, but they also fall into the basic concept of a *prohibition.* You cannot discriminate, but you do not have to take affirmative action to find handicapped people and bring them into your company.

With that brief introduction and overview, I would like to go through some of the trouble spots in the EEO laws so that you can avoid them.

SELECTION PROCESS

The selection process is one of the most important places where you can run afoul of the EEO laws. You simply have to evaluate people fairly. We all know that is subjective, but nevertheless, the law and theory are very clear. If you reject employees because they are black or because they are female or because you do not like their national origin or religion, you are very likely to wind up in big trouble. The EEO laws specifically allow attorneys' fees, thus creating a built-in incentive for people to bring lawsuits. If you discriminate against a black or a female and that person gets a lawyer and sues you, you are going to be liable not only for the damages suffered by that person, but also for the attorneys' fees that were generated in the lawsuit. In the case of the single plaintiff, it is possible that the attorneys' fees could be larger than the damages.

It is very important to understand that this applies to *each* and *every* job. Suppose, for example, you say that you are not prejudiced against minorities and you certainly do not mind having women in the company, but for certain jobs you want a certain kind of person. You want a white male to be your traveling sales representative, a female to be your secretary, a male (either white or black) to run some of the machinery in your plant because it is a very dirty job and you do not think women would like it, a woman to be the receptionist because you think that looks nicer, etc. *All of these are clearly illegal.* You must apply the equal employment opportunity antidiscrimination laws each time you hire somebody. As a practical matter, there are no exceptions to this rule.

The fact that your customers happen to like a particular kind of employee does not make any difference. Some of the airlines tried to raise this argument in the case of male flight attendants. They conducted surveys and found that the majority of their customers wanted female flight attendants. That did not even get them to first base. Customer preference is totally irrelevant.

MEASURING PEOPLE'S ABILITY

When you hire someone, you obviously want to get the best person you can for the job. The law, simply stated, is that *you must measure the person for the job and not the person in the abstract.* Thus, almost any arbitrary requirement (such as a college degree) is extremely suspect. You may be able to justify it, but remember that the burden is going to be on you and it is a difficult one to meet. You must clearly define the job and its requirements and do the best you can to select the best person for the job. This you are entitled to do. EEO laws *do not* require you to hire unqualified people. What you cannot do is simply pull an arbitrary requirement out of the air and say that you will not consider anybody who does not satisfy your preconceived and perhaps arbitrary criterion.

There are certain obvious applications of this principle. If you need a secretary, you are entitled to require that the secretary type a certain number of words per minute and take shorthand at a certain rate, etc. If you need an accountant, you are entitled to require the person to have an accounting degree from a college. However, if you need a sales representative and you want to say that you are only going to hire someone who has a college degree, you are going to have a problem. You are going to have to show that a college degree is a job-related requirement. Frankly, I do not know whether it is or not, but I do know that it is going to be *extremely difficult* for you to prove your case in court, and that the law imposes the burden on *you* to prove it.

There are elaborate rules regarding all forms of tests. These rules say, in substance, that if you give a test and it screens out an abnormally higher number of minorities than white males, the test is discriminatory, and the burden is on you to prove that it is job-related. Except in obvious cases such as typing tests for secretaries, this is extremely difficult, if not impossible. The criterion for abnormally higher rejection rates is 80 percent. Thus, a test will be discriminatory if it rejects more minorities than nonminorities by a factor greater than 80 percent. This is very important—let us see how it works.

EXAMPLE: You have 10 white male applicants and 10 black applicants. You give them all a test, and all 10 white males pass but only 7 of the blacks. The passing rate for white males is 100 percent, but for black males, it is 70 percent. You put the 70 percent over the 100 percent and you get 70 percent. Since the requirement is 80 percent, the test is discriminatory. It screens out a disproportionately high number of blacks. If eight blacks had passed the test, it would be all right. If the test does not pass muster under this rule, you must validate it. That is almost impossible except for obvious job-related things. Thus, if this job involved inspecting and required the use of a micrometer, and the test measured whether the applicant could read and use a micrometer, I think it would be all right, because this is a clear situation. Just be sure the test actually measured the ability to use and read a micrometer. On the other hand, suppose the job involved general factory work and the test you gave was a reading test. That would not be an obvious job requirement. You would have to validate the test. You would have to show, by the Equal Employment Opportunity Commission's highly burdensome regulations, that the ability to read was a legitimate job requirement.

The use of any paper-and-pencil test is a danger point. I recommend that if you use any such tests, you obtain legal counsel as to their permissibility under the EEO rules. If you are on the wrong side of this rule, a plaintiff has a ready-made case against you, and you are practically defenseless.

EQUAL PAY

Equal pay for equal work is another high-risk area. If you pay males more than females for equal work, that is a clear violation of the law, and the females can, and often have, brought costly suits against the employer for back pay. You simply must pay equal pay for equal work. You must look to the substance of the work. If you call a female employee a secretary and pay her $800 a month when in reality she is an administrative assistant or even an executive assistant, and then you hire a brand-new, bright-eyed white male out of college and give him a fancy title and pay him $1600 a month but it turns out that he does the same thing your "secretary" has done for many years, you may have to explain that in court. Many equal pay cases involve essentially these facts.

Another highly sensitive area is "female jobs" where, because of history and inertia, females comprise the majority, if not all, of the people doing that work. Testing and inspection in a factory can be prime examples. If you have a large group of females working in the same kind of job, and it turns out to be a lower-paying job than others in your factory, you should look into this situation to make sure there is no discriminatory reason for it.

Still another problem is different titles, but equal work. There have been many cases in the banking industry where white males would be given the designation of "trainee" and would be paid higher wages for essentially teller work. Females would be paid less, would be called tellers, but would actually be doing the same work as the males. If you have a training program, it must be legitimate and nondiscriminatory. Males and females must have equal access to the program, and the program must really lead to positions of increased responsibility.

TREATMENT OF PREGNANT FEMALES

Under the equal employment opportunity laws, discrimination on account of pregnancy is equivalent to discrimination on the basis of sex and is prohibited. Thus, you *cannot* discharge a female because she becomes pregnant, and you *cannot* require a female to take an unpaid leave of absence on account of pregnancy before it is medically required. Thus, you must, as a practical matter, allow pregnant females to work right up until the date their own doctor says they should stop, or until they stop voluntarily.

Further, you *must* consider pregnancy to qualify for any short-term disability benefits you have—including salary continuation. Thus, if you would pay your secretary for 6 weeks off work for a broken leg, you would have to do the same for 6 weeks off work for pregnancy.

The rules on treatment of pregnant females are quite complex, but they have been reduced to a set of guidelines and interpretive questions and answers published by the EEOC. At the end of this chapter, under "Help from the Government," that is one of the documents I recommend you obtain.

HEALTH CONSIDERATIONS

At the present time, the federal law does not contain any antidiscrimination requirements against handicapped people except in the context of federal contractors. Many states, however, do have such requirements. Again, the principle is to measure the person for the job. If a person has a handicap which does not necessarily prevent him or her from doing the job you have available, you cannot discriminate against that person. Since this is a subject of state law, I will not go into it. I would, however, suggest that before you have a policy of requiring prospective employees to take a physical examination before you hire them, you ask your lawyer if your state has an antidiscrimination law for handicapped people. If it does, you may be wasting your time and money in requiring the physical. Even if the physical turns up a problem, you may not be able to refuse to hire the person. Further, you may be digging yourself a hole here, because if you tell the person that he or she is hired subject to passing a physical, and the person does not pass the physical, the burden is squarely upon you to defend the reasons for your not hiring the person in the face of the relevant law.

YOUR EMPLOYMENT APPLICATION FORM

Many employment application forms I have seen are tickets for plaintiff's lawsuits. My advice is to design an employment application form which asks only for information which you need to evaluate an applicant—legally. Some employers put anything on an application form that they think they might want to know for any kind of vague and general reason. I have seen application forms which include the following items that in the view of the EEOC, which enforces these antidiscrimination laws, are discriminatory:
Do you own your own home?
Are you married?
What is your maiden name?
Questions about owning your own car.
Questions about how many dependents the person has.

The reason why all of these questions are viewed as discriminatory by the EEOC is that they have an adverse statistical effect on minorities. Minorities, partly because of past employment discrimination, do not own their own homes or their own cars in the same percentage as nonminorities. Consequently, if you ask such questions because you feel that persons who own their own home are stable and are going to stay in the community, and persons who own their own car are going to have an easier time in getting to work and are therefore going to have better attendance, you had better be able to prove it. So far, I have not seen anybody do it. In the overwhelming majority of cases, these kinds of questions on an employment application form will be one of the nails that puts the lid on the coffin in any lawsuit that might be brought against you. For example, if there is a single job for which a black male and a white male applied, and you chose the white male, the black male may have a very marginal case as to why you did not select him. On the other hand, if you have a bunch of these bad questions on your employment application form, that bad case turns into a good one, and you are very likely to become involved in a lawsuit where you have to pay back pay and attorneys' fees. I strongly recommend you examine your employment application forms and make sure the questions are entirely job-related.

One word of caution: Do not trust published forms, even from fairly reputable sources such as trade associations or chambers of commerce. They may be all right, but I have seen many recently drafted forms which purport to be free of legal difficulty and are not.

Another caution: You may need supplementary forms for special cases. Many questions are proper for one kind of job but not for another. For example, if you are hiring a person who is going to handle money, you can ask if the applicant knows of any reason why he or she might be denied bonding insurance coverage. That question would not be proper for persons who were not going to be bonded. Similarly, if you are going to hire a person to drive a motor vehicle for you, you can ask about past traffic violations, but you cannot ask this question if there is no legitimate reason for your knowing the answer.

PROMOTIONS

Substantially everything said above applies to promotions also. You must treat people equally on promotions just as you do in the case of the initial hires. Civil rights laws have progressed much past the stage where you could satisfy your obligations by hiring women and minorities but keeping them in lower-paid jobs. Today, all that will do is increase the magnitude of the judgment against you, because these minorities having the lower-paid jobs will constitute a class which has been discriminated against. If they institute suit, there will likely be a recovery on behalf of all the members of the class rather than simply for one person who was denied a promotion.

DISCHARGES

Discharges are very important events in terms of discrimination, because bad feelings may exist, and a fired employee may have an incentive to go see his or her lawyer. Whenever you fire somebody, you have to make sure that you can articulate a good business reason. That is my view and the practical result; it is not the law. Under American law, you can fire somebody for any reason whatsoever so long as it is not an illegal reason. Thus, if you want to fire somebody because you do not like that person, there is no reason under American legal principles why you cannot do so. On the other hand, if that person is a member of a protected group (and remember, the protected group is pretty large these days) and you cannot articulate a good business reason for his or her dismissal, that person is going to have an appealing employment discrimination case against you. He or she may bring suit and cause you to incur at least your own lawyer's fees and possibly additional cost if the judge or jury believes the other person instead of you. You can avoid this by making sure you act reasonably. Further, make sure you can articulate a good business reason.

This is not to say you have to put up with inferior performance on the job. It is only to say you cannot discriminate. If you have four people working for you, and two of them show up for work an hour late each day, you can certainly fire those two people. But what if you have four people working for you, two of whom are from minority groups and two of whom are not, and all four of them show up late every day and you fire only the minority people? That changes the facts. You must treat people the same. . . . If you are going to fire people for being late for work, you must fire everybody—minority, nonminority, male, female—just the same way. If you have a hard-and-fast rule that anybody who does not show up for work without having called in first gets fired, and you make an exception for your best worker—who incidentally is a white male—but you refuse to make an exception when a minority worker who is not performing well does the same thing, you are going to have a problem. You have discriminated. You have treated one person differently than the other, and whatever your internal motives, the court is very likely to say that race played some part in your behavior. It is usually enough to cause you to lose the case.

Since a discharge case is such a clear-cut event which can give rise to liability under the employment discrimination laws, I recommend that you make consideration of this subject your first priority whenever you are about to fire somebody. First of all, ask yourself if the person is a member of a protected group. To review, those groups are as follows: blacks, women, persons of Asian or Oriental origin, persons over 40, and possibly handicapped people, depending on your state law. If the person you are about to discharge is a member of a protected group, you want to be sure to ask yourself these simple questions:

1. Am I treating this person any differently than I have treated white males in the past?

2. Can I articulate and prove a valid business reason why I want to fire this person?

If the answer to either of these two questions is no, it might be worth a call to your lawyer. Remember, however, that your lawyer is on your side. He or she is going to believe what you say, and is not going to come in and audit your records to see if you really have treated minorities differently from nonminorities, or to see whether your statistical profile in the work force shows you have been putting women or minorities in the lower paying jobs.

On the other hand, the EEOC, or a private plaintiff, will do these things. If you tell your lawyer that the person is not doing a good job, that is a good enough reason to fire the person. On the other hand, if you tell that to a court, you are going to have to explain exactly why the person is not doing a good job, what you expected of the person, and what he or she has not done. Further, you are going to have to be able to introduce some evidence to prove what you say. In the case of many jobs, that is going to be difficult.

AGE DISCRIMINATION

The Age Discrimination in Employment Act protects workers between the ages of 40 and 70 against discrimination. Thus, all people—white, black, male, and female—between these ages are members of a protected group. The procedural requirements are somewhat less advantageous from the employee's point of view than in the case of race or sex discrimination. The bottom line, however, is the same. If you fire somebody because he or she is old, that person may sue you and collect a lot of money. If age is even one factor in your determination to dismiss a person, that is enough to cause a violation of the act.

In my experience, problems under the age discrimination law will come about when adverse economic situations cause you to have to reduce your work force. If you have 20 people and have to let two go, it may be very tempting for you to lay off two older workers who may not be as productive, aggressive, energetic, etc., as the younger ones. On the other hand, the following factors may complicate this decision.

1. The older workers may have more seniority than the younger workers, so you will have that going against you. While seniority is not legally binding except in the case of a labor contract, it does color a case quite a bit. If a judge finds that you have dismissed a worker who has 10 years' experience and kept one with only 2 or 3 years, you are going to need a little more evidence as to the business reason for dismissal.

2. It may be extremely difficult for you to objectively show that a person is "less energetic" or "less productive." If the employee in question is selling, working on piecework, or doing some other job in which you can measure his or her output by a certain amount of dollars or pieces, you can probably do it. In most jobs, however, productivity and quality of performance are very subjective things, and it may be difficult or impossible to prove your argument.

3. Another problem which I frequently encountered in age cases is

that management is careless in how they handle the dismissal. They may even mention the person's age, or there may even be a document which mentions retiring the "older workers" to make room for the younger ones. If you do this, you have made the plaintiff's case. Whenever you terminate someone, either by firing him or her for cause, by layoff for lack of work, or for any other reason, you must be very careful about the documents you create and what you tell the employee. I am not suggesting that you lie to anybody, but I do counsel against unnecessarily self-incriminating statements. I know it is hard to tell somebody that you are firing him or her because he or she is not as productive as the rest of the people in the company. It is hard to say that you have 10 workers, you have to lay the worst one off, and this person qualifies. On the other hand, if you try to smooth that over by some remark which is less offensive, you may very well cause yourself legal difficulties. For example, if you terminate someone over 65 because that person gets social security whereas the younger workers cannot, that is a clear violation of the law because the Age Discrimination in Employment Act protects people up to the age of 70. You may be a nice person, and you may not have hurt the worker's feelings quite as much as if you had told the truth, but you also may have a lawsuit, and you are probably going to lose it.

There is, of course, room for some subjectivity in determining whom you lay off during a work reduction. The key factor is to make sure that age (or race or sex or other minority status) plays *absolutely no* part in your determination. As a practical matter, the only way you can be sure of that is to have some legitimate business reason for taking the termination action.

WHAT ABOUT STATISTICS?

There are books written about the importance of statistics in employment discrimination cases. Basically, however, common sense is the rule. If you operate in a big city and have 50 people working for you, all of whom are white males, and you get a discrimination complaint from a female or a black who made an application to your company and was not hired, you are going to have a rather difficult time defending that case. You can talk all you want about qualifications, experience, etc., but you are going to have to settle that case. Keep in mind, however, that statistics have two important parts: One of them is the number of minorities that you have working for you, and the other is the availability of those minorities in the work force. In areas in which it is very difficult to find qualified applicants who are not white males, an all white male work force might not be a problem.

THE ECONOMICS OF TITLE VII LITIGATION

Employment discrimination cases brought by individual plaintiffs are not particularly attractive deals either for the plaintiff or for the plaintiff's lawyer. Let us say that an applicant who makes $12,000 a year applied to your company for a job. You did not hire that person; the person instituted a lawsuit claiming discrimination and won. It turned out that the person was out of work for 6 months. That is $6,000 damages, and you may have to pay it. Also, attorneys' fees can be recovered in this kind of a situation. Further, what if the employee, after having applied at your place for a job and been turned down, went down the street to a large company and got a job for $15,000 a year? There may not be any damages at all.

Further, Title VII litigation has a 180-day limitation. Someone who believes he or she has been discriminated against must file a charge with the appropriate state or federal agency within 180 days of the alleged discrimination. *For example, if you have discriminated against everybody for the past 10 years and you clean up your act during the next 180 days, you do not have any realistic exposure so long as nobody files a charge within that 180-day period.* For these reasons, single-plaintiff Title VII cases are not really attractive to many lawyers.

Further, the EEOC is not interested very much in these either. They are more interested in the larger cases, where they can allocate their limited resources to provide more openings and opportunities for more people. If the EEOC spends a lot of time negotiating with you concerning a 10-employee plant at which the turnover is only 10 percent a year, that is not much benefit for minorities as a whole. If they spend the same amount of time with a very large company that has a lot of job opportunities every year, they benefit the minorities more, and that is the approach they have taken. Thus, as a practical matter, EEO exposure to smaller companies is much less than it is to larger ones. EEO exposure to large companies is so severe that almost all have full-time staffs of many people, including lawyers and EEO specialists, to deal with this problem. For a small company, that is not necessary. However, the same rules apply, and, for a small company, a $10,000 back-pay award can be just as damaging as a multimillion dollar award to a larger one. On the other hand, as small business people, we do have to allocate our "worry resources" among a wide variety of things, and it seems to me that employment discrimination is something that you do not have to be too worried about *so long as you have the proper attitude and do not in fact discriminate.*

However, let us assume that someone does file a charge against you. *At this point, I recommend legal counsel.* You are starting here to build a record for subsequent actions. It may very well be that you can dispose of a discrimination charge at a hearing with your federal or state civil rights agency without much problem yourself. However, what if you cannot? You have built a record, and if you do not have a lawyer involved in the process, it might be a bad record. Private EEO cases by single plaintiffs are very easy to settle, and I recommend that you settle them promptly. On the other hand, I do not recommend that you try to settle them all by yourself without your lawyer.

Under current procedures, if someone files a charge of discrimination against you, the first round of problems will come from the state civil rights agency. Almost all states, except the southern states, do have state civil rights agencies. The state's civil rights agency will try to negotiate a mutually agreeable settlement. If that fails, the federal government, that is to say, the EEOC, will step in and try to settle the matter. If that fails, the aggrieved person will be issued a so-called right to sue letter by which the government says, in effect, that it has tried to reach a settlement, but cannot, and the person can get his or her own lawyer and sue you.

These hearings or conferences are relatively informal, and you do not *absolutely need* a lawyer to go along with you. It is not like going to court. There are no technical rules of evidence to worry about or technical procedures to cause you trouble. You simply go and tell your side of the story. On the other hand, you do need a lawyer in the background to make sure that you are taking the proper steps to keep a relatively small matter from developing into a large one. I definitely recommend that you consult counsel whenever a discrimination charge is filed, but the question of what role the lawyer should play is a little more complex and depends mostly on your own personal predispositions.

I *generally* recommend that you be the one who goes to the fact-finding conference and tries to make the settlement. However, this depends on your personality and desires. If you feel that you might get steamrollered by the EEOC representative—who may be a lawyer and who will definitely have considerably more experience in this sort of thing than you—or if you are so emotionally involved with the situation that you think you may get upset and be unable to reach a settlement even if a reasonable one is proposed, you should send your lawyer. The key thing to remember is that the decision you make should be based on these kinds of considerations and not fear of some kind of intricate legal maneuvering or strategy which only your lawyer can cope with. I would approach this like any other kind of hard bargaining session. Get your entire story in order, including a clear statement of all the facts involved. Then make the decision as to who should present that story on the basis of the best person for that job. It may be you; if you have a personnel person, he or she may be the best choice; and your lawyer is certainly an alternative. However, if you do send your lawyer, keep in mind that it might be an expensive deal. The lawyer is going to have to spend considerable time becoming familiar with *all* the facts of the situation, including how you have treated similar situations before.

I have seen many people try to stand on principle at these early stages and refuse to consider even a modest settlement if they believe the case has no merit. The typical pattern is that someone will file a charge and the employer will feel that he or she is being blackmailed. You get the old problem of "millions for defense but not one penny for tribute." The practical wisdom of this is highly doubtful. To be blunt, you may have to throw a few hundred dollars into the pot even in a situation where the plaintiff really does not have any case at all, in order to keep things from getting out of hand. This may make you mad, but it will save you a lot of money. Normally, the argument against this is that if you do it for one person, it is a blank check for every other minority or female in the community to institute a similar action. Theoretically, this argument has some appeal, but as a practical matter, it has not happened. Those companies which have settled cases at the early stages have generally avoided the monumental battles which can come about later on in litigation. Also, they have not been subjected to multiple unfounded allegations of discrimination. On the other hand, I have seen quite a few situations where relatively simple charges which could have been settled very economically at an early stage graduated into very expensive and drawn-out legal battles because the employer wanted to stand on principle.

STATE AGENCIES

One last matter which deserves some attention is dealing with the state employment discrimination agencies I alluded to above. Almost all states have such agencies, and the EEOC is required by law to defer to them to give them a chance to settle disputes. I cannot discuss each state's procedures in this book, so I would caution you to consult your counsel early. The minute you get a notice of an employment discrimination charge being filed against you in any agency—state, local, or federal—you should consult counsel. State procedures vary, and it may be necessary and appropriate to have your lawyer handle the matter at the state level. This is unusual, however; most state agency procedures are just as informal as if not more informal than the federal procedures.

In summary, then, here are some guides on handling EEO matters:

1. Once you get any employment discrimination complaint, immediate conversation with your attorney is recommended.

2. If you hire a substantial number of people during the course of a year, specific legal advice is essential. I would think that if you hired 20 or more people during any year, it would be imprudent not to have discussed your general practices and procedures with counsel.

3. Make sure your employment application form is clean.

4. Make sure you are careful and honest in all termination situations. State the *real* reasons for termination even if they involve telling the person he or she is not doing a good enough job. Make sure no termination decision is based—in whole or in part—on age, race, sex, national origin, or religion.

5. Understand your duties under any applicable state laws for handicapped people.

6. Always pay equal pay for equal work, and make sure you treat all people fairly and equally in employment-related matters.

7. Before imposing any discipline on anyone, make sure you ask yourself if you are treating all similarly situated employees the same.

8. Be alert to clusters of females or minorities in lower-paying jobs. If you have such a situation, make sure that it is not the result of unintentional discrimination against these protected groups.

9. If you use one or more written tests, except for *obviously* job-related tests such as a typing test for a secretary, discuss each test with counsel to see that it satisfies the government employee selection guidelines. Usually this will mean making sure a test does not screen out substantially more minorities or females than white males.

10. Do not have any arbitrary criteria which you cannot justify for a job. For example, do not require your secretary to have a college degree or your sales representatives to have a certain level of education. Remember the basic rule: You must measure the person for the job, not the person in the abstract.

HELP FROM THE GOVERNMENT

You will not be able to get a great deal of help from the government on the compliance aspects of equal employment opportunity. They are geared up to help employees file charges against you, not to help you comply with the rules. You can, however, obtain copies of the relevant laws and regulations from your local EEO office. I recommend that you obtain and read a copy of the Uniform Employee Selection Guidelines and the questions and answers interpreting them. There are also guidelines on how you must treat pregnant females in terms of rights to return to their job and benefits. This is a rather complex area, and I recommend you obtain and read the EEO guidelines and interpretative questions and answers on this subject. Additional recent guidelines from the EEOC, which I believe you should have, are Guidelines on Sexual Harassment, Guidelines on National Origin, and Guidelines on Religious Discrimination.

Other than getting free copies of the relevant laws, regulations, and guidelines, I do not recommend conferring with the EEOC on compliance. The EEOC is *not* a neutral impartial agency. They tend to be on the side of employees who claim discrimination. Deal with them as you would with an adversary in the purest sense of the word. It is definitely not like dealing with the Department of Labor or the Internal Revenue Service where you can get useful and reasonably impartial advice.

9
LABOR LAW

This is going to be a relatively short chapter, because I believe that labor law is an area where you need expert help. I would divide the expert help into two categories:

1. How should you operate your business in order to avoid a union organization attempt?

2. If there is a union organization attempt, what should you do?

Of course, if your business is already unionized, you will undoubtedly know everything I am going to say in this chapter and will already have a labor law advisor.

WHAT ARE THE IMPLICATIONS OF HAVING A UNION?

The reason I believe you should try to avoid union organization is that operating a small business is hard enough without the additional complications and restrictions on your flexibility which will be involved if you have a union and a union contract to contend with. I should add, however, that unionization is not all bad. It simply represents a way of running a business which, in my judgment, is not conducive to the success of a small business. There is too much "us" versus "them" atmosphere in a union shop. That may work all right in a large company, but in my experience, it has not done much to help small business.

On the plus side, if management is not one of your strong points, there is some merit in having a set of hard-and-fast rules for the workers to work by. In some cases, union people may be paid more than nonunion people, but this is not universally true. In fact, the opposite can be the case if you happen to be the generous type that likes to share the wealth with your employees and if your business has been successful. Also, in a union shop, you have a rather standard set of procedures for grievances, work rules, etc., and while these can be more rigid than in a nonunion shop, they do simplify things considerably if you are the type of person that has trouble saying no to employees' requests and therefore feel that you may be taken advantage of. For example, if you are having trouble with your employees coming in late and leaving early, and if you feel that you cannot deal effectively with this problem in an informal way, it may be very nice to have a union contract which says that the workday starts at a certain time and ends at a certain time and includes certain lunches and coffee breaks, so you do not have to impose this discipline informally.

Nevertheless, on balance, I believe small businesses are better off operating without a union because there will be more of a team spirit and because the inherent uncertainties involved in so many small businesses do not coincide very well with the fixed work rules and hours that typically become imposed on a company with a union contract.

In summary, then, the following are the implications of having a union.

1. There will be a written contract setting forth all the obligations of each party. Everything will be done by the book.

2. There may be an elaborate and formal grievance procedure which culminates in binding arbitration. You may wind up with some third party telling you how to operate your business in important respects.

3. Promotion practices are based almost entirely on seniority. It is much more difficult to fire poor performers, and it is very difficult to reward good performers.

4. The direct costs of bargaining are very substantial. Bargaining sessions can consume 20 to 50 hours of table negotiations, and there are many hours of homework and planning for each hour of actual negotiation.

5. The quality of work may decrease because the union protects inferior workers and there is little incentive for good workers.

WHY EMPLOYEES ORGANIZE

If you know the reasons why employees would like to have a union instead of negotiating with you personally, you will be quite far down the road to avoiding the problem. There is usually no single reason why employees want a union. The reasons are a combination of the following factors.

1. As the organization gets larger, communications do not develop, and the employees feel that they are not important and not being listened to. The union comes along, listens to the employees, and tells them that the union can communicate with management better than they can on an individual basis, and this is a very appealing argument.

2. There may be substandard working conditions or facilities, and the union can look at them and tell the employees that they can improve them through negotiations with management. Note that we are talking here about working conditions and facilities, not necessarily just low pay.

3. There may be no regard for seniority, with promotions being strictly on a merit basis. Seniority is generally appealing to workers because it gives them a sense of security. While nonunionized organizations emphasize merit, unions emphasize seniority. In fact, the union will emphasize seniority to the point where it is almost the sole factor in considering promotion and raises. Of course, this argument cuts both ways—your highly motivated and aggressive employees may not want to wait around for the requisite seniority to get raises and promotions. Nevertheless, seniority is a factor which unions use to appeal to the majority of workers, and it usually works.

4. There may be no grievance procedure or even any informal way for the employees to make their complaints known to management and get a fair hearing. This promotes frustration and is also something which the union can seize upon, because a union is, of course, able to provide a rather formal and fairly efficient grievance procedure.

5. Unequal treatment of employees is a very aggravating factor which unions sometimes seize upon. The union can insist upon equal treatment—based largely on seniority. Problems of inequitable discipline, lack of uniformity in work rules and discipline, favoritism, or discrimination are all things which the union can and does seize upon. Usually these factors are present when management has tried to respond contructively to its best employees. The union will generally protect the inferior employees, and there are usually more of the latter than of the former. Accordingly, even though it is rather basic human nature to reward the better employees and to bend the rules in their favor, such treatment can contribute to unionization or at least problems with the

morale of all other employees. (See also Chapter 8, "Equal Employment Opportunity.")

6. Union promises are a big factor. Unions are a business, and their business is to sell memberships. They are very good at it.

There are a number of signs that indicate a union organization attempt (or at least thinking about unions) might be present in an organization. These are the kinds of things you might want to be on the lookout for, and, if it seems appropriate, you may want to conduct a self-analysis to see why the employees might be unhappy. Some of the more common indications of thinking about a union rule are the following.

1. Technical questions from employees about their benefit plans or their pension plans. These can sometimes be prompted by union promises which tell employees that the union will be able to get them better benefits or pensions.

2. A more than normal amount of informal group meetings.

3. Rumors regarding unionism.

4. Union handbilling.

HOW TO REMAIN NONUNION

The key to remaining nonunion is sound personnel practices. Much of what the experts have to say in this area is simply common sense. Following is a list of some of the areas which are important.

1. A safe and healthy working environment.

2. A direct and efficient resolution of employee complaints. This does not mean that you have to do everything the employees say you should; it merely means you have to deal effectively with their complaints. If you cannot do something employees think you should, you should be able to articulate a reason why.

Do not be afraid to use personal preference as a reason. After all, it is your business. If an employee makes a proposal or suggestion which has merit but which you just do not want to implement for some reason, there is nothing wrong with saying that. Simply state that the proposal or suggestion is a good one and has merit. However, there are some other considerations which go the other way. Sometimes judgments come down to personal preference, and your personal preference is not to implement the suggestion. If you are constructive and do not abuse this argument, employees will understand it. The key thing is a fair hearing and discussion and your indication of appreciation of suggestions and ideas.

3. Provide meaningful and interesting work for employees. The difference between actual work and expectations is important. For example, in the case of secretaries or administrative assistants where, realistically, there may be a very limited career path, it would be a mistake to raise high expectations with glowing talk of unrealistic opportunities for promotion. Meaningful and interesting work is a very personal thing which depends upon each individual. So long as the employees are happy and feel that their work is meaningful to the company and that their legitimate expectations have been properly described, there should not be any problem.

4. There should be incentive for good performance.

5. There should be opportunities for growth.

6. There should be respect for each employee as an individual.

7. There should be consistent administration of discipline and criticism.

8. There should be up-to-date personnel policies.

9. There should be competitive salaries and benefits.

The above list is summarized from a wide variety of professional sources, and it is interesting to know that in the overwhelming majority of cases, the competitive salaries and benefits are placed last on this list. *You do not have to pay employees more than they are worth or more than the market value of their services in the community in order to avoid a union.*

A FAULT AND NEED ANALYSIS

One useful exercise is to look at a company in terms of possible faults and needs for improvement. Following are some of the areas which might be important.

1. The personnel administration and the staff. Do they function in a competent and efficient manner?

2. Is the supervisory staff good? Is the recruitment good? Is there training and involvement of the maximum number of employees in the decision-making process?

3. Look at the employment process itself. Are there good job descriptions? Do you have interview guidelines? Is there an orientation program? Do you have a probationary period and use it properly?

4. Do you have transfer and promotion policies which are based on merit and which are understood by the employees?

5. Do you get the maximum benefit you can out of a termination situation? For example, do you have an exit interview where an employee who is no longer with the company can tell you what he or she feels the problems with the company are? Do you know what your turnover statistics are, and do they show that any particular department has an abnormally high turnover rate or that your turnover statistics are worse than others in the same industry?

THE IMPORTANCE OF LOCATION

In my own personal experience, I must say that there is one factor which seems to be more important than those suggested by all the experts, and that is simply location. My own little business is in Chesterland, Ohio, which is a very small suburb in the far eastern portion of the greater Cleveland area. The people of Chesterland, Ohio are just not interested in unions. Unions are not particularly interested in the people of Chesterland, Ohio, because there are so few of them. While we try to operate our business according to the principles stated in this chapter, we are quite certain that even if we violated all of them, it would be extremely unlikely that any union would be interested in organizing our workers.

On the other hand, if we were located in downtown Cleveland, I believe the reverse would be true. It would be extremely difficult for us to run a substantial printing and publishing operation in downtown Cleveland without serious union organization efforts, no matter how much we paid the people or how we treated them.

THE UNION ORGANIZATION DRIVE

In my judgment, everything I have recommended up to this point you can and should do by yourself with the help of written materials. Except in unusual circumstances or if you have a lot of money to burn, I do not think that professional help is needed. The opposite is true in a union organization drive. It is a highly technical process, and you need a good labor lawyer *immediately.* There are, however, some things you should know so that you don't do something disadvantageous before you have the opportunity to talk to a labor lawyer.

What Do You Do When the Union Comes and Says That It Wants to Represent the Employees?

It is possible that the first you will know of a union organization attempt will be when the union comes to you and says that they have authorization cards from your employees, and they want to negotiate a collective bargaining agreement. Do not look at these cards. Simply have your secretary seal them in an envelope and put them in a safe place. Respond that you have a good-faith doubt as to whether a majority of employees want the union, and request an election. At this point, you must seek professional help. These first things, however, are very important, and if you are surprised, it would be very easy to do the wrong thing. Looking at the authorization cards would be a mistake, because after you do so, you might be accused of discriminating against employees who have signed union authorization cards. Also, asking for an election buys you time to explain why your company and the employees are better off without a union than with one.

The law says that you can request an election only if you have a good-faith doubt about whether the union does in fact represent a majority of the workers. The union may say it has cards from more than 50 percent of your workers, and therefore, your doubt is not "good-faith." Do not pay any attention to that argument. The law also says that it is illegal to bargain with a union which does not represent a majority of the workers, and the only way to be sure is to have an election. Further, there are many complicating factors, including the definition of the appropriate bargaining unit. In fact, in many union contests, that definition is the *key*. A single union can represent only persons with a reasonably common interest. You need professional help to determine what kind of appropriate bargaining units you may have in your company.

Current union representation elections are running about 60 to 65 percent in *favor of employers.* If you do a good job of explaining to your employees why they are better off without a union than with one, you have a good chance of winning a representation election. Of course, you must take a realistic look at your situation. If there are simply too many problems to explain away, and if you know that the union has already obtained authorization cards from almost 100 percent of your employees, you will have an uphill battle. Nevertheless, you are entitled to request an election, and I suggest that you do so for the reasons mentioned above.

Labor Law—Practicalities—Theoretical Rules

Labor law is a very difficult area, because the practical, real-life world does not always coincide with the reported cases. Specifically, what you can and cannot do during a union organization drive is very difficult to ascertain, because it depends on your motives as well as the views of the labor lawyer you are talking to. Some labor law firms are very aggressive. Some recent legal periodicals have featured such law firms because they not only counsel employers as to how to avoid a union but also, if there is a union organization drive, give very aggressive counsel on what actions the company can take to tell its side of the story. Other law firms are much more conservative. They read the many cases—both of the court and the National Labor Relations Board—and point out to corporate management that almost anything they do has some chance of being characterized as coercive, threatening, or inflammatory, and therefore, an unfair labor practice.

The problem is that the law says that an employer cannot coerce its employees against joining the union. This coercion concept, however, is much more subtle than just physical coercion. For example, if you tell the employees that if they join the union, you will not pay Christmas bonuses anymore, or that if they join the union, you will go out of business or move your plant to another city, those would be "threats" and would be an unfair labor practice. If you engaged in these activities and then you won the election, the union would be able to petition the National Labor Relations Board to have a second election because of these unfair labor practices. Thus, the union would get two chances instead of one. That is the danger. If you go so far in telling your side of the story that someone could later say that you coerced the employees, there can be a charge filed with the National Labor Relations Board, and it can order a new election. The union is entitled, as you are, to a fair election without any coercion. Of course, the rules are the same on the other side. The union cannot coerce employees either. In the context of an initial organization drive, however, union coercion really only takes the form of physical coercion, and while it is not unheard of, it does not appear to be widespread.

Another complicating factor is that you have to judge the totality of your conduct as well as the totality of the union's conduct. To take some extreme cases, if the union were to conduct its organizational drive in a manner which was absolutely beyond reproach, it would take very little in the nature of strong words from you to convince the National Labor Relations Board or a court that you had engaged in coercion, threats, or unfair labor practices. On the other hand, if the matter became somewhat heated and both sides exchanged strong views, that would also be taken into consideration. Of course, you do not just look at any single sentence, word, or speech; you must look at the conduct as a whole. If you do that, and it looks as if you are coercing the employees rather than simply informing them of your side of the story, it is possible that if you win the election, it will be set aside and the union will be entitled to another one.

Absent some unfair labor practice (on the part of either the union or the employer), an election will be binding for 12 months. Thus, after an election, you are assured of 12 months' "peace."

With these general cautions, I think it is useful to set forth a checklist of certain dos and don'ts which represent things that are generally agreed to be permissible or not in an organization drive. Keep in mind, however, that we are dealing with a complex area where professional judgment plays a large part. I do not recommend that you substitute this checklist for good, solid, experienced labor counsel. I do recommend that you cross-examine your labor lawyer to make sure that you and he or she are on the same wavelength as far as the proper approach goes. There is nothing inherently good or bad about either conservative or aggressive advice. However, you should know which you are receiving. If your labor lawyer is telling you that if you follow his or her advice, you are going to be practically assured that there will not be a successful unfair labor practice charge filed, he or she will be giving you very conservative advice. Thus, you may not do a very effective job of telling your side of the story, and you may lose the election. On the other hand, if your lawyer tells you that he or she is giving very aggressive advice which extends to the limit the things you can and cannot do, and that you are running some risk of having an unfair labor practice charge successfully filed against you, you will probably be able to do a very good job of telling your side of the union-nonunion story, and you will have a much better chance of winning the election. The trade-off, of course, is that you will probably do some things which at least give rise to the filing of an unfair labor practice charge, and then you will have to defend these actions and run the risk that the board will overturn your successful election. I must confess that I do not have any good answers to this dilemma, but I do feel that it is extremely important that you and your lawyer discuss it so that both of you are operating on the same set of guidelines.

I have also included a brief description of the things you can expect a union to do if they want to organize your plant. As you can see, this list covers essentially the same considerations we mentioned before in our discussion of how to remain nonunion: Can the union offer the employees anything they don't have now? Can the union solve any of the employees' problems? Can the union offer better job security?

CHECKLISTS

The following checklists will do more than any narration I can give you to provide a flavor of what a union organization drive might involve.

Here Are Things You May Do

1. Tell employees what your negotiating position will be if they elect a union.

2. Make sure employees understand the benefits they have already.

3. Inform employees that the signing of a union authorization card does not mean they must vote for the union if there is an election.

4. Inform employees of the disadvantage of belonging to the union, such as the possibility of strikes, serving in a picket line, dues, fines, and assessments.

5. Inform employees that you prefer to deal with them rather than have the union or any other outsider settle employee grievances.

6. Inform employees what you think about unions and about union policies.

7. Inform employees about any prior experience you have had with unions and whatever you know about the union officials trying to organize them.

8. Inform employees that no union can obtain more than you as an employer are able to give.

9. Inform employees how their wages and benefits compare with unionized or nonunionized concerns.

10. Inform employees that the local union may be dominated by the international union, and that they, the members, will have little to say in its operation.

11. Inform employees of any untrue or misleading statements made by the organizers. You may give employees the correct facts.

12. Give opinions on unions and union leaders, even in derogatory terms.

13. Give your legal position on labor-management matters.

14. Reply to union attacks on company policies or practices.

15. Advise employees of their legal rights, provided that you do not encourage or finance an employee suit or proceeding.

16. Declare a fixed policy in opposition to compulsory union membership contracts.

17. Compaign against the union seeking to represent the employees.

18. Insist that any solicitation of membership or discussion of union affairs be conducted outside of working time.

19. Tell employees, if they ask, that they are free to join or not to join any organization so far as their status with the company is concerned. During a union organization drive you *must:*

(a). Administer discipline, layoffs, grievance, etc., without regard to union membership or nonmembership, or the employees involved.

(b). Treat both union and nonunion employees alike in making assignments of preferred work, desired overtime, etc.

(c). Enforce rules impartially, regardless of the employee's membership activity in a union.

Here Are Some Things You May Not Do

1. Attend any union meetings, spy upon employees, or engage in any undercover activity which would indicate that the employees are being kept under surveillance to determine who is and who is not participating in the union program.

2. Tell employees that the company will fire or punish them if they engage in union activity.

3. Lay off or discharge any employee for union activity.

4. Grant employees wage increases or special concessions in order to keep the union out.

5. Bar employee union representatives from soliciting employee memberships during *non*-working hours.

6. Ask employees about confidential union matters, meetings, etc. (Some employees may, of their own accord, walk up and tell of such matters. It is not an unfair practice to listen, but you must not ask questions to obtain additional information.)

7. Ask employees what they think about the union or a union representative.

8. Ask employees how they intend to vote.

9. Threaten employees with economic reprisal for participating in union activities. For example, you cannot threaten to move the plant, close the business, curtail operations, or reduce employee benefits.

10. Promise benefits to employees if they reject the union.

11. Give financial support or other assistance to a union or to employees, regardless of whether or not they are supporting or opposing the union.

12. Announce that you will not deal with a union.

13. Tell employees that the company will fire or punish them if they engage in union activities.

14. Ask employees whether or not they belong to a union or have signed up for a union.

15. Ask an employee, during the interview when you are hiring him or her, about his or her affiliation with a labor organization.

16. Make antiunion statements or actions that might show your preference for nonunion employees.

17. Make distinctions between union and nonunion employees when assigning overtime work or desirable work.

18. Purposely team up nonunion employees and keep them apart from those you think may belong to the labor organization.

19. Transfer workers on the basis of union affiliation or activity.

20. Choose employees to be laid off on the basis of weakening the union's strength or discouraging membership in it.

21. Discriminate against union people when disciplining employees.

22. By the nature of work assignments, indicate that you would like to get rid of an employee because of his or her union activity.

23. Discipline union employees for a particular action and permit nonunion employees to go unpunished for the same action.

24. Deviate from company policy for the purpose of getting rid of a union employee.

25. Take actions that adversely affect an employee's job or any pay rate because of union activity.

26. Become involved in arguments that may lead to a physical encounter with an employee over the union question.

27. Threaten a union member through a third party.

28. Threaten your workers or coerce them in an attempt to influence their vote.

29. Promise employees a reward or any future benefits if they decide against the union.

30. Tell employees overtime work (and premium pay) will be discontinued if they unionize.

31. Say unionization will take away vacations, or other benefits and privileges presently enjoyed.

32. Promise employees promotions, raises, or other benefits if they get out of the union or refrain from joining it.

33. Start a petition or circular against the union or encourage or take part in its circulation if started by employees.

34. Urge employees to try to induce others to oppose the union or keep out of it.

35. Visit the homes of employees to urge them to reject the union.

Here Are Some Things a Union May and May Not Do During an Organizing Drive

The union may:

1. Verbally attack the company, its supervisors, and all its practices.

2. Promise improved wages and benefits, including specific amounts if elected.

3. Threaten that the company will take away benefits, reduce wages, lay off employees, or close the plant if the union is not selected.

4. Ask employees about their union views or how they intend to vote.

5. Give assistance to employees in supporting the union.

6. Visit employees in their homes.

7. Give free dues to those who join the union early.

8. Promise that there will not be a strike if it is selected.

The union may not:

1. Harm or threaten to harm employees or their property.

2. Threaten employees who do not support it with economic reprisal if it is selected.

Union organizers who are not employees

In connection with impromptu visits by union representatives, your supervisors should be under instructions not to permit any strangers or visitors in the plant. They have no right there and can be told to leave and/or escorted out. The union can handbill at plant entrances on public property.

Employees who support or oppose the union must be treated equally. But you do not have to allow anyone to solicit during working hours, and you do not have to allow anyone to distribute literature in work areas, though anyone must be permitted to do so in nonwork areas of the plant during nonworking hours.

Union Organization Checklist

Following is a checklist of the things the union will do if it wants to undertake a substantial organization drive. A single union will rarely do all of these things, and for a small company, the entire organizational effort may simply consist of a union representative who stops at the entrance after work and asks the employees if they want to join the union. Nevertheless, I think it is useful to go through this checklist so you can see the kinds of things which are important. Keep in mind that they are equally important even if the factors exist only in the employees' minds and are not raised by the union.

1. *Planning*
   Be assured that the union will have thoroughly planned any substantial organizational efforts. They will have accumulated a lot of information about your plant location, its physical structure, starting and quitting times, the products you make, public transportation near the plant, and the eating and drinking establishments near the plant. They will also know about the labor history of the plant.

2. *Fact-finding*
   After the preliminary planning, the union will get right down to the employees and their problems. They will try to find the key

individuals in the plant who have leadership influence, or who have personalities which naturally draw people to them. At the same time, the union will want to find out all it can about working conditions, job descriptions, how complaints and grievances are handled, and what complaints the employees have. The union will get complete information about seniority practices, overtime, paid holidays, benefit programs, and the attitude of foremen and supervisors to employees.

3. *The plant organizational committee*
After the union has made several key contacts and has gotten all the necessary background material, they will want to build a core of union support within the plant. They will, of course, want a cross section of ages, races, and sexes.

4. *The first meeting*
After the "quiet" states described above, there will be a first meeting which all the employees are invited to attend to listen to the union's pitch. Here the union will start to reap the dividends from the investment in time to gather all the background information. They will talk in detail about your plant, your practices, and indeed, even about your individual foreman and supervisors—by name. They will make a lot of promises, but the responsible unions won't make unreasonable or wild promises. They will sound very believable and convincing. Remember, selling memberships is their business and they are very good at it.

After the first meeting, everything should be out in the open, and you will want to start considering the things listed before in our checklist for union organization drives. At this point, you should have expert help available.

SELECTED READINGS ON UNIONIZATION

BOOKS

Brooks, Robert R.: *When Labor Organizes,* Yale University Press, New Haven, 1937 (361 pages).
Dougherty, James L.: *Union-Free Management,* Dartnell Corp., Chicago, 1968 (152 pages).
Hughes, Charles L.: *Making Unions Unnecessary,* Executive Enterprises Publications, New York, 1976 (117 pages).
Jackson, Gordon E.: *How to Stay Union Free,* Management Press, Memphis, 1978 (105 pages).

ARTICLES

Anthony, R. J.: "When There's a Union at the Gate," *Personnel,* vol. 53, November 1976, pp. 47–52.

Brown, H. L.: "When the Union Comes Knocking How Do You Answer?" *Inland Printer/American Lithographer,* vol. 181, July 1978, p. 425.

"Business of Union-busting," *The Economist,* vol. 269, October 21, 1978, p. 46.

"Employer Pitfalls in Unionization Drives," *The CPA Journal,* vol. 47, August 1977, pp. 68–69.

Greer, C. R., and S. A. Martin: "Calculative Strategy Decisions During Union Organization Campaigns," *Sloan Management Review,* vol. 19, Winter 1978, pp. 61–69.

Hill, R.: "How Some Firms Are Managing Without Unions," *International Management,* vol. 34, June 1979, p. 49.

"How Union Organizing Can Be Prevented," *Drug Topics,* vol. 123, March 16, 1979, p. 12.

Imberman, A. A., and R. C. Lasher: "New Labor Law Amendments and Your Nonunion Plants," *Business Horizons,* vol. 21, August 1978, pp. 56–60.

Kilgour, J. G.: "Before the Union Knocks," *Personnel Journal,* vol. 57, April 1978, pp. 186–192.

———"Responding to the Union Campaign," *Personnel Journal,* vol. 57, May 1978, pp. 238–242.

Laner, R. W.: "How to Handle an Organizing Campaign," *Management World,* vol. 7, August 1978, pp. 20–24.

———"Why Employees Join Unions," *Management World,* vol. 7, July 1978, pp. 8–10.

"Management's Best Defense," *Institutions/Volume Feeding,* vol. 79, October 1, 1976, p. 55.

Rohan, T. M.: "Would a Union Look Good to Your Worker?" *Industry Week,* vol. 188, January 26, 1976, pp. 35–41.

Sullivan, F. L.: "Limiting Union Organizing Activity Through Supervisors," *Personnel,* vol. 55, July 1978, pp. 55–65.

"What to Do When the Union Knocks," *Food Service Marketing,* vol. 39, December 1977, p. 8.

Wilson, J.: "Thoughts on Union Avoidance," *Personnel Administrator,* vol. 22, June 1977, pp. 14–18.

10
FORMS, WARRANTIES, AND CREDIT

This chapter is devoted to the proper preparation and use of three important commercial forms, and a brief discussion of fair credit laws. The forms are the purchase order form, the sales order form, and the standard warranty form. These three forms are important to your business and have a high degree of "legal" content. Fair credit laws and their complexities are briefly discussed at the end of the chapter.

YOUR PURCHASE AND SALE ORDER TERMS AND CONDITIONS

No matter what your business, it is very likely that the overwhelming majority of all your business transactions are going to be sales of your product or service, or purchases of other products or services. Large companies have purchase order forms and sales forms which they use for this purpose. Small companies should also—though many do not devote sufficient attention to this subject.

Preparation of good purchase orders and sales forms is easy. They can be looked at in two parts. The first part is the *substantive* or business aspects of the deal. The second part is the terms and conditions, or, as they are sometimes called, the *boilerplate.* Mechanically, the process works out conveniently to drafting the front and back of your forms.

The front of your forms must, of course, satisfy your business requirements. There is certainly no shortage of purchase order and sale forms which you can look at to get ideas. Note, however, that it is not necessary to have elaborately printed multipart forms. *Forms prepared by typewriter and duplicated on standard duplicating machines are perfectly adequate.*

The back of the forms can be a complicated and technical subject. However, if you take a look at some terms and conditions from other companies, plus the ones reproduced in this chapter, you ought to be able to come up with a set which is right for your products or services.

Why Bother?

You have never bothered to read the fine print on the back of these forms—and you suspect others don't either. That is true. However, if you do take a look at this boilerplate, you can see that some fairly important things are covered. I think that devising a set of terms and conditions for your business is worth the effort, does not necessarily require a lot of legal time and expense, and will give you the following benefits.

1. The most important benefit is simply the discipline of thinking about the terms and conditions on which you are willing to do business. When you sell your product, when do you want to get paid? Cash on delivery, net 10 days? 2 percent, 10 days? etc. Is the normal transaction to be FOB your plant with freight to the seller's place of business added, or do you want to use a delivered price system?

2. By setting forth the terms and conditions of your sales, and hopefully some of your purchases, you can work towards a better deal in all these transactions. Remember that price is only *one* of the aspects of a deal. The others include most of the things on these forms, such as warranties, obligations to replace and repair, time to present claims, etc.

3. *Last,* but certainly not least, if you do get into a dispute with a customer or supplier, your terms and conditions may help you negotiate a better settlement.

What About the "Battle of the Forms"?

You may say, "Okay, I see that if I put good terms and conditions which are favorable to me on my forms, I may get some advantages. But will my vendors and customers stand still for this? Won't they have terms and conditions which are favorable to them on their forms?"

First of all, the customers and vendors are going to read your terms and conditions just about as frequently and carefully as you are going to read theirs—hardly ever, and then only the portion which deals with a specific problem.

Second, if your vendors or customers have terms and conditions which are favorable to them, and you have no terms and conditions favorable to you,

you will be doing business on *their* terms. If, on the other hand, you *both* do a good job with your forms, the inconsistent portions of the forms will cancel each other out, and you will both be left with the *general law.* Since the general law has been developed over the years to be fair to both purchasers and sellers, that is not too bad a result.

You may wonder, "If a vendor puts a burdensome or harsh clause in that fine, hard-to-read print on the back of his or her forms, could I be bound by it even if I never read it?"

That could happen. In 15 years of practicing law I have *never* read a case where the court did *not* look at what was written on these forms in order to reach a conclusion about the terms and conditions of a particular deal. I have never seen a case where the court said that the terms and conditions were too fine and therefore did not count. Of course, we are talking here about *commercial transactions* between *business* people. In *consumer* transactions, there are entirely different rules. In business transactions, there is no big brother out there to make sure you do not get taken advantage of. The law on commercial transactions is basically simple—the contract between two parties is what the documents say. There is almost complete freedom to contract. The law only steps in to supply contract terms where the parties either have not focused on the problem at all, or have not agreed.

What is meant by the "Battle of the Forms"?

Most commercial contracts are accomplished through exchanges of forms, with neither party reading the fine print on the other's forms until a dispute or problem arises. If both companies do a good job of drafting their forms to protect their interests, it is very likely that the forms will have different or conflicting terms on some fairly important points. However, this does not alter the fact that both parties intended there to be a contract; it just means that they did not agree on all the fine points.

What should the law do? The old law said that a contract was formed by an *offer* and an *acceptance.* The first person to issue a form was making an offer. That could be accepted by the other party *only* by an acceptance which was a *mirror image* of the offer. If the other party proposed different or additional terms, that was not an acceptance but a *counteroffer.* Therefore, in most commercial transactions there was no contract at all based on the exchange of forms. Usually this presented no problem because both parties performed. However, if a dispute arose before performance, business people were often surprised to find out from their lawyers that even though they thought they had made a contract, they really hadn't because no one had supplied an acceptance which was a mirror image of the other's offer.

In approximately 1960, the commercial laws were rewritten by a special group of lawyers and law professors in a *Uniform Commercial Code.* This has now been enacted in all states except Louisiana. The UCC says that the old law was bad on this subject, that business people intended to make a deal when they exchanged these forms even if the boilerplate on the back was different. It therefore wrote into the law a provision which deals with the exchange of conflicting forms. This provision creates somewhat of a lawyer's paradise, because if one party is on his or her toes and/or the other is asleep at the switch, an extremely advantageous (or disadvantageous) contract can be created merely by the exchange of appropriate forms without either party having negotiated or even thought about most of the terms.

The legalistics

This situation is created by the following provisions of the Uniform Commercial Code, which are worth reading carefully.

Section 2-207. *Additional Terms in Acceptance of Confirmation*

1. A definite and seasonable expression of acceptance or a written confirmation which is sent within a reasonable time operates as an acceptance even though it states terms additional to or different from those offered or agreed upon, unless acceptance is expressly made conditional on assent to the additional or different terms.

2. The additional terms are to be construed as proposals for addition to the contract. Between merchants such terms become part of the contract unless:
   a. the offer expressly limits acceptance to the terms of the offer;
   b. they materially alter it; or
   c. notification of objection to them has already been given or is given within a reasonable time after notice of them is received.

3. Conduct by both parties which recognizes the existence of a contract is sufficient to establish a contract for sale although the writings of the parties do not otherwise establish a contract. In such case, the terms of the particular contract consist of those terms on which the writings of the parties agree, together with any supplementary terms incorporated under any other provisions of this Act.

Basically, this provision was designed to accomplish two objectives. The first was to make certain that there was in fact an enforceable contract when normal business procedures were intended to create an enforceable contract. The provision was necessary to change the old mirror-image rule. The second objective was to establish certain ground rules to determine precisely what the terms of the deal were where the documentation was inconsistent.

Generally, the effect of this provision is that the additional terms contained in a response to an offer (whether to sell or to buy) become part of the contract. This happens *automatically* unless

1. the offer *expressly limits acceptance* to the terms of the offer,

2. the additional terms *materially alter* the offer, or

3. the offeree *objects* to those terms.

Naturally, a busy purchaser or seller cannot possibly read, evaluate, and make necessary objections to every form that comes across his or her desk. However, unless he or she does so, the result will very likely be a contract which is most unfavorable to his or her company. The "materially alter" language is not very useful for planning purposes because of its uncertainty. Here is where the forms come in. You want to *expressly limit* your offer to your terms. If the company personnel have an adequate arsenal of appropriate forms and a knowledge of their importance and how to use them, this problem can be minimized and, in many cases, turned into a distinct advantage for the company. Following is a brief discussion of a suggested technique to achieve this corporate advantage.

Forms

Forms are the basic weapon in this battle. Naturally, anyone participating in the fight must have ammunition. Following are the four basic forms which every corporate purchaser or seller should have:

Purchaser	Seller
Request for Quotation	*Quotation*
Purchase Order	*Sales Form*

What should the forms contain?

The object of the forms is to make sure the contract is on your terms, not the other party's. Therefore, you must use a form which establishes that the only deal is the deal you propose, and that if the other party proposes additions or changes, those additions or changes are of no effect and your form governs. Following are two suggested clauses which will usually accomplish the desired objective.

Terms for buyer's documents

Vendor's commencement of work on the goods described herein or shipment of such goods, whichever occurs first, shall be deemed an effective mode of acceptance of purchaser's offer to purchase contained in this purchase order. Any acceptance of this purchase order is limited to acceptance of the express terms of the offer contained on the face and back hereof. Any proposal for additional or different terms or any attempt by vendor to vary, in any degree, any of the terms of this offer in vendor's acceptance shall not operate as a rejection of this offer, unless such variance is in the terms of the description, quantity, price, or delivery schedule of the goods, but shall be deemed a material alteration thereof, which is hereby objected to by purchaser, and this offer shall be deemed accepted by vendor without said additional or different terms. If this purchase order shall be deemed an acceptance of a prior offer by vendor, such acceptance is expressly conditional on vendor's assent to any additional or different terms contained herein.

Terms for seller's documents

Any acceptance of the offer to sell contained herein is limited to acceptance of the express terms of such offer contained on the face and back hereof. Any proposal for additional or different terms or any attempt by buyer to vary, in any degree, any of the terms in buyer's acceptance by purchase order or otherwise shall not operate as a rejection of this offer to sell unless such variance is in the terms of the description, quantity, price, or delivery schedule of the goods, but shall be deemed a material alteration thereof, which is hereby objected to by the seller, and this offer shall be deemed accepted by buyer without said additional or different terms. If this document shall be deemed an acceptance of a prior offer by buyer, such acceptance is expressly conditional on buyer's assent to any additional or different terms contained herein.

When do you use the form?

An analysis of section 2-207 reveals that the statute gives a very slight potential advantage to the first party to submit an offer (of either purchase or sale). This is so because it is the terms of the first piece of paper which are used to base all further adjustments. If the second piece of paper has terms which are materially inconsistent with the first offer, those terms will have no force or effect *if the first document contained the magic language,* but there probably will still be a contract. However, if the first document did not contain the magic language, any additional terms in the second document *will become a part of the deal* unless they materially alter the original proposal or they are objected to within a reasonable time. Furthermore, in many situations, the offeree will do one of the following two things:

1. Expressly accept the offer or accept by a course of conduct (like starting work)

2. Send a confirmation document which does not have the magic language

If either of these occurs, the first offeror has his or her way entirely.

If the offeree is on his or her toes and sends you an acceptance which has the magic language making the acceptance expressly conditional on your acceptance of his or her additional terms, you have a square conflict. Then what happens? Generally, the rule is that the inconsistent terms simply cancel each other out, and the parties are left with:

1. the terms which they agree upon or which are not inconsistent, and

2. such other terms as are generally imposed by law.

Therefore, if you play the game right, you may wind up with your desires entirely, and the worst that can happen is that you wind up with as many of your terms as are not inconsistent with the other party's terms, and the remainder of the contract is governed according to general principles of law. If you either do not play the game at all or play it wrong, you may wind up with a contract almost entirely on the terms of the other party.

WARRANTIES

Warranties are an important subject worth some of your thought and time. There are two sides to the coin:

1. Make sure you focus on warranties whenever you are buying anything important for your business.

2. Make sure you clearly decide what warranties you are going to give on the products you sell.

On the first question of warranties on products you purchase, I would simply like to refer you back to the previous section, "Purchase Order Terms and Conditions." Naturally, you should specifically negotiate warranties on important products if your bargaining position allows you to do so. Remember that your warranty protection is a cost item. If you buy something with good warranty protection, it is worth more than that same product with less significant protection.

The same principle—only with much more importance—extends to the products you sell. In today's litigious climate, you simply must build the cost of warranties into your price. Also, it is important for you to remember that, if you do *nothing,* you will *automatically provide fairly good warranty protection by operation of law.* If you want to disclaim warranty responsibility, you must do so in clear and specific legally approved language. Since warranties are potentially so important, I recommend you seek specific legal advice concerning the warranties you give—or do not give. *The key is to make sure you understand what warranties you are giving for your products.* The lawyer can make sure the right legalese is used—but you have to make the business judgment and build the cost of that warranty into the product. I would like to offer you the following thoughts and guidelines on warranties which should help you assess the magnitude of this problem in your situation and discuss some appropriate solutions with your lawyer.

Do You Sell a Consumer Product?

If you sell a consumer product to *consumers,* you must comply with the Magnuson Moss Warranty Act. This statute was enacted in 1976 to provide a relatively uniform system of providing warranties throughout the nation and to make those warranties honest. Essentially, the law says the following:

- You do not have to give any warranty at all.

- If you do give any warranty, it must be *either* a "full warranty" or a "limited warranty." A full warranty is a rather good warranty which must satisfy strict legal requirements. You must know what those are for your product. A limited warranty is essentially any kind of warranty you want to give which does not measure up to the standards of a full warranty. The legal requirements for a limited warranty involve "disclosure." The warranty must be worded correctly, and your lawyer can help you.

- You still must consider the UCC. The Magnuson Moss Warranty Act did *not* supersede many important Uniform Commercial Code requirements. Many companies, including some large ones, have either elected to ignore this problem or done a legally inadequate job of drafting their warranties.

- Because of this problem, you cannot be sure that warranties you see from other companies do the job they seem to be intended to do. I have seen some which offer a limited warranty under the Magnuson Moss Warranty Act but do not adequately disclaim the UCC-implied warranties. Thus, a purchaser has both sets of warranties—and this may not have been intended.

In summary, then, if you sell a consumer product to a consumer, my advice is to seek legal advice on your warranty, because you are in a highly technical area.

Do You Sell a Product Which Could Injure Someone?

Essentially, the rule here is that you cannot disclaim responsibility for a defective product which causes a personal injury—no matter what. Warranties are good only to grant or limit *commercial rights.* They don't serve any useful purpose in limiting product liability exposure—in fact, the contrary is the case. If you give a warranty, and a breach of that warranty causes personal injury, that is one of the theories the injured person can use to recover damages from you.

What About the Commercial Situation?

If you sell products which are not consumer products or if you sell consumer products but do not give any warranty to the consumer, you don't have to deal with the Magnuson Moss Warranty Act, but you still must consider the UCC warranty provisions.

What Are the UCC Warranty Provisions?

The Uniform Commercial Code starts off with a key principle—*almost absolute freedom of contract.* The UCC does not require you to give any warranty whatsoever. However, certain warranties are implied unless you disclaim them. Further, you have to disclaim them by certain legally prescribed language. Here is a brief rundown of the UCC warranty provisions.

- Unless disclaimed, you warrant that the product does not infringe anyone else's patent and that you have title to it. Usually this presents no problem.

- Any statement you make about the product is an express warranty. Again, there is no problem so long as you say what you mean and mean what you say. If you sell a "3-foot square table," there is an express warranty that the table is 3 feet. If you sell a "1-horsepower motor," there is an express warranty that the product is a motor and generates "1 horsepower." *Anything* said about the product, *any* picture, *any descriptive literature* or brochure, or *any samples* create an express warranty.

- *Unless disclaimed,* there are *two additional warranties* which are *implied by the UCC:* the *implied warranty of merchantability* and

the *implied warranty of fitness for particular purpose.* The implied
warranty of merchantability provides that the product is fit for the
general use to which products of that kind are usually put; the
implied warranty of fitness for particular purpose provides that if
there is a specific purpose for which the product is going to be used
the product will be suitable for that purpose.

- In order to disclaim these warranties, you must follow certain
  technicalities. To disclaim the implied warranty of merchantability,
  you must use the word "merchantability." To disclaim the implied
  warranty of fitness for particular purposes, you must use clear
  language, although no precise words are required. In both cases,
  the disclaimers must be conspicuous—which means that they must
  be in larger type than the remainder of the document. (For an
  example of how to disclaim these warranties, see the sample terms
  and conditions of *sale.*)

- You can limit warranty exposure to the cost of the product. This
  is a very important provision, because, normally, a breach of warranty will allow the buyer of the product to recover not only the
  cost of the product, but all other damages which flowed from that
  breach. Example: Absent any disclaimer, if you bought defective
  film for your photographic trip to Europe, the manufacturer of the
  film could be liable not only to replace the film but also to give
  you another trip to Europe. With the proper disclaimer, they are
  liable only to replace the film.

For these reasons, I *strongly suggest* that you carefully consider drafting
forms which *disclaim* the implied warranties, and *limit* a purchaser's remedy
under any breach of warranty claim to replacement of the product. Of course,
this is subject to the requirements of the marketplace. However, remember
that without some limits, a very small sale can give rise to a very large
liability.

EXAMPLE: You sell gaskets. You provide some defective gaskets to a motor maker.
   The motor maker puts the defective gaskets into his motors and sells them
   before he finds out they were defective. There must be an expensive recall
   to fix the motors. With a disclaimer and limitation on warranties, you are
   liable to provide new gaskets. Without the limitations, you may be liable for
   the cost of the entire recall campaign.

The subject of warranties is very closely related to that of product liability,
so if this kind of problem is present in your business, I suggest you read
Chapter 12 in conjunction with this one.

Following are samples which illustrate these points:

- Purchase order terms and conditions
- Terms and conditions of sale
- Sample—Full warranty
- Sample—Limited warranty

TERMS AND CONDITIONS OF PURCHASE

1. ACCEPTANCE

   This order must be accepted as written and it must be accepted by Vendor by written acknowledgment mailed to Buyer, or by commencement of performance, within ten (10) days of the order's date. After acceptance, this order, with any attachments, will constitute the entire agreement of the parties. Any addition to, change in, modification of, revision of, or waiver of this order will be invalid and rejected unless specifically agreed to in writing by Buyer.

2. PRICES

   Buyer will not be billed at prices higher than those stated on the front of this order unless other prices are specifically agreed to in writing by both parties. Such prices will include all charges for packing, hauling, storage and transportation to the point of delivery. Vendor will pay delivery charges in excess of those that Buyer has agreed to pay. The prices stated will include all taxes except those which Vendor is required by law to collect from Buyer. Such taxes, if any, will be separately stated in Vendor's invoice and will be paid by Buyer unless an exemption is available. Vendor agrees that any price reduction made with respect to the items covered by this order subsequent to its placement but prior to payment will be applicable to this order.

3. DELIVERY

   Time is of the essence in this order and substitutions will not be accepted. The entire order must be shipped by the date requested, but it may not be shipped more than one week in advance of the time(s) specified herein without Buyer's prior approval. If Vendor's shipments fail to meet the delivery schedule, Buyer, without limiting any other rights or remedies that it may have at law or in equity, may direct expedited routing of such shipments and any excess costs incurred as a result thereof will be debited to Vendor's account. When more than one shipment is made against any order, the invoice and shipping papers accompanying the last shipment must indicate that it is the final shipment. Buyer will not be obligated to accept untimely, excess or under shipments, and such shipments in whole or in part may, at Buyer's option, be returned to Vendor, or held for disposition at Vendor's expense and risk. Buyer will not be liable for Vendor's commitments or production arrangements in excess of the amount or in advance of the time necessary to meet Buyer's delivery schedule.

4. RISK OF LOSS

Vendor will bear all risk of loss of all merchandise covered by this order until such merchandise has been delivered to the designated location.

5.   MODIFICATION OF ORDER

Buyer may modify this order at any time by submitting a written notice of new order to Vendor. If such modification affects the cost or time of performance and if Vendor makes a written claim for an equitable adjustment within thirty (30) days after receipt of notification of change, an equitable adjustment will be made by Buyer.

6.   INSPECTION AND TESTS

All goods ordered hereunder will be subject to inspection and testing by Buyer at all reasonable times and places, including the period of manufacture, and in any event prior to acceptance. Vendor agrees to permit access to its facilities at all reasonable times for inspection of goods by Buyer's agents or employees and will provide all tools, facilities and assistance necessary for such inspection at no additional cost to Buyer. It is expressly agreed that inspections and/or payments prior to delivery will not constitute final acceptance and that all goods will be subject to final inspection after delivery to Buyer. If the goods delivered do not meet the specifications or otherwise do not conform to the requirements of this order, Buyer will have the right to reject them. Goods which have been delivered and rejected in whole or in part may, at Buyer's option, be returned to Vendor for reimbursement, credit or replacement, or may be held for disposition at Vendor's expense and risk.

7.   WARRANTIES

Vendor warrants that all goods and services furnished hereunder will conform to applicable specifications, instructions, drawings, data and samples, will be merchantable, of good material and workmanship and free from defects, will be fit and sufficient for the purposes intended by Buyer, and will be free from all liens and encumbrances. These warranties will be in addition to all other warranties, express, implied or statutory. All warranties will survive acceptance of and payment for any and all goods ordered pursuant hereto and will run to Buyer and its customers.

8.   DRAWINGS AND SPECIFICATION REVIEW

If during the term of this order, Buyer's representatives review drawings, specifications or other data developed by Vendor in connection with the order and make suggestions or comments or approve such documents and data, such actions are only expressions of opinion by Buyer and will not serve to relieve Vendor of any of its responsibilities or obligations under this order.

9.   USE OF INFORMATION

Vendor agrees that all information furnished or disclosed to Buyer by Vendor in connection with this order is furnished or disclosed as a part of the consideration for this order, that such information is not, unless otherwise agreed to by Buyer in writing, to be treated as confidential or proprietary, and that Vendor will assert no claims (other than for patent infringement) by reason of the disclosure, reproduction or use of such information by Buyer, its agents, its assigns or its customers.

10. TOOLING

Unless otherwise specified in this order, all tooling and/or all other articles required for the performance hereof will be furnished by Vendor, will be maintained in good condition and will be replaced when necessary at Vendor's expense.

11. ADVERTISEMENTS

Vendor will not in any manner advertise or publish the fact that it has furnished, or contracted to furnish, the goods or services included herein without the prior written consent of Buyer. Vendor will not disclose the existence of or any information about this order to any party without the prior written consent of Buyer.

12. SUBCONTRACTING

Vendor agrees to obtain Buyer's prior written consent before subcontracting this order or any substantial portion hereof, provided, however, that this limitation will not apply to the purchase of standard commercial supplies or raw materials.

13. BUYER'S PROPERTY

Title to and the right to immediate possession of any property, including patterns, tools, jigs, dies and any other equipment or material, furnished to Vendor or paid for by Buyer will remain in Buyer. No articles made therefrom will be furnished by Vendor to any other party without Buyer's prior written consent. Vendor will keep adequate records of such property which will be made available to Buyer upon request, and will store, protect, preserve, repair and maintain such property in accordance with sound industrial practice, all at Vendor's expense. Unless otherwise agreed to in writing by Buyer, Vendor will insure Buyer's interest in such property against loss or damage by reason of fire (including extended coverage), riot or civil commotion. Copies or certificates of such insurance will be furnished to Buyer on demand.

In the event that Buyer's property becomes lost or damaged to any extent from any cause, including faulty workmanship and/or negligent acts by Vendor, its agents, or its employees, while in Vendor's possession, Vendor agrees to indemnify Buyer or replace such property, at Vendor's expense, in accordance with Buyer's request. At the completion of the goods requested by Buyer in this order for which Buyer's property was required, Vendor will request disposition instructions for all such property, or the remainder thereof, whether in its original form or in semi-processed form. Vendor agrees to make such property available to Buyer at Buyer's request, in the manner requested by Buyer, including preparation, packing and shipping as directed. Expenses for preparation for shipment will be for Vendor's account and shipment will be made F.O.B. Vendor's plant.

14. DRAWINGS AND DATA

Vendor will keep confidential all information, including designs, drawings, specifications and data, furnished by Buyer, or prepared by Vendor specifically in connection with the performance of this order, and will not divulge or use such information for the benefit of any other party. Except as required for the efficient performance of this order, Vendor will not make copies or permit copies of such information to be made without the prior written consent of Buyer. Vendor will not use, either directly or indirectly, any such information or any data derived therefrom for any purpose other than to perform this order without obtaining Buyer's written consent. Vendor will return all such data and information to Buyer upon completion by Vendor of its obligations under this order, or upon demand.

15. TERMINATION

Buyer may terminate the performance of work under this order in whole or in part at any time(s), by written notice to Vendor. Upon receipt of such notice, Vendor will, unless the notice directs otherwise, immediately discontinue all work and the placing of all orders for materials, facilities and supplies in connection with the performance of this order and will promptly cancel all existing orders and terminate all subcontracts insofar as such orders or subcontracts are chargeable to this order. Upon the termination of work under this order, full and complete settlement of all claims of Vendor with respect to the terminated work will be made as follows:

(i) As compensation to Vendor for such termination, unless such termination results from the default of Vendor, Buyer will pay to Vendor the percentage of the total order price corresponding to the proportion of the amount of work completed on the date of termination to the total work to be done as Vendor's full compensation for the work completed under this order; and

(ii) Upon Buyer's payment to Vendor in accordance with this paragraph, title to all equipment, materials, work-in-progress, finished products, plans, drawings, specifications, information, special tooling and other things for which Buyer has paid will automatically vest in Buyer.

Nothing contained in this paragraph will be construed to limit or affect any remedies which Buyer may have as a result of a default by Vendor.

16. DEFAULT—CANCELLATION

Buyer reserves the right, by written notice of default, to cancel this order, without liability to Buyer, in the event of any default on the part of the Vendor, the discontinuance of business by Vendor, or the sale by Vendor of the bulk of its assets other than in the usual course of business. If Vendor fails to perform as specified herein, or if Vendor breaches any of the terms hereof, Vendor will be liable to Buyer for all damages, losses and liability incurred by Buyer directly or indirectly as a result of Vendor's breach, and Buyer reserves the right, without liability to Buyer, upon written notice to Vendor, to cancel this order in whole or in part and/or to obtain the goods ordered herein from another source with any excess cost resulting therefrom to be chargeable to Vendor. The remedies provided in this paragraph will be cumulative and in addition to any other remedies provided at law or in equity.

17. FORCE MAJEURE

Neither party hereto will be liable for defaults or delays due to Acts of God, or the public enemy, acts or demands of any government or governmental agency, strikes, fires, floods, accidents, or other unforeseeable causes beyond its control and not due to its fault or negligence. Each party will notify the other in writing of the cause of any such delay within five (5) days after the beginning thereof.

18. COMPLIANCE WITH LAWS

Vendor agrees to fully observe and comply with all applicable Federal, State and local laws, rules, regulations and orders pertaining to the production and sale of the goods ordered, and, upon request, Vendor will furnish Buyer certificates of compliance with such laws, rules, regulations and orders.

19. EQUAL OPPORTUNITY

Executive Order No. 11246, as amended, relative to Equal Employment Opportunity and all other applicable laws, rules and regulations, including Title VII of the Civil Rights Act of 1964, are incorporated herein by this specific reference. In addition, if this purchase is, or is deemed, to be issued under a government contractor, all applicable laws, rules and regulations relating to the hiring of disabled veterans and veterans of the Vietnam era and to the hiring of individuals with physical or mental handicaps are incorporated herein by this specific reference.

20. GOVERNMENT CONTRACTS

If this order is placed, directly or indirectly, under a contract of the United States Government or any State or other governmental authority, then all terms and conditions required by law, regulations or by the Government Contract with respect to this order are incorporated herein by reference. To the extent that the terms and conditions of this order are inconsistent with any such required terms and conditions, the required terms and conditions will prevail and be binding on both Buyer and Vendor. Vendor agrees, upon request, to furnish Buyer with a certificate or certificates in such form as Buyer may require certifying that Vendor is in compliance with all such terms and conditions as well as any applicable law or regulation. Upon request, Buyer will make available to Vendor copies of all pertinent terms and conditions required by any such Government Contract.

21. NOTICE OF LABOR DISPUTES

Whenever Vendor has knowledge that any actual or potential labor dispute is delaying or threatens to delay the timely performance of this order, Vendor will immediately give written notice thereof, including all relevant information with respect thereto, to Buyer.

22. INDEMNIFICATION

Vendor agrees to indemnify and hold harmless Buyer, its successors, assigns, customers and users of its products, against all suits at law or in equity and from all damages, claims and demands arising out of the death or injury of any person or damage to any property alleged to have resulted from the goods hereby ordered, and/or resulting from any act or omission of Vendor, its agents or employees, and, upon the tendering of any suit or claim to Vendor, to defend the same at Vendor's expense as to all costs, fees and damages. The foregoing indemnification will apply whether Vendor or Buyer defends such suit or claims and whether the death, injury or property damage is caused by the sole or concurrent negligence of Vendor or otherwise.

To the extent that Vendor's agents, employees or subcontractors enter upon premises occupied by or under the control of Buyer, or any of its customers, or suppliers in the course of the performance of this order, Vendor will take all necessary precautions to prevent the occurrence of any injury (including death) to any persons, or of any damage to any property, arising out of acts or omissions of such agents, employees, or subcontractors, and except to the extent that any such injury or damage is due solely and directly to Buyer's negligence, will indemnify, defend and hold Buyer, its officers, employees and agents, harmless from any and all costs, losses, expenses, damages, claims, suits, or any liability whatsoever, including attorney's fees arising out of any act or omission of Vendor, its agents, employees or subcontractors. Vendor will maintain and require its subcontractors to maintain (1) public liability and property damage insurance including contractual liability (both general and vehicle) in amounts sufficient to cover obligations set forth above, and (2) worker's compensation and employer's liability insurance covering all employees engaged in the performance of this order for claims arising under any applicable Worker's Compensation and Occupation Disease Acts. Vendor will furnish certificates evidencing such insurance which expressly provide that no expiration, termination or modification will take place without thirty (30) days prior written notice to Buyer.

23. PATENT INDEMNIFICATION

Vendor will indemnify and hold harmless Buyer, its successors, assigns, customers and users of its products, against all suits at law or in equity and all loss, liability and damage, including costs and expenses, resulting from any claim that the manufacture, use, sale or resale of any goods supplied under this order infringe any patent or patent rights, and Vendor will when notified, defend any action or claim of such infringement at its own expense.

24. ASSIGNMENT

Neither this order nor any rights or obligations herein may be assigned by Vendor nor may Vendor delegate the performance of any of its duties hereunder without, in either case, Buyer's prior written consent.

25. CONTROLLING LAW

All questions concerning the validity and operation of this order and the performance of the obligations imposed on the parties under this order will be governed by the laws of the State of _____, U.S.A.

26. REMEDIES

The remedies provided herein will be cumulative and in addition to any other remedies provided by law or in equity. A waiver of a breach of any provision hereof will not constitute a waiver of any other breach hereof.

27. LANGUAGE

All correspondence pertaining to this order, or to any of the terms and conditions covered by this order, will be in the English language.

STANDARD CONDITIONS OF SALE

1. DELIVERY

Unless otherwise specified on the reverse side hereof, Seller will deliver all products to Buyer F.O.B. Seller's factory. Seller reserves the right to make partial deliveries and to ship products as they become available. Delivery dates are approximate and will be calculated from the date that Seller has received all information necessary to permit Seller to proceed with work immediately and without interruption.

Seller reserves the right to supply the products and/or services ordered by Buyer from any of its world-wide manufacturing facilities.

If any or all products are not delivered when ready due to the request of Buyer or cannot be delivered when ready due to any cause referred to in the "Delays" Article hereof, Seller reserves the right to invoice Buyer at any time thereafter and to place such products in storage. In such event, (1) Seller's delivery obligations will be deemed fulfilled and title and all risk of loss or damage will thereupon pass to Buyer, (2) any amount otherwise payable to Seller upon delivery will be due and payable upon presentation of Seller's invoices and its certification as to such cause, and (3) all expenses incurred by Seller such as for preparation for and placement into storage, handling, storage, inspection, preservation, and insurance will be due and payable by Buyer upon submission of Seller's invoices.

If Buyer wishes to pick up products from Seller's designated manufacturing facility, such pickup must be made within three (3) working days after Buyer has received notice from Seller that such products are ready to be picked up. If Buyer fails to pick up the products within the three (3) day period after receiving the notice from Seller, Seller may deliver the products to Buyer at Buyer's expense.

2. PRICES

The sales price(s) for products will be the list or posted price(s) of Seller in effect at the time of delivery, and will include the cost of Seller's usual factory tests and inspections. The cost of packing and crating in accordance with the standards of Seller is an additional charge and will be added to the sales price(s).

Unless otherwise agreed to by Seller and Buyer in writing, prices applied to this order are firm for the duration of the order.

3. TAXES

All prices are exclusive of any applicable U.S.A. federal, state or local sales, use, excise or other similar taxes. All such taxes will be for Buyer's account and will be paid by Buyer to Seller upon submission of Seller's invoices. If Buyer is exempt from any applicable sales tax but fails to notify Seller of such exemption or fails to furnish its Sales Tax Exemption Number to Seller in a timely manner and Seller is required to pay such tax, the amount of any such payment made by Seller will be reimbursed by Buyer to Seller upon submission of Seller's invoices.

Any taxes (including income, stamp and turnover taxes), duties, fees, charges, or assessments of any nature levied by any governmental authority other than of the U.S.A. in connection with this transaction, whether levied against Buyer, against Seller or its employees, or against any of Seller's subcontractors or their employees, or otherwise, will be for Buyer's account and will be paid directly by Buyer to the governmental authority concerned. If Seller is required by law or otherwise to pay any such levy and/or fines, penalties, or assessments in the first instance, or as a result of Buyer's failure to comply with any applicable laws or regulations governing the payment of such levies by Buyer, the amount of any payments so made by Seller will be reimbursed by Buyer to Seller upon submission of Seller's invoices.

4. PAYMENT

    Unless Buyer and Seller otherwise agree to terms other than those specified herein, payment will be made in U.S. Dollars at _____ as follows:

    (i)   On orders by shipment to countries other than the U.S.A., payment on all sales over five thousand U.S. Dollars (U.S. $5,000) will be made through the medium of a Letter of Credit to be established by the Buyer at its expense including any bank confirmation charges. All Lettters of Credit will be in favor of and acceptable to Seller, will be maintained in sufficient amounts for the period necessary to meet all payment obligations, will be irrevocable and issued, or confirmed, by a bank in _____ satisfactory to Seller within fifteen (15) days after acceptance of any order, will permit partial deliveries and will provide for pro-rata payments upon presentation of Seller's invoices and Seller's certificate of delivery F.O.B. Seller's factory, or of delivery into storage with certification of cause therefor, and for the payment of any termination charges.

    (ii) On all other orders payment will be made within thirty (30) days after the actual date of Seller's invoice(s).

    (iii) A monthly interest charge at the rate of one and one-half percent (1½%) or the maximum legal rate, whichever is less, will be assessed on all past due payments.

If Buyer fails to fulfill any condition of this Article, Seller may suspend performance and any costs incurred by Seller as a result thereof will be paid by Buyer. Seller will be entitled to an extension of time for performance of its obligations equal to the period of Buyer's non-fulfillment whether or not Seller elects to suspend performance. If such non-fulfillment is not rectified by Buyer promptly upon notice thereof, Seller may terminate performance and Buyer will pay Seller its termination charges upon submission of Seller's invoices.

5.   RISK OF LOSS AND TITLE

For non-export sales, risk of loss and title to products will pass to Buyer at the time of delivery specified in Article 1 hereof. Buyer will pay, or reimburse Seller for, all freight and in-transit insurance costs from time of delivery.

For export sales, Seller reserves the right to request that the Buyer agree that title to, beneficial ownership of, right of possession to, risk of loss on, and all property rights in products will remain with Seller and pass to Buyer at the port of entry of the ultimate country of destination (but prior to unloading or customs inspection at such port) specified on Buyer's order and/or declared as a country of ultimate destination on Seller's invoices.

Neither (i) the time, method, place or medium of payment provided for herein, or any combination of the foregoing, nor (ii) the manner of consignment provided for, whether to, or to the order of, the Buyer or its agent, will in any way limit or modify the rights of Seller, as the owner of the products, to have control over and the right to possession of the products until the title thereto passes to Buyer as provided for above. The term F.O.B. (Free on Board) or other commercial abbreviations, if used on any documents related to the transaction contemplated herein, will not be deemed to relate to the time when or the place where the ownership of and responsibility for the products is transferred from Seller to Buyer.

Buyer will pay all freight and insurance costs from the point of delivery specified in Article 1. In-transit insurance to the point that title passes to Buyer as provided above will be purchased for Seller's account and will be in an amount in U.S. Dollars not less than the aggregate prices of products delivered hereunder. Any insurance proceeds collected by Buyer for Seller's account will be promptly remitted to Seller in U.S. Dollars. The insurance policies purchased by Buyer will be for the benefit of Seller, whether or not Seller is named as an insured in such policies, until title and risk of loss to products passed to Buyer pursuant to this Article 5. Where possible the policies will provide that they are for the benefit of Seller and/or Buyer "as their interests may appear." Seller agrees that any insurance proceeds which Seller may receive in excess of amounts payable by Buyer for the products will be promptly remitted to Buyer.

6.   EXPORTS

Seller reserves the right, with respect to any and all goods purchased for export pursuant to these Standard Conditions of Sale, from time to time, to request and obtain from Buyer a written statement or statements certifying that such goods were in fact exported within one (1) year of the date of Seller's invoice(s) therefor.

7.   TESTING AND ACCEPTANCE

Prior to the delivery of any products, Seller will perform its standard factory acceptance test applicable to such products, and, upon request by Buyer, Seller will certify in writing that the products have satisfied the requirements of such test. Such certification will be in the form of Seller's standard quality control stickers or stamps. Buyer will be deemed to have accepted the products upon satisfactory testing, and title thereto, will pass to Buyer in accordance with the terms of Article 5 hereof.

8.   LIMITED WARRANTY

Seller warrants that products manufactured by Seller, when properly installed, used, and maintained, will be free from defects in material and workmanship. Seller's obligations under this warranty will be limited to repairing or replacing, at Seller's option, the part or parts of the products which prove defective in material or workmanship within one (1) year from the date of delivery, provided that Buyer gives Seller prompt notice of any defect or failure and satisfactory proof thereof. Products may be returned by Buyer only after written authorization has been obtained from Seller, and Buyer will prepay all freight charges to return any products to Seller's factory, or any other repair facility designated by Seller. Seller will deliver replacements for defective products to Buyer freight prepaid to the destination provided for in the original order. Products returned to Seller under this warranty will become the property of Seller. With respect to any product or part thereof not manufactured by Seller, only the warranty, if any, given by the manufacturer thereof, will apply. Seller's obligations under this warranty will not apply to any product which (1) is normally consumed in operation, or (2) has a normal life inherently shorter than the warranty period stated herein. **THE FOREGOING WARRANTIES ARE IN LIEU OF ALL OTHER WARRANTIES, WHETHER ORAL, WRITTEN, EXPRESS, IMPLIED OR STATUTORY. IMPLIED WARRANTIES OF MERCHANTABILITY AND FITNESS FOR A PARTICULAR PURPOSE WILL NOT APPLY. SELLER'S WARRANTY OBLIGATIONS AND BUYER'S REMEDIES HEREUNDER ARE SOLELY AND EXCLUSIVELY AS STATED HEREIN.**

With respect to products purchased by consumers in the United States for personal use, the implied warranties, including but not limited to the warranties of merchantability and fitness for a particular purpose, are limited to twelve (12) months from the date of delivery.

In those states which do not allow limitations on the duration of an implied warranty the above limitation will not apply. Similarly, in those states which do not allow the exclusion or limitation of consequential damages, the above limitation or exclusion will not apply. This limited warranty gives consumers specified legal rights and they also will have all other rights provided by law.

9.   PATENTS

If Buyer receives a claim that any product or part thereof manufactured by Seller infringes a United States patent, Buyer will notify Seller promptly in writing and give Seller all necessary information and assistance and the exclusive authority to evaluate, defend and settle such claim. Seller, at its own expense and option, will then (i) settle or defend against such claim, or (ii) procure for Buyer the right to use such product, or (iii) replace or modify the product to avoid infringement, or (iv) remove it and refund the purchase price less a reasonable amount for depreciation. Provided such timely notice has been given by Buyer, should any court of competent jurisdiction hold such product to constitute infringement, Seller will pay any costs and damages finally awarded on account of such infringement and, if the use of such product is enjoined, Seller will take, at its option, one or more of the actions described in (ii), (iii) or (iv) above. With respect to any product or part thereof not manufactured by Seller, only the patent indemnity, if any, given by the manufacturer thereof will apply. The foregoing indemnity will not apply to any product made to the specification or design of Buyer. The rights and obligations of the parties with respect to patents and all other industrial property rights are solely and exclusively as stated herein.

10.   LIMITATION OF LIABILITY

The total liability of Seller (including its subcontractor) on any claim, whether in contract, tort (including negligence) or otherwise, arising out of, connected with, or resulting from the manufacture, sale, delivery, resale, repair, replacement or use of any product will not exceed the price allocable to the product or part thereof which gives rise to the claim. In no event will Seller be liable for any incidental or consequential damages including, but not limited to, damages for loss of revenue, cost of capital, claims of customers for service interruptions or failure of supply, and costs and expenses incurred in connection with labor, overhead, transportaiton, installation or removal of products or substitute facilities or supply sources.

11.   INDEMNIFICATION

Buyer will indemnify Seller and hold Seller harmless from and against any liability, damage, loss, expense, claim or judgment arising from injury (including death) to any person (whether an employee of Buyer or any other person) or damage to any property, however caused, whether by Seller's sole or concurrent negligence or otherwise, arising from the sale, resale, repair, replacement or use of any products delivered pursuant to this order.

If requested by Seller, Buyer, at its own expense, will defend any claim, suit or action which is brought against Seller and is within the indemnification set out in the preceding paragraph provided that Seller promptly gives Buyer notice of such claim, suit or action, furnishes a copy of all documents and instruments served upon Seller in connection therewith and reasonably cooperates with Buyer in such defense. Seller, at its own expense, will have the right to be represented in such defense by advisory counsel of Seller's selection. If Seller does not request Buyer to defend any such claim, suit or action, Seller, at its own expense, will undertake the defense thereof and Buyer, at its own expense, will have the right to be represented in such defense by advisory counsel of Buyer's selection.

Buyer will pay any judgment finally awarded in any claim, suit or action which is brought against Seller and is within the indemnification set out hereinabove, whether Seller or Buyer directs the defense thereof, and Buyer agrees to pay any amounts payable in settlement or compromise of any such claim, suit or action, provided that Buyer agrees in writing to the settlement or compromise amount and to the terms of settlement or compromise.

12.   NUCLEAR USE
Buyer and third parties will not use any product or part thereof in connection with any activity or process involving nuclear fission or fusion or use or handling of any nuclear by-product material, as those materials are defined in the U.S. Atomic Energy Act of 1954 (as amended), unless Seller's written consent has been obtained prior to such use, and until such time as Buyer, at no expense to Seller, will have arranged for insurance coverage, indemnities and waivers of liability, recourse and subrogation, all acceptable to Seller, and all fully adequate in the opinion of Seller, to protect Seller (and its subcontractors and suppliers) against liability of any kind whatsoever whether in contract, tort (including negligence) or otherwise.

Seller will not be obligated to deliver the products until such indemnities, insurance and waivers have been procured and are legally operative in Seller's favor, failing which Seller may rescind the sale without liability for damages of any nature.

13.   DELAYS
The date on which Seller's obligations are to be fulfilled will be extended for a period equal to the time lost by reason of any delay arising directly or indirectly from (1) acts of God, unforeseeable circumstances, acts (including delay or failure to act) of any governmental authority (de jure or de facto), war (declared or undeclared), riot, revolution, priorities, fires, floods, strikes, labor disputes, sabotage or epidemics, (2) inability due to causes beyond Seller's reasonable control to timely obtain instructions or information from Buyer, necessary and proper labor, materials, components, facilities, or transportation, or (3) any other cause beyond Seller's reasonable control.

The foregoing extension will apply even though such cause(s) may occur after Seller's performance of its obligations has been delayed for other causes.

If delay resulting from any of the foregoing causes extends for more than sixty (60) days and the parties have not agreed upon a revised basis for continuing the work at the end of the delay, including adjustment of the price, then either party, upon thirty (30) days written notice, may terminate the order with respect to the unexecuted portion of the work whereupon Buyer will pay Seller its termination charges.

14.   GOVERNMENTAL AUTHORIZATIONS
Buyer will be responsible for the timely obtaining of all required authorizations, including Export Licenses, Import Licenses, Exchange Permits and all other governmental authorizations, even though such authorizations may be applied for by Seller. Buyer and Seller will assist each other in every manner reasonably possible in securing such authorizations as may be required. Seller will not be liable if any authorization is delayed, denied, revoked, restricted or not renewed and Buyer will not be relieved thereby of its obligations to pay Seller for its work.

All sales hereunder will at all times be subject to the export control laws and regulations of the United States Government and any amendments thereof. Buyer agrees that it will not make any disposition, by way of trans-shipment, re-export, diversion or otherwise, except as said laws and regulations may expressly permit, of U.S. origin goods purchased from Seller, other than in and to the ultimate country of destination specified on Buyer's order and/or declared as the country of ultimate destination on Seller's invoices.

15. DEFAULT—CANCELLATION

Seller reserves the right, by written notice of default, to cancel this order, without liability to Seller, in the event of any default on the part of the Buyer, the discontinuance of business by Buyer, or the sale by Buyer of the bulk of its assets other than in the usual course of business.

16. GENERAL

(i) Any order resulting herefrom will in all respects be construed and be given legal effect in conformity with the laws of the State of _____, U.S.A.

(ii) These Standard Conditions of Sale supersede all prior discussions and writings and constitute the entire agreement between Buyer and Seller with respect to the terms and conditions governing all orders. No waiver or modification of these Conditions will be binding upon Seller unless made in writing and signed by a duly authorized representative of Seller.

(iii) Seller's obligation hereunder will be dependent upon Seller's ability to obtain the necessary raw materials.

(iv) The remedies provided herein will be cumulative and in addition to any other remedies provided by law or equity. A waiver of a breach of any provision hereof will not constitute a waiver of any other breach hereof.

(v) All correspondence pertaining to this order, or to any of the terms and conditions covered by this order, will be in the English language.

(vi) All prices are subject to change without notice and may be subject to any increase which may be in effect on the date of shipment.

(vii) Any provisions in any purchase order, quotation, acknowledgment, or other forms or contract documents applicable to sales of Seller's products which are inconsistent, or in conflict, with any of the provisions herein are hereby objected to and will be deemed to be inapplicable to such sales.

SAMPLE WARRANTIES

Warranties are a technical subject which require legal counsel. You can help your lawyer by thinking about your situation and suggesting approaches. You can also help by gathering form warranties from other companies/products.

Note that my interview with Mr. Robert J. Crump in Chapter 16 lists warranties and contracts as a place where he was often consulted *too late*. Do not make the same mistake.

The same product can have a rather complex series of warranties. For example, a lawn mower may have a 2-year warranty, but for the first year, the engine would be protected by a 1-year warranty from the engine maker. Similarly, an appliance may have a full warranty on some parts and only a limited warranty on others. A tool might have a full warranty for a relatively short period and then a limited warranty thereafter. A product which must be installed might have a full warranty on the installation but only a limited warranty on the product itself. There is considerable flexibility in structuring your warranties, and the following are only two relatively simple examples. If you are alert to the problem, you can collect a fairly good sample of other companies' warranties by merely saving them from your normal household purchases.

Example of a Full Warranty

CAUTION: There are many restrictions imposed by the Federal Trade Commission on limitations which can be placed in a full warranty. At this time, those are only in proposed form. Warranties are a very technical subject which requires legal counsel—especially where consumer products are involved.

Your (well-known vacuum cleaner) is warranted in normal household use, in accordance with the instruction book, against original defects in workmanship for a period of one year from date of purchase. In commercial or rental use, the period of warranty is ninety days. This warranty provides, at no cost to you, all labor and parts to place this appliance in correct operating condition during the warranty period.

Warranty service can only be obtained by presenting the appliance to one of the following authorized warranty service outlets.

(Factory Service Centers)
(Authorized Warranty Service Dealers)

This warranty does not cover pickup, delivery, or house calls; however, if you mail your appliance to a factory service center for warranty service, transportation will be paid one way under this warranty.

While this warranty gives you specific legal rights, you may have other rights which vary from state to state.

If there are any questions concerning this warranty or the availability of warranty service outlets, write or phone.

Example of a Limited Warranty

NOTE: A limited warranty is used where you do not want to satisfy the technical requirements for a full warranty. Because you are limiting your warranties, it is essential to consider both the UCC and the Magnuson Moss Warranty Act. Otherwise, you may find that you have limited your obligations under the Magnuson Moss Warranty Act, but the buyer still has remedies under the express or implied warranty provisions of the UCC. We have seen many "limited warranties" which do not appear to take this into consideration. Following is one which seems to do a good job.

We warrant this (instrument) to be free from defects in workmanship or material for a period of one year from date of purchase. During the warranty period, such defects will be repaired or the defective instrument will be replaced, at our option, without charge. This warranty does not cover damage through accident or misuse.

ALL IMPLIED WARRANTIES, INCLUDING BUT NOT LIMITED TO WARRANTIES OF FITNESS AND MERCHANTABILITY, ARE HEREBY LIMITED IN DURATION TO A PERIOD ENDING ONE YEAR FROM DATE OF PURCHASE.

Some states do not allow limitations on how long an implied warranty lasts, so the above limitation may not apply to you. This warranty gives you specific legal rights, and you may also have other rights which vary from state to state.

Repair or replacement will be made at our option if this instrument is returned postpaid to:

FAIR CREDIT LAWS

The 1970s saw the development of a vast body of law relating to consumer credit. Keep in mind that this is *consumer* credit. It only applies if you are giving credit to a consumer. If you are in another type of business that operates in a commercial atmosphere—such as wholesaling or manufacturers who sell to wholesalers or retailers—these credit rules do not apply.

I have some very simple advice for any small business which desires to sell to consumers on credit. *Don't.* The plain fact of the matter is that the government has made this just too complicated and risky for a small business. Should you desire to do so anyway, the second piece of advice is to make sure you see a good consumer credit lawyer. These laws and regulations are just ungodly complex and technical. They are so technical that they prescribe the exact words you must use to state your interest charges and the exact size and kind of type in which certain words and numbers must appear. Further, if you extend credit to someone and he or she does not pay you, and you have the audacity to try to collect, there is another law called the Fair Debt Collection Practices Act which says in effect that you have to be gracious about it. Otherwise the deadbeat who did not pay you has a cause of action against you instead of vice versa.

All the credit laws are enforced by the Federal Trade Commission, and, should you desire more explanation of what they provide, you can call your local FTC office and they will send you not only copies of the statute but also relatively good and understandable brochures as to what those statutes say. The relevant statutes, in case you want to ask for material by name, are the following.

1. The *Truth In Lending Act,* which contains all the provisions about how you have to compute the annual percentage rate and spell it out in the documents in certain prescribed ways.

2. The *Equal Credit Opportunity Act,* which was designed to assure females equal access to credit regardless of their martial status.

3. The *Fair Credit Billing Act,* which tells you how you have to deal with complaints about bills that you send your customer.

4. The *Fair Debt Collection Practices Act,* which restricts the techniques you can use to collect from people who do not pay you.

5. The *Fair Credit Reporting Act,* which gives consumers the right to see their credit files and correct any erroneous information which might cause them to have credit denied in the future.

Keep in mind that all of these apply only if *you* are issuing the credit. The reason I suggest you not bother is that there are so many alternative ways of granting people credit. For example, if you honor a credit card, that credit company is extending the credit, and you are completely off the hook on all these laws. Thus, you can grant consumers credit by honoring Visa, Master Charge, American Express, Diners' Club, or other credit cards without any concern whatsoever for these laws—they are the credit card company's problem. True, it is going to cost you a little money, but, on the other hand, running a credit department yourself is going to cost you money also.

In summary, then, the bottom line is very clear. Steer clear of granting consumers credit yourself. If you have to grant consumers credit in your business, do so either by bank cards or by some other credit card system. If you must grant consumers credit and if you cannot use someone else's system, be prepared to spend a rather substantial amount of money in legal fees for complying with the numerous federal requirements on extension of consumer credit.

11

OCCUPATIONAL SAFETY AND HEALTH

The requirements of the Occupational Safety and Health Act can be divided into two different categories. The first category is the technical or substantive requirements of the act. These are such things as proper machine guarding and grounding of electrical outlets. Your lawyer is not going to be too much help to you here. The second category is the legal rights and obligations imposed upon you by the act. These can be briefly summarized as follows:

EMPLOYEE DISCIPLINE

I believe the most important thing that you should know about the Occupational Safety and Health Act is that it contains a *criminal* penalty for a willful violation which results in the death of an employee. The second most important thing you should be aware of is that it is illegal to discharge or discipline an employee for refusing to do work which that employee reasonably believes exposes him or her to an immediate and serious risk of harm. It is also illegal to discriminate against any employee because that employee may have complained to the Occupational Safety and Health Administration (OSHA) about a safety violation.

There have been quite a few recent cases which show how these problems interact. The typical fact pattern is that employees will refuse to do some work which they legitimately feel exposes them to an unreasonable risk of harm. So far, all of the cases apparently have been legitimate on the part of the employees. Many of the cases involved requests to work in high places where either the scaffolding or the thing the employees were supposed to stand on was unsafe. One case involved going up on high catwalks outside in the dark during bad weather. The employers disagreed with the employee as to the safety of the job and ordered the employee to do it anyway. The employee still refused to do the work, and was either discharged or disciplined. The employee then filed a compliant with OSHA, and the case went to court. The courts have held that in these kinds of situations, so long as the employee's belief is genuine and reasonable, the employee cannot be disciplined or discharged for refusing to do work which he or she believe is dangerous. That, however, in my judgment, is only a very small part of this problem. True, the employer has lost a case and been obliged to pay back wages to the employee, but that is only a small amount of money. What if the employee had actually done the hazardous work over objection, an accident happened, and the employee had fallen to his or her death? The Occupational Safety and Health Act requires that you file a notice with OSHA any time there is a workplace accident which results in the death of an employee or in the hospitalization of five employees. Thus, there definitely would have been an inspection, and the OSHA inspectors would have had as one important item for consideration whether to institute *criminal* actions against the *corporate individuals* who ordered or were responsible for ordering this employee to perform the dangerous work. True, OSHA would have had to find some standard or regulation which was violated, but this would be relatively easy to do in many cases.

In summary, then, the most important thing to keep in mind under the Occupational Safety and Health Act is that you must take employee complaints about safety problems very seriously, and you must not discharge or discriminate against any employee for raising safety questions. Above all, I believe it would be foolish to order an employee to perform work unwillingly which he or she reasonably believes is hazardous.

You should keep in mind that we are talking about rather serious problems here. If an employee is exposed to some relatively minor safety hazard or one which is not immediate, such as excess noise levels or dust in the air, he or she cannot refuse to do the work. The employee's legal remedy is to file a complaint with OSHA, cause an inspection to be made, and have the problem resolved that way. It is only where time pressures do not permit this type of administrative response that the employees are within their rights to refuse to perform the work.

RECORDS AND REPORTS

Your next set of legal obligations under OSHA is to file reports in certain restricted circumstances and to keep records. These are relatively simple requirements, but they are important, and you must not only do them but also take extreme care not to falsify them. One of the calamities discussed in Chapter 15, "Miscellaneous Calamities That Can Send You to Jail," is filing false information with the government. Thus, for example, if you lie to an OSHA inspector, or if you give incorrect information when you file a report of an accident which results in death, that can not only get you into trouble with OSHA, but also cause a *criminal* prosecution *for that reason alone.* The basic reporting requirements are simply to notify OSHA if there is an accident which results in a death or hospitalization of five or more employees. There is no annual or routine kind of reporting. It is only in one of these serious accident cases that you have to actually file a document with OSHA.

There are also record-keeping and posting requirements. You must keep a "log of occupational safety and health injuries," which is essentially what the name implies: an ongoing log of all the incidents which have given rise to any employee injuries or health problems. You also have to post a summary of this log annually at each of your locations. There is a second form called the "supplementary record of occupational injuries and illnesses" which you must maintain. It is simply a one-page form which explains in a little more detail how each of the accidents which you listed on the log occurred. In the case of employee exposure to certain chemicals, medical records are required.

In many states, similar information is required to be kept under the workers' compensation law. Sometimes there is a single set of forms which can be used to satisfy both requirements. There is also a posting requirement which obligates you to display an occupational safety and health poster informing workers of the existence of OSHA, the fact that they have rights, and the fact that if they have any complaints, they can go to their OSHA office and discuss them.

OSHA INSPECTIONS

I would like to turn now to the OSHA inspections. The Occupational Safety and Health Act allows occupational safety and health inspectors to enter your plant, without notice and without any warrant, and conduct a "wall-to-wall" inspection. This is one of the most controversial features of the law. These unannounced inspections were thought to be unconstitutional. Certainly, it would be unconstitutional to allow the police to come into your home unannounced and conduct a search unless they had a search warrant or unless you consented. Employers thought that the same thing should apply to the business location. Federal inspectors should not have carte blanche access just because they feel like coming in and snooping around.

After a number of cases, the Supreme Court did decide that this was, in fact, the rule. Occupational Safety and Health Act inspectors *do not* have the authority to enter your premises *unless* they have a *search warrant* or unless you *voluntarily grant them permission* to do so. This has given rise to considerable disagreement among lawyers as to whether it is more desirable to force OSHA inspectors to get a warrant or to cooperate voluntarily. Generally, OSHA can get a warrant to enter your premises; it is only a matter of delay. To be sure, there are exceptions—OSHA must apply to the nearest federal district court. There are hundreds of federal district courts and even more federal district court judges. Each has his or her own ideas as to when a search warrant should be issued. In some cases, federal district courts have refused to issue the warrant because OSHA has failed to show any probable cause for thinking that there was a violation. In other cases, OSHA inspectors have been denied access to a plant and never gone to court to get the warrant. In other cases, OSHA has gotten the warrant, but not come back to inspect the plant. It appears from discussing this matter with many different lawyers that these situations are in the minority—but it is a significant minority. Most of the time, OSHA will ask for and receive a warrant if it is denied access to the plant. In most of these situations, OSHA inspectors will in fact come back and inspect the plant. Thus, it is possible that if you ask them to get a warrant, the only thing you will do is delay the inspection a few days and cause them to be very mad when they come back.

The overwhelming majority of *large companies* seem to be granting OSHA inspectors access to their plant voluntarily without insisting on a warrant. However, in the case of small business, I just do not know what the statistics show. Certainly, there are many lawyers representing small companies who take the position that their clients should not allow an OSHA inspector into the plant unless the inspector has a warrant. Other lawyers think this is a waste of time and energy and simply counsel their companies to do a good job on employee safety and let OSHA conduct its inspections. My advice is between the two extremes.

1. I do not think you should welcome the OSHA inspector with open arms and invite him or her into your plant to issue you citations.

2. I do not think that, unless there are special circumstances, you should automatically declare legal war on OSHA if one of their inspectors arrives at your plant.

3. I do think you should understand the extent to which OSHA applies to your plant, and if it is substantial, have an OSHA lawyer available. Since you will need an OSHA lawyer available to respond to emergencies, you might as well ask that lawyer for his or her views on inspections and warrants. Keep in mind, however, that the decision is for *you,* and the best *legal* answer might not be the best *business* answer. After all, you have public relations and employee relations to consider also.

4. Remember that you do not need a *definite and unalterable* action plan before the OSHA inspector arrives. You can wait until the inspector arrives and then discuss the matter with the inspector.

Here are some questions to ask *before* you grant access to the plant.

a. Why is the inspector there?
b. Has any employee filed a complaint (you do not want the name of the employee that filed a complaint, you just want to know if a complaint has been filed)?
c. What parts of the plant does the inspector want to see?

After you know these facts, you can make a much better judgment of what to do than simply deciding beforehand without knowing the circumstances. For example, if the inspector said that an employee had filed a complaint about a particular machine and all the inspector wanted to do was inspect that machine, you have a very different situation from one where the inspector says he or she has no particular reason for wanting to inspect your facility—your name just came up, and he or she wants to go through the whole facility on a wall-to-wall inspection which he or she estimates will take 3 days.

Also, remember that you do not have to make any decision right then. You can call your OSHA lawyer. If your OSHA lawyer is not available, you can ask the OSHA inspector to either wait or come back later. You can even ask for 2 or 3 days to discuss the matter with your lawyer. The OSHA inspector will almost always go along with this, because it will take that long to get the warrant anyway. However, if a serious employee complaint is involved, the inspector may say that you can have your 2 or 3 days, but he or she must get a warrant so that when he or she does come back, you will have to let him or her in.

Of course, these couple of days have secondary benefits. Not only can you go through your plant and remedy possible safety problems before the inspector comes back and cites you for them, but you can also make sure that your forms and records are up to date, that the plant is generally in good order from a housekeeping standpoint, and that appropriate people in the plant know about the forthcoming inspection.

I do not recommend asking OSHA inspectors to get warrants unless you are willing to get your lawyer involved in the inspection. When you start to get technical like this, you definitely need good legal advice at every stage of the inspection.

YOUR RIGHTS DURING THE INSPECTION

Once you grant the inspector permission to enter your facility without getting a warrant, that does not mean you cannot change your mind. Of course, everything that the inspector sees while on your premises with your permission and everything the inspector sees while he or she is being escorted out the door after you have changed your mind are possible subjects where citations can be issued. The only time you would want to change your mind is if you granted an inspector access to your facility and he or she started what you believe to be an extremely burdensome and nit-picking investigation, and you wanted to get your lawyer involved. Most of the time, OSHA inspectors are not this way. In the overwhelming majority of cases, an OSHA inspection will not be too much of a problem to you. He or she may find a few safety violations, and there may even be a citation and some penalties. These, however, will be rather modest. OSHA penalties are generally not large—on the order of hundreds of dollars rather than thousands. Many cases involve penalties of less than $100. Of course, there may be many violations, and in total the amount of penalties may drift into the low four-figure range, but that is the exception rather than the rule. Imminently hazardous situations can, however, generate substantial penalties.

During the inspection, the following ground rules apply:

1. Technically, the inspector is a guest in your plant (unless he or she has a warrant). You have the right to stop the inspector from doing anything you object to. This, however, is somewhat akin to asking for a warrant—a strict insistence on all your legal rights at every stage. I do not recommend this unless you have previously consulted your lawyer and have a clear set of ground rules and procedures.

2. In most cases, you will not elect to insist on your legal rights in this manner and will allow the inspector certain liberties, which might include talking to your employees in private or taking pictures.

3. If the inspector arrives with a warrant, his or her authority will be spelled out in the warrant. You should read it, and I think you should get legal counsel promptly. If the inspector has gone to the trouble of getting a warrant without first asking you to grant access to the plant voluntarily, you can be sure OSHA thinks there are serious problems.

4. In many cases, the OSHA inspector will want to take air samples or make measurements of the noise levels in your plant. If this occurs, you should take exactly the same measurements at exactly the same time. If you have these kinds of situations, you are getting into a more technical set of problems, and expert legal and industrial hygiene help is probably called for.

5. The inspection will always begin with an "opening conference," at which time the OSHA inspector will want to see your records. These will include the OSHA forms discussed above as well as any other required forms or records relating to one of the many

chemicals which OSHA regulates. Medical records of your employees might also be requested but this is rare. The OSHA inspector will inform you of your basic legal rights, and will ask for an employee representative to accompany him or her. If your shop is unionized, or if you have a safety committee, you probably have such a person. If not, the inspector will simply talk with employees during the inspection.

6. The inspection will usually concentrate on either safety problems or health problems, depending on your particular operation. Most inspectors will be generally knowledgeable about all safety and health matters, but particularly knowledgeable about either safety (things like machine guards) or health (things like air contamination or noise or chemicals). OSHA will probably know quite a bit about your business before they send an inspector and will, therefore, be able to make a decision as to which type of inspector would be most appropriate.

7. After the walk-through inspection, there will be a closing conference where the inspector will tell you informally about any problems that were observed. If the inspector has observed a serious hazard which is severe enough to ask for immediate corrective action, he or she may ask you to shut down a particular operation until the problem is corrected. On the other extreme, if there are minor problems which can be corrected easily (such as housekeeping violations), he or she may also ask you to correct them immediately and not write them up at all. In between these two extremes are the kinds of violations which are not too serious, but which do take some time to correct. In occupational safety and health jargon, this is called the "abatement period."

One of the most productive things you can do during the closing conference is to try to negotiate a reasonable abatement period. Keep in mind that the OSHA inspection process is basically a negotiation process, and to some extent at least, you can persuade the inspector to give you enough time to fix a violation so that you do not have to contest a citation merely for that purpose. Also, there may be problems that you know about that the inspector does not. For example, the inspector might have noticed a particular machine guard which he or she feels is inadequate, and you may have already spent considerable time and effort trying to design a better one. In such a case, you should certainly tell that to the inspector so he or she can take this into consideration. Perhaps the machine guarding question is a little more difficult than the inspector had thought, and he or she will allow you more time for abatement.

8. After the inspector leaves, he or she will go back to the OSHA office and discuss this matter with his or her immediate superiors. Within a month or so, OSHA will issue you any citations which they feel are justified. Once you receive a citation, you have only 15 days to object to it. Otherwise, it becomes final and you can no longer object. Thus, it is very important to examine that citation immediately and determine whether or not you want to make any objections. If you do, you have to do so very promptly, and I strongly suggest consultation with your lawyer at this point. I am not saying that you should have your lawyer handle the entire process, because it is something that you or your employees can probably do. On the other hand, it may be more efficient for your lawyer to do it, and in any event, your lawyer should review the work. Remember that contesting an OSHA citation is just like any other administrative proceeding. It is rather technical, and you are building a very important record. These are the kinds of things which your lawyer can help you with.

THE ON-SITE CONSULTATION PROGRAM

In the late 1970s, OSHA instituted a program where their inspectors would voluntarily go through your plant without a formal inspection. Before that time the only way an OSHA inspector could help you was by a formal inspection. This meant that if the inspector saw a violation, he or she was required by law to issue you a citation. There was no such thing as informal consultations or informal help. However, in response to widespread criticism, principally from small businesses, OSHA changed their rules, and this is no longer the case. OSHA can, and is indeed happy to, have an inspector visit your plant and have a "mock-OSHA inspection." If the inspector sees a violation, he or she will just tell you about it, but will not issue you any citations or make you pay penalties. Further, the whole thing is confidential. No records are kept or follow-up inspections made to see that you have, in fact, corrected any problems. Further, if you have a "regular" inspection later on, there is no connection between that and the informal one. In short, there is nothing to lose.

There is one very minor hitch. If the inspector sees something which is "imminently hazardous," he or she will ask you to correct that problem immediately. In that situation, he or she may even issue you a citation and, if the problem is serious enough, may ask you to shut down the operation until the problem is corrected. Except, however, in the case of one of these imminently hazardous problems—which I assume you could spot yourself—

there is no downside risk of having one of these voluntary OSHA on-site consultations. They are performed by OSHA without any cost to you whatsoever.

When the voluntary on-site consultation program was first announced, there was some uneasiness about it. Admittedly, the concept of calling up a federal inspector and asking him or her to come out and go through your plant seemed like unnecessarily asking for trouble. However, experience has not proved out these first fears. I know of no complaint that OSHA has misused this on-site consultation program. The OSHA on-site consultation program may not be necessary or appropriate for everyone, but I do think it is useful in some cases and worth your careful consideration. It is certainly an inexpensive and efficient way to obtain expert technical advice on safety problems.

SPECIAL TROUBLE SPOTS—NOISE AND CARCINOGENS

I believe that OSHA is an overly maligned agency. In general, I feel that their inspections are reasonable, that the people are reasonable, and, in the overwhelming majority of situations, that an OSHA inspection will deal with technical safety problems which you can negotiate yourself and where you will not need legal help. There are, however, two exceptions: noise and carcinogenic chemicals. When the subject turns to noise or carcinogens, OSHA just goes berserk. Common sense is thrown to the winds.

On the noise question, OSHA says that you *must* use every engineering control possible to reduce noise to the levels they say are acceptable, even if earplugs would do the job just as well. Further, there is considerable disagreement within OSHA and the courts as to whether there is *any* appropriate cost-benefit analysis. OSHA itself says that there is practically none. They say unless you prove that engineering controls would be so expensive that they would put you into bankruptcy, you have to implement them. This is true even though they may or may not reduce the noise to the required levels. The Occupational Safety and Health Review Commission has recently said that *some* cost-benefit analysis is appropriate, but it was an exceedingly confusing opinion. There are three commissioners, and each wrote a separate opinion. The Supreme Court has yet to address this question directly. If you have a noise problem in your plant, I suggest that you have an OSHA lawyer actively involved in your compliance program, because this subject can be extremely important to you. As a general matter, the courts are much more reasonable than OSHA, and legal help will be extremely beneficial to you from an economic point of view. In some cases, your lawyer may be able to save you from catastrophic compliance costs.

OSHA's position that you must use engineering controls before personal protective equipment also applies in other areas, such as air contamination.

You must reduce air contamination in your plant by engineering controls before you start to use respirators. OSHA's reason for this approach is that they do not believe people will wear or use the personal protective equipment. Thus, if you have these kinds of problems, it is also appropriate to have good legal advice available to you.

On carcinogens, OSHA has again taken an extremely unrealistic position. Essentially, the problem is scientific. No one knows for sure what is carcinogenic and what is not. OSHA wants to take an extremely conservative view and ban all chemicals which might be carcinogenic. This is true regardless of the evidence of carcinogenicity or the costs. They have not had 100 percent success in court. However, the issues involved are complicated and far from settled. If you use chemicals in your business which are suspected of being carcinogens, you need an OSHA lawyer on your team. The same is true for toxic chemicals such as lead, asbestos, or berillium.

SPECIAL RULES FOR SMALL BUSINESS

The Occupational Safety and Health Act applies to *all* businesses even if they only have one employee. However, in response to criticism from small business, Congress has restricted OSHA from actively enforcing its requirements on small business. For example, at this time, the record-keeping requirements are not applicable if you have 10 or fewer employees. Similarly, OSHA is not supposed to inspect your facility if you have 10 or fewer employees unless there is a serious problem manifested by an employee complaint or an accident which has resulted in a death. In the future, it is likely that these kinds of exemptions or modifications of OSHA requirements for small business will continue and possibly expand. It is a rather rapidly developing area. However, finding out if you are covered by OSHA and if so exactly what provisions apply or do not apply to you is rather easy and inexpensive. You can just call up your local office and ask. They will be glad to tell you and send you a copy of any appropriate directives or regulations which spell the rules out in more detail.

HELP FROM THE GOVERNMENT

OSHA is one of the most helpful government agencies. They not only have the on-site consultation program mentioned above, but do an excellent job of preparing useful brochures which explain to you and your employees exactly what your rights and obligations are. Of course, OSHA will also give you copies of the law, the regulations, and the standards. I suggest you take advantage of this service and ask for this material. Following is a list of things I would ask for at this time, but keep in mind that OSHA is always generating new pamphlets and revising existing ones. A personal visit or a telephone call to your local OSHA office will provide you quite a bit of free and useful information.

The publications on the list are all free. Many of them would be useful in training or safety sessions and could probably be obtained from OSHA in quantity for this purpose. Usually, your local OSHA office is the best place to get them.

OSHA Handbook for Small Businesses.   Publication No. 2209, 1979, 51 pages.
> Good discussion, applicable to both small businesses and individual facilities of larger companies. Contains general discussion of procedures for compliance plus good, understandable checklists.

Record Keeping Requirements Under the Occupational Safety and Health Act of 1970.
> Contains the relevant record-keeping forms and instructions. Forms are Form 200, Log and Summary of Occupational Injuries and Illnesses; and Form 101, Supplementary Record of Occupational Injuries and Illnesses.

OSHA Inspections: How You Can Help—A workbook and guide.   Publication No. 3023, 1979.
> Booklet is meant for employees to help OSHA inspector, but is also useful information for employers.

OSHA Health Inspections: How You Can Help—A workbook and guide.   Publication No. 3024.
> Same as above, except concentrates on health inspections instead of safety inspections.

The following are good pamphlets averaging about 30 pages in a 3 × 7 inch format. They are typically meant for employees, but provide useful information for employers—especially for safety sessions or training programs.

Worker's Rights Under OSHA.   Publication 3021.

Job Safety and Health: OSHA Inspections Are Only the Beginning.   Publication 3029.

You Have a Right to Protect Your Life on the Job; That Right Is Called ELEVEN-C.   Publication 3032.

Job Safety and Health: Answers to Some Common Questions.   Publication 3024.

Health and Safety Committees: A Good Way to Protect Workers.   Publication 3035.

The Target Health Hazards.   Publication 2051.

General Industry OSHA Safety and Health Standards Digest.   Publication 2201.
A short and small (4 × 5 inches, 50 pages) digest of most important general industry standards.

Construction Industry OSHA Safety and Health Standards Digest.
Same as above for construction industry.

12
PRODUCT LIABILITY

WHAT IS THE PROBLEM?

The two kinds of companies which face the largest product liability problems are manufacturers of capital goods which are used by employees of other companies (lift trucks, metal working equipment, power presses, etc.) and manufacturers of consumer goods which have shown a high degree of hazard to the consumer (lawn mowers, hand power tools, bicycles, ladders, boats, etc.). These kinds of companies have had tremendous problems getting product liability insurance at any reasonable cost—even if their claims history has been 100 percent clear. The problem of product liability created quite a stir in the mid- to late 1970s—rising to the point of near-crisis. Largely, this was the result of a relatively small, but still significant number of horrible example-type cases, most of which involved a variation on one or more of the following themes.

1. A capital goods manufacturer would point to a case where someone was injured using a piece of equipment it had made many years ago and which might have been resold, rebuilt, and even misused by the employees. The employee who was injured on the machine could not sue the employer, because workers' compensation would preclude that. The injured employee could, however, sue the maker of the piece of equipment alleging that it was defective because it did not have proper guards, was not designed properly, etc. Many of these cases were successful—as they could well be today.

2. Small manufacturers of consumer goods which have proved to be frequent sources of injury to consumers have had their insurance canceled and been unable to obtain new insurance at any premi-

um, or if insurance was offered, it was offered only at a high cost. Sometimes, an insurance company would quote a premium which was one to one and a half times the coverage. In other words, for $50,000 of coverage the premium might be $80,000. The insurance company then would be assuming that there would be 1.6 losses of the maximum amount each year in order to justify this kind of premium. Some small companies never had any claims at all, and therefore questioned the rate-making processes of the insurers in setting these kinds of rates.

3. Very large companies which could afford self-insurance or could afford to establish captive insurance companies were not hurt as much as smaller companies. Lobbyists for small companies felt that Congress ought to enact laws which would reverse this trend.

4. Some insurance companies had been turning to a "claims made" basis. This means that the insurance applies on the date a claim is made, not necessarily on the date the injury was caused or the date the product was made or sold. Some insured companies had been surprised by this because it was not fully explained to them. They felt that it was unfair—especially when coupled with the insurance company's right to cancel the insurance. If a claim is made which looks like it might be the first of a series, the insurance company might cancel the insurance, and no new insurance would be obtainable. The insurance company that had previously accepted the premiums—perhaps for many years—would be off the hook except for the small number of claims which were instituted before the policy was canceled.

The law on product liability cases is extremely bad for defendants. Essentially, the courts in almost all jurisdictions have, under one theory or another, taken the view that an injured plaintiff ought to be able to recover from *either* the manufacturer or the seller of a defective product which caused the injury. Further, the meaning of "defect" has been expanded to include almost anything imaginable, including foreseeable misuse by the plaintiff, improper labeling or warning, or even claims made by the maker of a product that the product was "safe" when it was capable of causing an injury.

There are some other, social factors which have also made the picture bleak. Juries tend to award large amounts as damages when a person is injured. It is common to have verdicts in the mid-six-figure range, and verdicts over a million dollars are becoming common. Another social factor is that Americans are becoming more litigious. When I graduated from law school in 1966, product liability suits were fairly common. Ten years before that they were rather rare, and 10 years after that, there was a virtual flood of them. Today, if a consumer is injured, the first thing he or she thinks about is whether he or she can sue someone for the injuries. Usually, a lawyer will be able to develop a claim against someone, and if the injury is real, there will almost always be a recovery. A person who comes into court with a lost arm, permanent disfigurement, or paralysis is going to leave with a lot of money. It's just that simple. Very few juries are going to send such a person home empty-handed when the defendant is an impersonal corporation which everyone on that jury is going to assume is covered by an even more impersonal insurance company.

DO YOU HAVE THE PROBLEM?

The first thing you have to do is understand if there is any circumstances whatsoever where your product could cause personal injury to others. Even if you are simply in a retail or wholesale operation, you still have to be concerned, because the plaintiff can sue *either* the person who sold the product or the company which made the product. For example, many cases involve suits against grocery stores alleging personal injury caused by the explosion of bottles of pop. The plaintiff can sue the grocery store, and the grocery store can, if it so desires, join the maker of the soft drink in question in the lawsuit. This does, however, place the burden on the grocery store, and you could envision a situation where a plaintiff would be able to recover from the grocery store but the grocery store would not be able to recover from the company that sold it the product in question. One of the basic principles of product liability law is that *an injured consumer* cannot have his or her rights cut off by any kind of contract. Thus, no matter what kind of contract, disclaimer, etc., is involved, if a *consumer* is injured, he or she is very likely to be able to recover. *The rule is exactly the opposite, however, in a commercial situation.* A store, being a business enterprise, is not a "consumer." If you buy things from a manufacturer pursuant to a contract which limits the manufacturer's liability *to you* in the event of a personal injury, that contract is certainly valid. The manufacturer cannot cut off its obligation *to the consumer,* but the consumer does not have any obligation to sue the manufacturer—the consumer can simply elect to sue you because you are handy and locally available. The first step, then, is to assess your level of risk. It would be a good idea to discuss this with your lawyer, because there are many legal implications in determining that risk.

I am sure you have all read newspaper accounts of persons injured by products which really do not seem hazardous. Such cases include the following:

- Liability based on fingernail polish catching fire when a cigarette ignited the fumes.

- Liability based on clothing catching fire if the clothing was not coated with flame-retardant materials. Further, the major flame-retardant material was determined to be a potential carcinogen by the Consumer Product Safety Commission, causing many recalls of products which used it.

- Liability based on a lawn mower injury where the injured consumer was using the lawn mower to trim hedges.

- Liability for an oven based on an injured woman who fell when the oven door collapsed while she was standing on it to clean the kitchen.

- Liability for injuries caused when the roof of a car collapsed when the driver ran the car into a ravine, based on the theory that the roof should have been strong enough to stand up if the car rolled over in an accident.

- Liability for loss of an eye when an auto mechanic used a screwdriver for a chisel and when he hit it, a piece of metal broke off and went into his eye.

Remember that all these kinds of cases are *very common.* Would you have thought that a six-figure verdict could be rendered against you because of a screwdriver that you either made or sold? These examples show clearly that you *must* discuss this subject with your lawyer to assess your level of risk. You can also get useful information from your trade association and your insurance broker.

HOW CAN YOU MINIMIZE THE PROBLEM?

While you cannot eliminate the product liability problem, there are a number of things you can do to minimize it. Following are some examples—each of which is rather technical and should be discussed with your counsel.

Your Forms

Make sure, to the maximum extent possible, that transactions are governed by forms prepared by you, not the other company's forms. This brings into play the entire "battle of the forms" process which is discussed in Chapter 10. While you cannot cut off any consumer's rights by doing this, you may be able to cut off rights of intermediaries, or you may be able to give yourself additional rights against other people involved in the transaction—for example, your suppliers.

Express Warranties

Evaluate all express warranties. A breach of warranty is one of the theories that a plaintiff can use to bring a successful product liability claim. The kind of warranty you give, of course, is a mixture of legal, financial, and marketing considerations, but do not forget the product liability aspect. Also, do not forget that "warranties" is an extremely broad term—they include any promise you make about your product or, indeed, even a description of your product.

Your Written Materials

Consider your warnings, your instruction booklets, your advertisements, and any other written statements that go along with your product. Many lawsuits have been based not upon the product itself but on a failure to warn of a defect, or some misstatement or failure to describe a hazard in the literature that went along with the product.

Consider Insurance

You will have to consider your insurance coverage both with your lawyer and with your insurance advisor. Following are some suggestions.

1. Do not select an insurance carrier on the basis of cost alone. Make sure the carrier has a practice of ethical dealings with the public and has adequate claims-servicing facilities for your company— including expertise in the product or products you sell.

2. Participate actively in the discussion of any reserves. Review these at least quarterly.

3. Participate actively in all major claims, and discuss them with the insurance carrier. Do not just assume that once a claim is presented it is the insurance company's problem.

4. Make sure you get any available technical assistance from your insurance company. You are paying for it and might as well take advantage of it.

Records

Records are both a problem and an opportunity. If you have good records to show exactly how products were tested, how specific reports of injuries were evaluated, etc., that might help you. On the other hand, it might also hurt you, because it would show a prior knowledge of the hazard in question. The worst thing that you can have are documents which show that you knew about an alleged hazard and did nothing to correct it. The multimillion-dollar verdict in the case against a large auto-manufacturing company (involving an alleged defect in the design of one of its models, causing it to catch fire when hit from the rear) was based in large part on the fact that internal company documents disclosed a knowledge of this danger and, allegedly, a failure to make the relatively minor change which would have minimized the danger.

Get Legal Counsel

Make sure you have access to a good product liability lawyer. Chances are that if you are a small company, you will want to depend upon the insurance company's lawyers to actually handle the defense of any claims. On the other hand, that does not mean you should not have your own lawyer to monitor the cases and also to provide you with advice on how problems can be minimized.

Price

In my view, this is the most important aspect of product liability. Product liability exposure is a cost, and you should make sure you understand that cost and have built it into the price of your product. Further, rights against your suppliers, or indemnification from your suppliers, is valuable, and the reverse is also true. If your suppliers will not indemnify you from product liability claims based on their products, they are not entitled to the same price as companies who will. Do not get caught in the middle. Don't say that, from a marketing point of view, you simply cannot insist on disclaiming product liability responsibility from your commercial customers (remember that you cannot disclaim it as far as the consumer is concerned), but that you do not have the bargaining position to make your suppliers stand behind their products. That places *you* on the product liability hot seat. If you end up in this position, you simply must have adequate insurance, and you must price your products according to this risk. Remember, it is something which can strike from out of the blue. One day you look at your history and find that you never had a problem. The next day you get served with papers on a lawsuit where a person has been injured—perhaps in a bizarre type of accident—and wants damages in the millions of dollars.

Prevention

Of course, your first line of defense on the product liability front ought to be simply to make safe products. We all know this is a goal which is virtually unattainable—but that does not mean you should not strive to come as close as you can. Your lawyer can help you minimize your exposure, but cannot do very much in the area of helping your business operation, other than pointing out litigated cases involving your products or similar products and alerting you to dangers which have already caused injuries.

In summary, then, I recommend that the product liability question be placed on your agenda of things to discuss with your lawyer if you feel that it is even remotely a problem for you. Your insurance advisor should also be involved in this discussion. Unfortunately, unless the present situation changes, if you really do have a serious product liability problem, your insurance advisor may have difficulty in placing insurance which is cost-effective. Your lawyer can also be of only limited help, because while he or she can tell you how to minimize exposure, he or she cannot eliminate the exposure altogether, and in a small company even one lawsuit can literally wipe the business out.

I do not have any very good solution to this problem. It has been studied by numerous federal agencies and task forces of interested people and they have not figured out any solution either. It is an inherent problem of small business. That is the place where even a single catastrophe can put you out of business, where unreasonable insurance coverage just is not realistic, and where self-insurance is not a viable alternative.

This is a rather rapidly developing area of the law. In early 1980 the Department of Commerce issued a model product liability law which would minimize some of the problems. This has not, to date, been enacted in any state. On the other hand, some states have enacted limited pieces of legislation which reduce—but do not completely eliminate—the problem. Unfortunately, state legislation is a very poor way to deal with this problem. If your products are likely to be sold in any state, you can be sued in any state, and it will be the law of that state which governs. Thus, for planning purposes, it really does not do you much good to know that some states may have favorable laws so long as other states have unfavorable ones. At this time, the law in almost all major industrial states is still extremely adverse to defendants and extremely favorable to the injured plaintiffs in these kinds of cases.

THE CONSUMER PRODUCT SAFETY ACT

The Consumer Product Safety Act was enacted in 1972 to establish an independent regulatory agency with extremely broad powers to protect consumers from unreasonable risk of injury from hazardous products. The agency has the authority to set safety standards for consumer products and to ban those products showing evidence of undue risk of injury. The Act covers consumer products, but defines a consumer product very broadly as "any article or component part thereof—whether American-made or imported—manufactured or distributed (1) for sale to a consumer for use in or around a permanent or temporary residence or a school, in recreation or otherwise; or (2) for the personal use, consumption, or enjoyment of a consumer in or around a permanent or temporary household or residence or a school, in recreation or otherwise." The reason I mention this law is to make small business owners aware of the following important things:

1. If you make or sell a consumer product, you simply must be aware of this law and know whether anything you sell is subject to any Consumer Product Safety Act standards. Your lawyer can help you—so can the Consumer Product Safety Commission in Washington.

2. The act contains a very important notification provision which provides that if you make or sell a consumer product which you think may cause a serious risk of injury, you must notify the Consumer Product Safety Commission. Failure to do so can cause serious civil penalties and, in extreme cases, criminal penalties.

The relevant provision of the Consumer Product Safety Act on the notification provision is as follows:

Section 15(b). Every manufacturer of a consumer product distributed in commerce, and every distributor and retailer of such product, who obtains information which reasonably supports the conclusion that such product—
    (1) fails to comply with an applicable consumer product safety rule, or
    (2) contains a defect which could create a substantial product hazard as described in subsection (a)(2)
shall immediately inform the Commission of such failure to comply or of such defect unless such manufacturer, distributor, or retailer has actual knowledge that the Commission has been adequately informed of such defect or failure to comply.

The definition of "substantial product hazard" in subsection (a)(2) referred to above is as follows:

(2) a product defect which (because of the pattern of defect, the number of defective products distributed in commerce, the severity of risk, or otherwise) creates a substantial risk of injury to the public.

There are elaborate regulations under this provision, and I suggest that anyone involved in the manufacture or sale of consumer products obtain a copy from his or her lawyer and read and understand them. You simply cannot ignore this requirement. If someone sues you alleging that he or she has been seriously injured by one of your consumer products, or if a customer writes you and says that there was a "near miss" on a potentially serious injury caused by a defect, you must not only decide what your monetary risk might be and what you should do to minimize it, but also address this notification requirement. Again, the key thing is not to do anything foolish such as finding out about a serious problem and then sweeping it under the rug and hoping no one will ever find out. It is almost impossible to incur criminal penalties under the substantive provisions of the Consumer Product Safety Act. You have to fail to do something the commission tells you specifically to do. However, in cover-up cases, the prosecutions are not under the substantive law; they are under the other criminal laws which make obstruction of justice, conspiracy, and making false statements to the government a crime.

The bottom line on the Consumer Product Safety Act is this:

1. Make sure you know about it and what requirements apply to you.

2. Make sure that if the law applies, you appreciate the implications of the notification requirement and consult your lawyer any time you think it *might* be applicable.

13

INTELLECTUAL PROPERTY

The term "intellectual property" includes patents, copyrights, trademarks, and trade secrets. In many small businesses the value of intellectual property is overlooked. It can, however, be one of the company's most valuable assets and is something which deserves your attention. A frequent source of legal difficulty for small businesses arises out of employees who leave the company and either go to work with a competitor or start up their own small business in competition with their former employer and with the use of trade secrets or proprietary information gained at their former employer's expense. While I do not have any magic legal tricks to prevent this from happening, I do have some advice which will minimize the danger and at least make it harder for someone to improperly appropriate your intellectual property.

Another all too frequent problem is that a small business will spend a lot of money on a product only to find that because of another company's patent or trademark protection, much of its effort cannot be turned into profit.

PATENTS

The best-known of all of the intellectual property rights is the patent. Patent laws are federal; there is *one* United States patent law which applies in *all* jurisdictions, and there are no state patent systems. There are, however, numerous foreign patent systems. The United States patent law provides essentially that any person who invents a product or process can obtain a patent on it. The two principal kinds of patents are product patents, covering actual physical products, and process patents covering the processes by which the products are made. A given article can be subject to both a product patent governing the finished product and a process patent governing the manufacturing process.

A very important aspect of patent law has to do with improvements or modifications. A normal chair presents an easy way to illustrate this. Suppose that someone had an idea for a seat with four legs. The first person with this idea could obtain a patent. The patent would simply recite that the inventor claimed rights on a configuration containing a seat with four legs used for sitting. Then, suppose someone else came along and put a back on that configuration. That person could obtain a patent on a seat with four legs as modified by inclusion of the back. Suppose someone else came along and decided that it would be a good idea to put arms on the configuration and obtained a patent on a seat, four legs, and back and arms. You can see how this process would go on, and you can also see what the end result would be. By far, the biggest market would be for a chair with back and arms, but no single person would have patent rights on this. The person who invented the first configuration of the seat with four legs would have a very good and valid patent, but, because the product was rather crude, it would not have a very large market. The next person, who improved it with the back, would have a little larger market but could not make the chair himself or herself until after getting a license from the person with the basic four-legs-and-seat patent. Thus, the process of improvement would go on and on, and each person improving the product would have to get a license from the other people whose patents were used in the improvement process. By the same token, the people who had the basic patents would obtain some benefit, through royalties, by allowing people to improve the product and obtain a larger market.

Suppose, however, that our second inventor—the one who thought of putting the back on the chair—failed to realize either that a license was necessary in order to use the basic seat or that a patent was necessary in order to protect his or her improvement. In the first case the inventor might go through a lot of time and expense to market the chair with a back only to end up subject to a costly patent suit for infringement of the basic seat patent. In the second situation, our third inventor, who made the chair very marketable by adding the arms, would not be obliged to pay the person who invented the back any royalty. The third inventor would be able to market the chair with arms merely by paying the first royalty to the holder of the basic seat patent.

The moral of the story is, of course, that if you are designing, manufacturing, or selling a proprietary product, you want to make sure that it does not infringe anyone else's patent, and if you have added something to make it better than the competition, you want to be sure to get a patent on that improvement so that you can protect yourself against infringement and participate in later improvements.

There are, of course, a number of questions which can arise under the patent laws. For example, what kind of invention will justify a patent? Most courts say that there must be something new and substantially different from the "prior art" in order to justify a patent. How much is "substantially different"? The criterion seems to be that that which would have been readily apparent to a craftsman is not new or novel, but something that goes beyond that is. Obviously, this is a subjective area.

Another question is, if you have a patent on an article, may somebody else manufacture one which is only a little bit different? Again, this is a subjective area, and the test is whether the difference in the product which is alleged to infringe your patent is *substantial*. If you make a certain product and paint it red, and a competitor makes the same product and paints it green, the mere fact that one is red and one is green will not protect the competitor from a claim of infringement. On the other hand, if the competitor changes the product in a way which makes it substantially different from yours, there will be no infringement even if the product is used for essentially the same thing. To pursue our chair example, if someone designed a seat with three legs instead of four, that would not infringe the patent governing a seat with four legs. Even though both of these items could be called a stool and each would serve substantially the same function, there is enough difference between a three-legged stool a four-legged stool to justify two different patents. On the other hand, if the original patent holder claimed a seat 12 inches around with legs 12 inches long, and someone else simply made the legs slightly longer or shorter but kept the basic configuration, that would not be substantially different, and the second person would infringe the basic stool patent.

Since the patent rights are granted by the federal government, they cannot be taken away when your employees leave. If you have a patent for one of your products, whoever makes that product without a license from you would be guilty of infringement. If employees left to form a competing company and started making the same product, they would be guilty of infringement, just as strangers would be if they simply copied your product.

On the other hand, the question of exactly who invented something in the business or employment relationship is sometimes unclear. If you will re-member our illustration of improvements, you can see how the problem would arise. Suppose, for example, that you had the basic patents when an employee joined your company, and the employee worked for you for a few years, during which time various improvements were added to the product. If everyone is working together in a harmonious relationship, there usually is not any great incentive to decide exactly who invented an improvement and to get a patent in the name of that person. On the other hand, when somebody leaves, this changes the situation drastically, and if you have not protected yourself before the falling out, you may find that your employee can either get improvement patents which rightfully belong to you or, at a minimum, create substantial confusion in the patent office and greatly in-crease your costs and difficulty in obtaining the patents you deserve. The usual remedy for this problem is to have *all* employees sign a form which requires the following:

1. The employee will assign to the company all rights to any invention made during the course of employment.

2. The employee will prosecute or assist in the prosecution of any patent application. The agreement usually provides that the company will pay all expenses.

3. If any patents are issued, the employee will assign them to the company.

Most companies have *all* their employees sign this kind of agreement upon initial hiring. For example, even though I worked as a corporate attorney, I was required to sign such an agreement for the company I worked for when I was hired. The secretaries in the legal department were also required to sign the form. This is good practice, because it is difficult to know in advance which employees will come up with patentable ideas. The agreement must be reasonable, or it will not be enforceable. It must limit its application to inventions made during the course and scope of the employee's work; it cannot cover inventions made on the employee's own time. This can be a troublesome area, because sometimes employees get their corporate and personal work so mixed up with each other that it is difficult to tell whether an invention was made on company time using company equipment or on the employee's personal time.

If you do not have your employees sign such a contract, any disputes will have to be resolved by general legal principles. These provide that in the case of an employee who was hired to invent, such as a research engineer, the law will impute an agreement substantially like that stated above, so that all inventions made during employment which relate to what the employee was hired to do for the company will have to be assigned to the employer. If, on the other hand, the employee was not hired to invent, this will not be the case. The invention will belong to the employee but will be subject to a *shop right* by the employer. A shop right is the right of an employer to use an invention without infringing even if the employee is later granted a patent.

For example, if an employee in your shop devises a better way to perform a certain operation and later gets a patent on that method, you as the employer will be allowed to use it, because it was developed in your shop. You will have a shop right to use that improved method. The employee, on the other hand, will be the owner of the patent and will be entitled both to license it if he or she desires to do so and to obtain all the royalties. If the employee invents something *entirely* on his or her own time, using his or her own equipment and facilities, the invention and any subsequent patents belong entirely to the employee, and the employer has no greater right than anyone else to those inventions.

Obviously, the subjectivity inherent in all of this plus the likelihood that the precise facts (Did the invention occur during company time? on company property? Was it the kind of thing the employee was hired to do?) will be less than 100 percent clear in most cases dictates the desirability of preparing for this problem by the use of invention assignment agreements. A sample is included.

Infringement

Infringement is simply the unauthorized use of an invention. It is not necessary that the infringers know they are infringing. Indeed, this is perhaps the biggest advantage of a patent over a trade secret. The concepts of inducing infringement and contributory infringement are also worth mentioning. Inducing infringement is just what the name implies. The law provides that "whoever actively induces infringement of a patent shall be liable as an infringer." Contributory infringement refers to the sale of parts or components of a patented product. The law provides that "whoever sells a component of a patented product constituting a material part of the invention, knowing the same to be especially made for use in an infringement of a patent, shall be liable as a contributory infringer."

A patent grants the owner of the patent the right to make, use, and sell the patented article. Thus, you can be guilty of infringement if you *either make, use,* or *sell* an article which is patented.

If you are found to be guilty of infringement, there will usually be two remedies. The first will be an injunction to stop you from continuing the infringement, and the second will be an award of damages for past infringement. You can usually negotiate out of the injunction by getting a license from the patent holder, but at this point, where you have already been judged by a court to be guilty of infringement, your bargaining power is not very good. Further, there is no offset for the amount that you have spent in promoting the article. For example, if you are selling an article which infringes someone else's patent and you have spent a lot of money on an advertising campaign, that is not taken into consideration except to the extent that you have increased your sales—and liability is usually based on the number of articles sold. In some cases, liability may be based on the profits you made, but whatever the rule, you must assume that if you are found to have infringed a patent, the method of calculating the damages will be the one that awards the largest amount of damages to the patent holder.

Perhaps even more significant than royalties and damages will be the cost of defending the suit. Patent suits are notorious for being extremely costly.

Licensing

Let us turn the situation around a bit and assume that you have the patent. Essentially, there are two ways you can benefit from the patent. One is to use the patent as a club to keep anyone from competing with you in the manufacture, use, or sale of the patented article. The other is to license people to use the patent and make a profit through royalties. There is no "right" or "best" approach, and different companies take different approaches. However, assuming you decide to license the patent, there are some very important things you ought to know.

Patent licenses are usually rather long and elaborate documents, and they ought to be prepared by counsel. Thus, you will be making a substantial investment in legal time, and you ought to be sure that the benefits to be obtained warrant this investment.

Second and most important is that *patent licenses have given rise to some of the most disastrous litigation that I know about.* Generally, the pattern is that a company will license another to use its patent. The licensee will default or not perform the license agreement in the terms expected by the licensor, and the licensor will then institute a lawsuit. The licensee will then defend on the following grounds:

1. The *patent is invalid.*

2. The defendant will probably *counterclaim* for alleged *antitrust violations* which can entitle the defendant to recover three times the actual damages plus attorneys' fees.

3. There will be an allegation of *patent misuse* which would possibly subject the licensor to damages plus the loss of ability to enforce the patent in the future.

In short, patent licenses are not something you want to enter into lightly, and even more importantly, they are not something you want to institute a lawsuit on without very careful analysis of all the pros and cons and possible legal pitfalls.

Patent Quality

In popular thought, a patent is a patent. Unfortunately it is not quite that simple. All patents look alike in the sense that they have two parts: disclosures and a set of claims. The disclosures simply disclose the invention, and are the price you pay for the patent. After the patent expires (usually after 17 years), you will have disclosed your invention, and the rest of the world will be entitled to use it without regard to your patent. The claims are the exact items which are entitled to patent protection. Naturally, the broader your claims the better your coverage. However, if your claims are too broad, the likelihood is enhanced that the court will determine that your invention really did not justify the claims, and therefore the patent was invalid.

In the United States a large portion of litigated patents are eventually determined to be invalid. A brief look at the process by which patents are issued shows why this is the case. In order to obtain a patent, you have to file an application that discloses the invention. This then goes to the patent office, where one of its examiners looks over the "prior art," which is a combination of previously issued patents and materials published in technical journals. If the patent examiner does not find any prior art, the patent office will issue your patent. Usually, however, the matter becomes somewhat complicated, and there is a process of negotiation whereby the patent examiner and the patent applicant negotiate what kind of patent might be available and what kind of claims ought to be allowed. *All this applies to every patent.* Of all the patents issued, however, only a small fraction turn out to be commercially valuable. Thus, when you file a patent application, in most cases you really do not know how much the patent will be worth to you if and when it is issued, and, therefore, it is a little difficult to judge how much time and effort to expend in preparing the application and in negotiating with the patent office about the claims and disclosures.

On the other hand, if the patent is important enough to be involved in litigation, it must be a *very valuable* one. In this kind of a situation there may be many hours of legal time spent in finely combing all of the prior art and generally flyspecking the whole process. This kind of all-out effort is bound to turn up things which were not turned up in the original patent application, and therefore, many patents are, upon court scrutiny, determined to be invalid.

If the patents you have are of dubious validity (statistically your odds are about 50-50 in court), do they really do you any good? Can you really sue someone for infringing your patent? As we saw above, one of the most prevalent sources of antitrust counterclaims is patent suits in which one company alleges that another company infringed a patent, and the defendant company counterclaims for many millions of dollars on the basis of an antitrust violation. Thus, if you sue someone for infringing your patent, you risk a multimillion dollar counterclaim plus the possibility that your patent might be termed invalid.

An Approach to Patents

I do not want to sound negative about patents and patent licensing—quite the contrary. I think that a company is best served by getting patents where it can, and after it gets those patents I see no reason why it should not make as much money out of them as possible by licensing. On the other hand, I have seen some situations which have caused wasted effort and much anguish because of the lack of a proper approach to patents.

On the one extreme I have seen companies spend a lot of money on patent lawyers, patent applications, and the other miscellaneous fees and expenses which are involved in getting patents without any clear and coherent approach as to exactly what they were going to do with those patents. In some cases, I am afraid this has resulted in quite a waste of money. Patent lawyers are expensive, and patent matters can take up a lot of their time—not to mention your own. Before you spend this time and money, it seems to me desirable to have some plans as to how you are going to get some benefit from it. If the only benefit you expect to obtain is to be able to sue someone else who comes knocking at your door telling you he or she has an infringing product, I think you are probably kidding yourself.

At the other extreme, I have read a *disturbingly large* number of cases which seem to point out very clearly that companies have been much too quick on the trigger to slap a patent infringement suit on somebody. In far too many of these cases, the net result is that the *defendant* (the company you are suing) winds up with *at least* a judgment that your patent is invalid and possibly damages of its own in the form of an antitrust counterclaim. Thus, at a minimum, a proper approach to patents includes a *careful* review by counsel as to the legal merits of the case.

This latter point raises a very important issue about use of lawyers in the context of patents. Your general corporate lawyer will not be able to get a patent for you. Patents are a very highly specialized area of the law. Patent lawyers have two areas of expertise which corporate lawyers do not. One is familiarity with the patent office and how to get a patent, and the other is familiarity with the technical aspects of your invention. Thus, if you are going to get patents, you are going to have to get a patent lawyer, and, in the overwhelming majority of situations, that lawyer is going to be someone else besides your corporate lawyer.

On the other hand, most patent lawyers do not have the expertise, experience, and judgment of corporate lawyers when it comes to other matters such as litigation, counterclaims, and antitrust. My suspicion is that business people and patent lawyers have gotten together to decide whether to institute a patent infringement suit against someone and have made that judgment purely on the basis of the technical merits of the patent. Experience has shown time and again that this is not a good approach. You must involve a general corporate lawyer also, and that general corporate lawyer must be one with experience and expertise in litigation and antitrust.

The 1-Year Rule

A patent can be granted for anything you invent within 1 year after it is "reduced to practice." So, for example, if you invent a new kind of attachment to a metal working machine to do a specific process, you have 1 year after you have finally perfected that new attachment to get your patent. There are two obvious problems:

1. Exactly when you perfected the device (or reduced it to practice) is likely to be the subject of some debate.

2. If you use the device yourself for more than 1 year after you have perfected it, you will not be able to get a patent at all. You will have precluded this method of coverage, and you will be restricted to trade secret protection.

Thus, the decision on whether you want to get a patent on something is not one which can be postponed indefinitely. You have to make the decision rather promptly because of these two factors. It is much better to be conservative and file your application early than to chance some second-guessing as to when you might have reduced your invention to practice and how long you used it yourself before you filed the patent application.

In summary, then, if you have inventions which you think might deserve patent protection, your first job is to find a patent lawyer. Usually, your general corporate counsel is the place to start—he or she probably knows several patent lawyers who help his or her other clients. Next, you and your corporate counsel must sit down with the patent lawyer and discuss not only the merits of the invention, but what you intend to do with it. You must decide if you are going to license others. If you feel that bringing suit on the patent against a potential infringer is a possibility, you must make sure your general corporate lawyer is involved in that determination before the suit is filed. You are entitled to a rather clear idea from patent counsel as to the cost of patent protection, and you have to decide whether the costs are worth any potential benefits. Last, but not least, you should have invention assignment forms executed by all your employees.

COPYRIGHTS

Copyright laws are fairly straightforward and do not present a problem for business people unless they sell a product which must be protected by the copyright law (e.g., publishers, advertising people, companies that assemble catalogs or directories, and record companies). Of course, if you happen to be in one of those businesses, you should have a good copyright lawyer and make sure that your products are afforded all possible protection under the copyright laws.

If your business involves copyrights only tangentially, it will be very easy for you to obtain copyright protection yourself. On the other side of the coin, if you refrain from copying other people's copyrighted information, you will not have any problems with them asserting their copyright against you.

The Mechanics of Obtaining a Copyright

In the case of written material you claim a copyright by simply including the copyright notice on your material. The copyright notice has three elements:

1. The copyright symbol "©", the word "copyright," or the abbreviation "copr."

2. The year of first publication.

3. The name of the copyright owner.

If you look at the beginning of this book, you can see that on one of the introductory pages, there appear the words "Copyright 1981 by McGraw-Hill, Inc." A similar phrase would be all you would need to copyright any written materials. Some publishers go on to include the rest of the language that McGraw-Hill uses ("All rights reserved," etc.), and I suppose this does have some advantage for a big company like McGraw-Hill, whose products are the copyrighted books. For most purposes, however, you do not need those details. All you need is the simple phrase consisting of the word "Copyright," the year of publication, and then the owner of the copyright.

Under the old law, the copyright notice had to appear on the page immediately following the cover page, and if it was omitted from even one issue, the copyright was lost. Now, however, these technicalities have been greatly relaxed. The copyright notice can appear anyplace on the material that reasonably informs the reader that it is copyrighted, and if the notice is omitted from no more than a relatively small number of copies, the copyright protection will not be lost. An innocent infringer, however, who copies the work unaware of the copyright because the notice was not included, is protected from liability for infringement.

There is a common-law copyright recognized in almost all states. Thus, if someone writes a book, article, etc., and does not attempt to claim the federal copyright protection, there still may be a copyright on that work. From the point of view of the person generating the work, reliance on common-law copyright is ill-advised, because it is so easy to use the federal copyright law. However, when you look at the other side of the coin—i.e., Can you copy something?—you do have to keep in mind that the fact that the federal copyright notice has been omitted from a document does not necessarily mean that you are free to copy it—especially if you are going to copy it and sell it for profit or try to palm it off as your own work without giving any credit to the author.

Copyrights can be registered with the U.S. Copyright Office by depositing a copy, paying a modest fee, and filling out the appropriate registration form. There is a separate registration procedure for written materials and other forms of protectable material such as phonograph records. Registration of your copyright can be important in litigation, but you can register it any time. Most small companies do not bother with the federal registration for non-commercial works.

A valid copyright will give you the exclusive right to use the work and to authorize others to do the following:

1. Reproduce it.

2. Prepare derivative works based on the copyrighted work.

3. Distribute copies to the public by sale, lending, or otherwise.

4. In the case of literary, musical, dramatic, and similar works, to perform them for profit or display them publicly.

Also, of course, the copyright will give you the right to sue anybody who infringes the copyright.

Under the old law, a copyright lasted for 28 years. Under the 1978 copyright amendments, however, it has been extended for the life of the author plus another 50 years.

The possible remedies for infringement are rather severe. They include an injunction to make the infringing party stop infringing and damages for past infringement. They also include lost profits which the copyright owner might have obtained, possible impounding of infringing articles, costs and attorneys' fees, and, in extreme cases, criminal penalties.

Fair Use

One of the most difficult questions under the copyright law is the concept of fair use. The proliferation of copying machines is, of course, the cause for most of the concern. Indeed, one of the principal items of discussion during the legislative debates on the 1978 copyright amendments was the extent to which photocopying should be allowed. Since the old law was enacted long before these machines were invented, there was no provision dealing with the problem. The new law attempts to codify the law of fair use as it emerged in several cases decided under the old law. Unfortunately, most of the cases involving the fair use question do not involve normal corporate operations.

The new copyright law did a fairly good job of listing the general kinds of considerations which were relevant in determining what was fair use and what was not, but these are very difficult to use to come up with hard-and-fast conclusions. The relevant portion of the law which lists the important factors is quoted below:

> . . . The fair use of a copyrighted work, including such use by reproduction in copies . . . for purposes such as criticism, comment, news reporting, teaching . . . scholarship or research, is not an infringement in copyright. In determining whether the use made of a work in any particular case is a fair use the factors to be considered shall include—
> (1) The purpose and character of the use, including whether such use is of a commercial nature or is for nonprofit educational purposes;
> (2) The nature of the copyrighted work;
> (3) The amount and substantiality of the portion used in relation to the copyrighted work as a whole; and
> (4) The effect of the use upon the potential market for or value of the copyrighted work.

In summary, it seems that we have a simple, commonsense test of fair use. While this is very flexible, it also presents difficulties for planning purposes, because different people are obviously going to have different ideas of what is fair. In the context of a business operation, it seems to me that the following guidelines provide good practice—although because the area is so subjective, different attorneys might have different views on these guides.

1. There is absolutely no cost or risk involved in protecting material which you generate by copyright. Therefore, I suggest that, as a matter of course, any catalogs that you prepare and spend a lot of time on should be copyrighted by putting the copyright notice on it as explained above.

2. It is not necessary to register copyrights with the copyright office unless and until you want to sue somebody for infringement. Therefore, in the overwhelming majority of cases, assuming you are not in the publishing business, I suggest that you simply use the copyright notice and do not bother spending the time and effort necessary to register copyrights with the U.S. Copyright Office.

3. In buying material and using it yourself, I suggest that you take a commercial view of fair use. For example, if you buy a subscription to a periodical, you can duplicate various articles, or indeed,

a complete issue on some occasions, for use *within your own organization*. There may be some technical arguments as to the extent of the fair use exception under the copyright laws, but I know of no case, nor any circumstance whatsoever where a publisher has objected to a subscriber's making copies of something for internal use. At the other extreme, if you *systematically* make copies of other people's copyrighted material and thereby clearly deprive the copyright owner of additional subscriptions which he or she would otherwise have, or if you use copyrighted material in something you are going to *sell for profit yourself,* I think you are asking for trouble.

4. Be especially careful of catalogs and other similar materials which may have been compiled at some expense by other companies. Many times these catalogs will have so-called trap lines, which are ficticious items of information designed to trap someone who was simply copying the information. If a competitor of yours has put together an excellent catalog and spent a lot of time and money gathering the necessary information, you cannot simply copy it yourself and save all that time and money without running a risk under the copyright laws. This, of course, runs both ways, and that is why I suggest that you copyright everything that you spend a lot of time and money preparing. You may want to use trap lines also.

5. There may be some slight advantage in copyrighting advertisements. We will discuss this point further under the trademark section of this chapter. In some situations it might be desirable to include the copyright notice on any advertisement you prepare if it seems possible to you that a competitor may want to try to use it. For example, a lawyer who was putting on seminars on product liability cases developed an excellent advertisement in the form of a very short article about the important aspects of minimizing product liability exposure. It was a mail-order–type advertisement consisting of a half a dozen pages or so, and I noticed it was copyrighted. The lawyer obviously had spent a lot of time in developing that ad, and did not want other people to be able to use his work to promote competitive seminars.

6. There are some things which cannot be copyrighted, such as United States government publications, which are in the public domain. Also, statutes, cases, congressional history, congressional debates, and all such things which are generated by the government agencies generally cannot be copyrighted. However, it is

possible to copyright the arrangement of those things on a page. Thus, if a publisher has gone to the trouble of setting particular statutes in type, you cannot capitalize on this time and expense by simply cutting the page out of the published work and using that for duplication. You can, of course, retype the material and use it freely.

7. Ideas cannot be copyrighted. Therefore, if someone writes an article and copyrights it, you are certainly free to read that article, digest it, take the ideas from that article and other sources, and weave them into your own material without any copyright problems. On the other hand, if someone has copyrighted an article, you cannot simply rephrase it or change minor words and claim it as your own. Exactly where the line is to be drawn is not clear. However, a little common sense will give the appropriate answer in most of these cases.

TRADEMARKS AND TRADE NAMES

The federal trademark law is the Lanham Act, sometimes called the Trademark Act, which was adopted in 1946. While it has been amended on several occasions, it would be fair to say that the law is generally the same now as then.

The legislation provides for a federal registration system of trademarks used in interstate commerce, and that federal registration gives the registered owner of the trademark certain procedural rights should the owner decide to sue another company for infringing that trademark or trade name. On the other hand, the registration does not give a great many substantive rights. *Substantive rights are obtained in a trademark by using the mark.* Thus, it is the *use* of the mark, *not the registration* of it, which gives you most of your rights.

When Should You Register Your Mark?

Why, then, does anyone bother to register trademarks? If we consider the following three examples, we can see the kinds of cases where registration of a trademark would be appropriate and where it would be a waste of time and money.

1. Let us first consider the local store situation. This could be any store, but for purposes of illustration, let us assume that you have developed a way to manufacture inexpensive replicas of old spinning wheels and other antiques and want to sell them locally in a store under the trade name "Oak Wheel Reproductions." You

have your trade name "Oak Wheel Reproductions" set forth in a distinctive style of type. You have a die made, and you have it burned into all of your items. You also have a sign at the front of your store which displays this trademark. Should you bother to register the mark?

If you are going to sell the products locally, there would not appear to be any advantage in registering the mark. By using the mark and advertising it in your city, you will have obtained all the rights you need to stop anyone else from using that mark in your city to sell competitive goods. However, there would be nothing to prevent someone from selling competitive goods bearing that same mark in another city. The theory is that you have used your mark and thereby obtained rights in it in the area where you have actually used it, but you have not obtained any rights anywhere else.

2. Suppose we change our example from a store that you opened to sell things that you make yourself to a pilot program to sell the same things which you manufacture on a relatively large scale and hope to sell in a broader geographical area. Here you will be spending a substantial amount of money on advertising in the local area in hopes that you can sell your product in other locations in the future. If you do not register the mark, you may find that someone beat you to the punch in another city or another state. *This, then, is the classic and most important situation where registration of your mark is necessary.* It will prevent you from spending a lot of money only to allow someone else to capitalize on it before you do.

3. Pursuing our example, suppose that you are a national furniture company and want to establish a new line and introduce it nationwide. You are going to embark on a nationwide program of advertising "Oak Wheel Reproductions" in all major cities. Here there would be little to be gained by registering the mark because your actual use of the mark in all of the major markets would give you sufficient rights to prevent anyone else from selling competitive goods with that mark. On the other hand, a nationwide advertising campaign like this costs so much money that it tilts the scales in favor of registration. The registration fees are substantial when weighed against the revenues of a small local shop but insubstantial when weighed against the advertising costs and promotional expenses for a nationwide campaign. In this situation, almost all major companies will register the mark even though

they know that the increased rights they get by registration are more procedural than substantive.

In summary, then, if your business is such that you are talking about a small local area and you are sure that you are going to use your trademark and trade name in your area and are not going to want to expand into other major cities or states, there is not much point in spending money for attorneys' fees and registration costs to register your trademark. By the same token, if it is a pilot program and you intend to expand it, it is almost imperative that you register the mark.

When Should You Conduct a Trademark Search?

The other side of the trademark registration coin is trademark infringement. If someone else registers your "Oak Wheel Reproductions" mark in another city, you still have the right to use that mark in your city. Again, use is much more important than registration. Since you will know who is advertising products similar to yours in your own city, you do not have to spend the money for a trademark search. On the other hand, if this is only a pilot program, you are going to want to know about other trademark registrations so that when you expand your product, you will not run into problems. That is where a trademark search becomes very important. For a relatively modest amount (approximately $300 to $500), you can have a professional trade-mark-search company search all of the registered marks for those which may be confusingly similar to yours. If you run across someone else who has used your "Oak Wheel Reproductions" mark in another city but has not used it nationally and has not registered it, you are not in too much trouble. Only one city is off limits to you. On the other hand, if someone has registered the mark nationally, you are going to be under some restriction in your future use. You can still use it in your own city because the other person has not acquired any rights by use. On the other hand, you are not going to be able to register your mark because of the other person's prior registration, so when you start expanding, you are likely to run into competition from the other person, and his or her rights on the mark are going to be superior to yours in the new areas. It is very important that you know this and weigh the risks involved before you spend a lot of money promoting a mark which you cannot register nationally.

In summary, then, if you are going to be using a trademark or a trade name, you want to ask yourself the question, Where am I going to want to use this mark? If the answer is, in a very small geographical area where you know the situation firsthand, there is no need to register the mark yourself or to conduct a trademark search. On the other hand, if there is a realistic possibility that you will expand your use of the mark into other areas, both a registration and a search would probably be justified. Assuming the matter does not get too complicated, you are talking about $2,000 to $2,500 for both the registration and the search.

TRADE SECRETS

A trade secret is anything which you use in your business, which gives you a commercial advantage, and which is not generally known. Commonly, trade secrets are thought of as secret formulas or top-secret processes for manufacturing esoteric things. They are not limited to these things. A customer list, a mailing list, a list of qualified vendors, and a list of customers who pay their bills as opposed to those who do not are all extremely valuable trade secrets. Financial information can also be a valuable trade secret. The prices you pay for components in your products, the wages you pay your employees, the total cost of each product, your overhead expenses, and your capital resources are all things which competitors might like to know and which would help them hurt you. To the maximum extent possible, you want to prevent this from happening.

As we discussed in our patent section, one of the biggest potential trouble spots for losing trade-secret information is employees leaving your company and either starting their own business or going with a competitor. Therefore, in addition to having employees sign an invention assignment form as we discussed in the patent chapter, I always recommend having the employee sign a confidentiality or nondisclosure agreement. I have included a sample drawn from a relatively large company which had extremely valuable trade secrets of this classic type. You may not need something this elaborate. On the other hand, it is easier to take things out of the form then to add them in, so I think you can use the form to some advantage. As in the case of all forms, it is much better if you can obtain specific legal advice from your own lawyer as to how the form might be tailored to your own circumstances.

Another way to inadvertently disclose your trade secrets is through supplying information to your vendors. In some cases, this is necessary, because you will have to give the vendor enough information for him or her to supply you with the proper kinds of products. In this situation, I recommend a nondisclosure agreement carefully spelling out exactly what kind of trade-secret information you are supplying and exactly how it will be protected. I have included several forms which deal with this point from several angles so you can see the differences. One form is to use where you are giving your confidential information to the vendor, another is for cases where the vendor asks you to sign an agreement holding his or her information in confidence, and the third is for a joint exchange of confidential information. Obviously, these forms take different positions, and you must be careful to use the proper form in the proper circumstance. Of course, these examples are intended to facilitate working with your lawyer—not to be simply copied.

Note the specificity with which the nondisclosure form covering your information deals with the relevant considerations. Don't be bashful. Spell all these things out. You should know who in the vendor's company is going to have access to the information, how that access is going to be granted, etc. In my judgment, it is *entirely inadequate* to simply write a short cover letter stating that a package of confidential information is trade secret and you expect the vendor to treat it as such. That is much too vague. If the information is worth protecting at all, it is worth going those extra steps to make sure the vendor understands that he or she (and perhaps other named persons in the vendor's company) is the *only* one who is granted access to the information, that no copies should be made, that the copies should be returned to you, etc.

In short, unless you are going to do this right, I question whether it is worth bothering with at all. The reason for this approach is partly legal—if you do not do a good job, a court is likely to say that you didn't exercise enough care over the information to bring it up to the status of a legal trade secret. The major reason, however, is simply that most people honor agreements they sign. If you spell out everything in the agreement as to exactly what is going to happen with your information and how you are going to get it back, in the overwhelming majority of circumstances, it will turn out that way. On the other hand, if you leave the entire matter so vague that you cannot reasonably expect the other party to understand exactly what his or her responsibilities are, I do not think you are in much of a position to complain if the other party is careless with your data.

The other half of the trade-secret problem is receiving information from other companies in confidence. There are two parts to this half. One is a commercial-type arrangement, and the other is receipt of unsolicited ideas. In the commercial setting, there is every reason to believe that you will get some benefit from the information, and the only question is how much trouble you should go to in order to protect the information. As you can see from the form, I have limited your obligations in this kind of situation to treating the information with the same degree of care as you treat your own information. If you undertake a higher degree of care, be sure to exercise that higher degree, because if you do not, you can be subject to many dollars of damages if you lose the other party's trade secret. These are usually negotiated documents—the other party has lawyers, too. The key thing to remember is that this is an important and sensitive area. Read all the documents and make sure you understand and abide by them. Essentially, the same thing is true for exchanges of information, except that here the obligations of both parties are in the same piece of paper. That makes it a little difficult to say that you want a low degree of care for you to exercise concerning the other party's information and the reverse for the other party in the case of your information. You must hit a politically acceptable medium, and I have tried to do that in the suggested form.

The last area I would like to discuss is the receipt of unsolicited ideas. The experience of most large companies has shown that unsolicited ideas are not very valuable. They either are something you already knew or are not worth doing. They can, however, be productive of litigation. Suppose, for example, someone gives you an idea which merely duplicates something you already have in process. When you finally come out with your new product using this idea, the person who submitted you the idea is going to think you stole it, and you are then going to have to prove that you thought of it first yourself. This can be costly and difficult. For that reason, most large companies either will not accept unsolicited ideas at all or will do so only pursuant to a letter agreement similar to the one I have included.

In summary, you are likely to be in one of two situations regarding industrial property. The subject may be very important to you, in which case a patent, trademark, and copyright lawyer is going to be a very important part of your team. The key thing here is to pick a good one who will provide you good, economical, and efficient service. Everything I talked about in Chapter 1 about selecting your general lawyer would, of course, be applicable, with one very important addition. Your patent, trademark, and copyright lawyer will have to work hand in hand with your general corporate lawyer, so they will have to get along well. In fact, the best way to find a good intellectual property lawyer is to have a good general corporate lawyer who will recommend one. If your business is not such that you need an intellectual property lawyer, the items that I discussed in this chapter probably will not cause you much of a problem if you keep in mind the precautions I have suggested.

SUMMARY

To briefly review, ask yourself the following questions.

1. What is my patent situation? Do I have adequate protection for my own patents? Am I sure I am not infringing anybody else's?

2. What is my copyright situation? Do I have anything that I should copyright? If so, have I placed the copyright notice on it? Am I sure when I prepare my catalogs and other materials that I am not infringing someone else's copyright? Have I obtained permissions when I have copied things out of other people's catalogs, or do I have some exposure to the trap line problem?

3. Am I using a trademark, and should it be registered? Am I spending a lot of money to promote my mark in hopes that I can expand

it in the future? If so, did I have a trademark search and register my mark so that I can do this without legal difficulties?

4. What is my trade-secret situation? Do I have any (keeping in mind that customer lists and financial information can be considered trade secrets)? If so, have I taken the rudimentary steps necessary to protect them, including having my employees sign nondisclosure agreements, being careful about information I give to vendors, and using agreements with vendors and others whenever I do have to disclose proprietary information? Have I protected myself from the unsolicited-idea trap by refusing to accept unsolicited ideas unless I have a protective letter absolving me from any responsibility?

EMPLOYEE INVENTION AND CONFIDENTIAL INFORMATION AGREEMENT*

[THE COMPANY NAME]
XYZ, INC.

XYZ's special competence in its various fields of endeavor is the secret of its growth, and provides the source of both career opportunities and security for employees throughout the Company. Career opportunities for XYZ people have been a Company tradition not only because of the generally high competence of XYZ personnel, but also because of Company growth. Such growth depends to a significant degree on the Company's possession of proprietary information—not generally known to others—more and better information than others have about research, development, production, marketing and management in XYZ's chosen fields.

To obtain such information and use it successfully, XYZ spends considerable sums of money in research and product development, product improvements, the development of marketing methods, and service to its customers. Many XYZ people make major contributions. This results in a pool of information which enables XYZ to conduct its business with unusual success, and thus with unusual potential for its employees. However, this potential exists only as long as this information is retained proprietary within XYZ. Once generally known, this information gives no advantages to XYZ, its employees or its stockholders.

In effect, all XYZ employees have a common interest and responsibility in seeing that no one employee accidentally or intentionally siphons off or distributes to non-XYZ people any part of this pool of information.

---

*NOTE: This form covers *both inventions* and *confidential information*. The drafter can divide these into separate forms if it is thought appropriate. If the agreement is not signed at initial employment, be sure it is supported by consideration.

To help protect you, all other employees and the Company against such a possibility, this Employee Agreement has been prepared for your signature and the Company's so that we have a common understanding concerning our mutual responsibilities in this connection. Please read it carefully so that you may understand its importance.

Employee's Last Name	First Name	Initial

Inventions

1. I will promptly disclose in writing to the Company all inventions, discoveries, developments, improvements, and innovations (herein called "Inventions") whether patentable or not, conceived or made by me, either solely or in concert with others during the period of my employment with the Company, including, but not limited to, any period prior to the date of this agreement, whether or not made or conceived during working hours which,
   (a) relate in any manner to the existing or contemplated business or research activities of the Company, or
   (b) are suggested by or result from my work at the Company, or
   (c) result from the use of the Company's time, materials, or facilities
   and that all such inventions shall be the exclusive property of the Company.

2. I hereby assign to the Company my entire right, title and interest to all such inventions which are the property of the company under the provisions of paragraph 1 of this Agreement and to all unpatented inventions which I now own except those specifically described in a statement which has been separately executed by a duly authorized officer of the Company and myself and attached hereto and I will, at the Company's request and expense, execute specific assignments to any such invention and execute, acknowledge and deliver such other documents and take such further action as may be considered necessary by the Company at any time during or subsequent to the period of my employment with the Company to obtain and defend letters patent in any and all countries and to vest title in such inventions in the Company or its assigns.

3. I agree that any invention disclosed by me to a third person or described in a patent application filed by me or in my behalf within six months following the period of my employment with the Company shall be presumed to have been conceived or made by me during the period of my employment with the Company unless proved to have been conceived and made by me following the termination of employment with the Company.

Confidentiality

1. I will not during or at any time after the termination of my employment with the Company use for myself or others or divulge or convey to others any secret or confidential information, knowledge or data of the Company or that of third parties obtained by me during the period of my employment with the Company and such information, knowledge or data includes but is not limited to secret or confidential matters,
   (a) of a technical nature such as but not limited to methods, know-how,

formulae, compositions, processes, discoveries, machines, inventions, computer programs and similar items or research projects,

(b) of a business nature such as but not limited to information about cost, purchasing, profits, market, sales or lists of customers, and

(c) pertaining to future developments such as but not limited to research and development or future marketing or merchandising.

2. Upon termination of my employment with the Company, or at any other time at the Company's request, I agree to deliver promptly to the Company all drawings, blueprints, manuals, letters, notes, notebooks, reports, sketches, formulae, computer programs and similar items, memoranda, customer's lists and all other materials and all copies thereof relating in any way to the Company's business and in any way obtained by me during the period of my employment with the Company which are in my possession or under my control.

I further agree that I will not make or retain any copies of any of the foregoing and will so represent to the company upon termination of my employment.

3. The Company may notify anyone employing me or evidencing an intention to employ me as to the existence and provisions of this Agreement.

4. The invalidity or unenforceability of any provision of this Agreement as applied to a particular occurrence or circumstance or otherwise shall not affect the validity and enforceability or applicability of any other provision of this Agreement.

5. This Agreement shall inure to the benefit of and may be enforced by the Company, its successors or assigns and shall be binding upon me, my executors, administrators, legatees, distributees and other successors in interest and may not be changed in whole or in part except in a writing signed by a duly authorized officer of the Company and myself.

I agree to comply with and do all things necessary for the Company to comply with provisions of contracts between it and any agency of the United States Government or contractors thereof. This includes but is not limited to all provisions relating to invention rights or to the safeguarding of information pertaining to the defense of the United States of America.

SAMPLE UNSOLICITED IDEA LETTER

Thank you for offering to show us your idea. As I am sure you must realize, our company receives many such suggestions, and experience has shown us that in most of these cases, the idea presented has already been considered by us. Accordingly, we are unable to accept your proposal unless you are willing to agree to the following conditions:

1. If appropriate, provide that samples cannot be returned to the submittor.

2. Provide that compensation will be paid only if the company, in its sole

discretion, deems it appropriate, and only then in such amounts as the company, in its sole discretion, deems appropriate.
3. Provide that the company accepts no reponsibility for holding any information in confidence.

FORM 1. CONFIDENTIALITY AGREEMENT WHERE YOU ARE GRANTING ANOTHER COMPANY ACCESS TO PROPRIETARY INFORMATION

This agreement shall evidence the terms and conditions on which _____ _____ shall be granted access to certain proprietary information of our company.

Whereas Clauses or Purpose Clauses

Whereas or purpose clauses are important. They should set forth the reasons why you are granting the information. It is impossible to think of every possible contingency, and a recitation of the basic purpose of the transaction gives both parties and the courts, if necessary, some framework within which to resolve any future problems. Do not, however, put important substantive or procedural provisions which you intend to rely on in the whereas clauses. Some courts do not consider this to be technically a part of the agreement.

Definition of Information

Be sure to describe carefully what information is being transferred. Be sure the definition includes two things:

1. A careful itemization of exactly what information is covered— including both written information and information which may be disclosed orally at certain meetings or when the other party goes through your plant.

2. A general definition of all other information which shall be disclosed in conjunction with the relationships between the parties regarding this aspect of business.

Do not limit the scope of the agreement to certain specific documents unless that is clearly appropriate.

Obligation of the Other Company

In consideration of our disclosing the above information to you, you agree that you will hold all such information in trust and confidence, that you will refrain from using it for any purpose except that which is expressly contemplated by this agreement. Further, you will abide by the following restrictions:

1. No copies will be made of any of the written information supplied.
2. Only the employees of your company listed below shall be granted access to this information, and each of them shall be required to sign a copy of this agreement.
3. At the conclusion of our discussions or upon demand by us, all the information shall be immediately returned, including any written notes which you may have made regarding the information.
4. This information shall not be disclosed to any consultant retained by you except upon our prior written approval, which shall be conditioned on such consultant's signing a copy of this agreement and agreeing to be bound by it.

Public Information

Your company shall have no obligation with respect to any item of information (1) known to your company prior to receipt from our company, or (2) generally known in the industry prior to such receipt or (3) after the same is published or becomes generally available in the industry through no act or failure on your part.

Termination

The termination clause affects only discussions between the parties, the project they are working on, etc., *not* the confidentiality provisions. Therefore, in some cases you will not want any termination clause at all. If you do, one like the following is suggested.

This agreement shall expire _____ from the date hereof, but may be terminated prior to expiration by either party giving 30 days prior written notice to the other party; provided, however, the obligations to protect the information shall survive such termination and shall continue forever.

Scope of Agreement

No rights or obligations other than those expressly recited herein are to be implied from this Agreement. No license is hereby granted, directly or indirectly, under any patent or for any of the information disclosed.

FORM 2. YOUR COMPANY IS ASSUMING CONFIDENTIAL OBLIGATIONS

This agreement shall evidence the terms and conditions on which _____

_____ shall be granted access to certain proprietary information of your company.

Whereas or Purpose Clauses

Whereas or purpose clauses are important. They should set forth the reasons you are granting the information. It is impossible to think of every possible contingency, and a recitation of the basic purpose of the transaction gives both parties and the courts, if necessary, some framework within which to resolve any future problems. Do not, however, put important substantive or procedural provisions which you intend to rely on in the whereas clauses. Some courts do not consider this to be technically a part of the agreement.

Definition of Information

When you are receiving information, make sure you undertake obligations only with respect to clearly identified and labeled information.

1. Identify specific documents or files by name and label each piece of information.

2. If meetings are involved, specify the meeting and who was there, etc.

3. Try *not* to put a catchall clause in this form.

Obligation of Our Company

For a period of _____ from the date hereof, we will refrain from using your information in connection with the manufacture or sale of products or services, and we will exercise the same degree of care for your information as we use for our similar information. However, you agree that we will not be liable for any unauthorized disclosure which may occur in spite of such care.

Public Information

We will have no obligation with respect to any information (1) known by us prior to receipt from you, or (2) generally known in the industry prior to such receipt, or (3) independently developed by us, or (4) after substantially the same information is published or becomes available to others without restriction through no act or failure to act on our part, or is received by us from a third party having no obligation to you with respect to the information.

Manner of Disclosure

Information subject to this agreement shall be disclosed to us in written form and marked with the legend (your company proprietary information) or an equivalent conspicuous legend. No sheet or page of any written material shall be so labeled which does not contain proprietary information. We will have no obligation with respect to any written material which is not so labeled, or any information disclosed orally unless a written summary of such oral disclosure is delivered to us within 15 days of the oral disclosure specifically identifying the items considered proprietary.

Duration

   This agreement shall expire _____ but may be terminated prior to expiration by either party giving 30 days prior written notice to the other party; provided, however, the obligations to protect proprietary information in accordance with this agreement shall survive such termination.

Additional Rights

   No rights or obligations other than those expressly recited herein are to be implied from this Agreement. No license is hereby granted, directly or indirectly, under any patent.

FORM 3. BOTH PARTIES HAVE CONFIDENTIAL OBLIGATIONS

   This agreement shall evidence the terms and conditions on which your company and our company shall exchange certain confidential information.

Whereas or Purpose Clauses

Whereas or purpose clauses are important. They should set forth the reasons you are granting the information. It is impossible to think of every possible contingency, and a recitation of the basic purpose of the transaction gives both parties and the courts, if necessary, some framework within which to resolve any future problems. Do not, however, put important substantive or procedural provisions which you intend to rely on in the whereas clauses. Some courts do not consider this to be technically a part of the agreement.

Definition of Information

   The information subject to this agreement shall be information dealing with _____. Such information shall mean that which (1) originated with or is otherwise within the knowledge of one company and not others, (2) currently is protected against unrestricted disclosure to others, and (3) pertains directly or indirectly to the project the parties are working on. With respect to information made available by you to our company, the obligations of this agreement shall extend only to information in any specifications, drawings, reports, or other writings existing prior to the date of this agreement, as your company has specifically identified by listing the same on Exhibit A attached hereto.

Duration

   For a period of _____ from the date hereof, both of our companies will refrain from knowingly using proprietary information received from the other party in connection with manufacture or sale of products or services, and to prevent dissemination to third parties, each party will exercise the same degree of care as it employs for protection of its own proprietary information.

Public Information

No obligation will exist under this agreement with respect to any item of information (1) known to the recipient prior to receipt from the other party, or (2) after substantially the same information is published or becomes available to third parties without restriction through no act or failure to act on the part of the recipient, or (3) after substantially the same information becomes available to the recipient from a third party having no obligation to hold such information in confidence.

Manner of Disclosure

Proprietary information made available in written form by one party to the other will be conspicuously marked with an appropriate legend. No sheet or page of any written material will be so labeled which is not, in good faith, believed to contain proprietary information. A recipient of information hereunder will have no obligation with respect to (1) any portion of any written material which is not so labeled, or (2) any information received orally unless a written summary of such oral communication specifically identifying the items of proprietary information is furnished to the recipient within 15 days.

Additional Rights

No rights or obligations other than those expressly recited herein are to be implied from this Agreement. No license is hereby granted, directly or indirectly, under any patent.

14

YOUR LAWYER AND YOUR INSURANCE

All small businesses should have a competent insurance advisor. On the other hand, the reason you need insurance is to protect against risk, and what we usually mean here is legal risk. You want to protect yourself against someone suing you. That means that your insurance program ought to be discussed with your lawyer so that you know what your realistic exposures are and what kind of insurance you need. Following are some things that any insurance advisor will tell you. You do not even need to discuss them with your lawyer.

We all know that the automobile is the source of a lot of potential liability. Not only must you have your own cars insured, but you must be sure that anyone driving a car on company business—even if it is his or her own car—has adequate insurance also. Be sure to discuss this with your employees and your insurance advisor. It is possible that you can obtain a blanket coverage so that even if your employees do not have enough coverage, your insurance will respond. However, you must clearly identify this problem and make sure you know what kind of coverage you have or do not have. *If you do not have some kind of overriding blanket coverage, you must make sure that no employee does anything for you unless that employee has demonstrated to you that he or she has adequate insurance.* If you send an employee to the post office and the employee runs somebody over, and it turns out that the employee does not have adequate insurance, you are going to be liable. That employee is performing duties for you in the course and scope of his or her employment, and the law will clearly impose a secondary obligation on you. Of course, the primary obligation is on the employee, but that does not do you much good if the employee has little insurance and not much money. Automobiles, then, are such a frequent source of difficulty that you must be absolutely sure that any automobile used in your business is adequately protected.

Of course, you need the normal array of insurance on your premises to protect against liabilities for slips and falls, etc. You should be protected against fire, vandalism, theft, etc., in whatever amounts seem appropriate under the circumstances.

The second level of coverage is those risks which are peculiar to your business. You should discuss these with your lawyer and insurance agent together. These are the areas where the insurance agent will tell you that a particular type of policy is available and ask you if you want it. The decision as to whether you want that coverage will, in part, depend upon your realistic legal exposure. For example, in our little business it would be possible to obtain a policy of "publisher's errors and omissions coverage" which would protect us if we should libel someone or if we should be incorrect in some statement of law and someone were to rely on that to his or her detriment. I have elected not to procure such insurance, because I do not think that is a realistic exposure. The kinds of legal things that I write about simply do not lend themselves to libel claims. Anything I say about a named individual or a company is something which is already reported in a public document, such as a court case, legislative history, or a federal regulation. There is simply no realistic exposure to a libel suit.

Similarly, my publications are of the newsletter variety or the digest variety and are not intended to be definitive statements of the law. They are simply my own analyses and recommendations which are directed toward other corporate lawyers. There simply is no realistic exposure to me based upon some claim that we did not discuss some important problem that perhaps we should have.

Similarly, I could procure a "valuable paper" insurance policy which would protect manuscripts for books such as this and for all the other writing that we do. If all of those papers were in one place and if we had a fire, we would indeed be out of business, and this kind of insurance would be an absolute necessity. But there is a rather simple way to deal with this problem: Make sure that you have copies of things at various different locations. In my own situation, for example, my mother keeps a complete copy of our list of subscribers and everything we write at her house. There is also a complete copy in our home as well as in our editorial offices in downtown Cleveland. The possibility of all three of these places burning down all at once is remote. I have also elected, then, to forgo this kind of coverage.

Each situation, of course, will be somewhat different, but these illustrate the general approach you should take. First, understand clearly what your legal risks are and whether insurance is available and, if so, at what cost. These are the kinds of situations that you should discuss jointly with your lawyer and insurance agent. Second, whenever insurance is proposed to cover some catastrophe, ask yourself if there is some other way to cover that same catastrophe in a more efficient and economical manner. Perhaps something as simple as keeping a duplicate set of records off-premises could save you a lot of money in insurance premiums.

Generally, it is not necessary—and I would think it would be inappropriate—to have your lawyer review your insurance contracts. Frankly, if you cannot trust your insurance agent to review these for you, I think you need a new insurance agent. Insurance agents are generally compensated by commission, and they should do the job for you without any extra out-of-pocket expenses on your part. Your lawyer should be used to identify and quantify risks but not to pour over insurance documents and make sure that they say what the insurance agent said they said.

A final thought about insurance: You probably should have the same insurance advisor for both your individual and your corporate insurance. The reason is that these can be so interconnected. Disability, health, and life insurance are prime examples. I think it is obvious that in today's world we all need adequate disability and health insurance, and also a certain amount of life insurance. On the other hand, there are a number of ways for the owner of a small business to obtain this coverage. It can be done through a corporate policy or policies, individual policies, or a combination of the two. The key thing is to make sure you understand exactly what insurance you have, how much it is costing you, what you are protected against, what you are not protected against, and the tax treatment of the premiums.

This last point raises the ever-present tax dragon and points out the necessity of having your tax advisor familiar with your insurance picture. If your corporation buys some of this insurance, it may have tax consequences to you. For example, a corporation can provide all of its employees with $50,000 worth of group term life insurance without any tax consequences to the employees. The corporation can deduct the premium, and there is no requirement that the employees report this premium on their income tax return. On the other hand, if the insurance is greater than $50,000, there is a requirement that the employees pay a tax on the premium attributable to the difference. Similarly, if a corporation provides you with disability or health insurance, that may or may not be taxable to you, depending upon exactly how it is done. A recent change in the tax law beginning in 1980 did take away one of the available perks for the owners of a small business. It is no longer possible to have your corporation directly pay any excess medical expenses which are not covered by the corporate insurance plans. Before 1980 it was possible to establish a special plan whereby certain key officers or directors would have a reimbursement program. The company would pay any medical expenses which might not be covered by insurance. Now, however, that is no longer possible unless you do it for everybody in the company.

The interaction between insurance and taxes is complex. The point I want to stress here is simply that your tax advisor may have some useful ideas for you if you make sure that he or she is aware of all the insurance that you have personally and that the corporation provides you.

One exception to my general feeling that you do not need a lawyer involved in your insurance program other than to assess the kinds of risks you face and help you quantify them would be where you have to fill out a rather elaborate application for insurance and where the facts seem a little complicated. Keep in mind that an application for insurance really is a set of promises and warranties. If you say something incorrect on that application, and if it is important, the insurance company can seize upon that misstatement to get off the hook on the basic policy. In such situations I recommend that you go over the actual insurance application that you are going to submit to the company with your insurance advisor, and, if it seems at all appropriate, it might be worth a few dollars of your lawyer's time also. If you should want product liability insurance, you would probably have to submit a rather detailed application, and it might be worth a legal review.

Directors and officers' liability insurance is available to large companies to safeguard the directors and officers against personal claims of mismanagement or improper business decisions. Generally, it is not available to small companies.

Insurance against environmental problems is also a difficult subject. The bottom line is that you probably cannot get any meaningful insurance protection. Almost all general liability policies have a "pollution exclusion clause" which is fairly broad. Nevertheless, if you do have exposure to environmental matters it may be worth discussing with both your lawyer and your insurance agent.

To summarize the legal advice I would give on insurance matters:

1. Any insurance agent can provide you with insurance coverage on just about any possible calamity that you can think of except your own mismanagement. A first-rate insurance advisor can think of additional possible calamities that you never thought of and suggest insurance policies for those, too. You may find it in your best interest to discuss your realistic legal exposure with your lawyer before spending money on some of these policies.

2. Insurance often has tax implications.

3. Special kinds of insurance (e.g., product liability, environmental, officers and directors' liability) may require a fairly elaborate application. A legal review of the application to make sure there is nothing the insurance company can use to get off the coverage hook may be worthwhile.

4. Legal involvement in your insurance program should be extremely modest. If you and the insurance advisor do your homework and present a suggested program to your lawyer, a couple of hours of your lawyer's time to get his or her advice is all that would be required.

15

MISCELLANEOUS CALAMITIES THAT CAN SEND YOU TO JAIL (White Collar Crime)

I have reserved this chapter of the book for a very brief discussion of miscellaneous calamities that can really bring the wrath of the federal government or state enforcement officials down upon you. These are things to avoid at all costs. There is no cost-benefit analysis, no risk weighing, no mitigating circumstances, and no excuse for getting tangled up in any of these matters.

I speak not from a moral standpoint. I speak only from a practical business point of view. The reason is simple. If you happen to get involved in one of these matters in a serious way, you are very likely to end up losing your bank account to the lawyers and losing your business due to diversion of your own attention to these matters rather than to your business. Adverse physical and psychological consequences are also a distinct possibility—these are traumatic experiences.

TAX

I have spoken briefly in this book about tax planning. I have suggested an *aggressive point of view*. Wherever there is a doubt, resolve it in your favor. If there is an opportunity to structure any business deal to minimize taxes, I am all for it. However, there is a line between tax avoidance, which I and all other business counselors strongly advocate, and tax evasion, which is where you go to jail. The following things are likely to cause a serious risk of criminal prosecution, assuming substantial amounts of money are involved. "Substantial" probably means a couple of thousand dollars of tax for each of two or more tax years.

1. Deliberately not reporting substantial amounts of income, and taking steps to hide the unreported income.

2. Knowingly putting substantially erroneous information on your tax return.

3. Claiming deductions for nonexistent expenses, such as people on the payroll who do not exist, or payments to fictitious organizations.

4. Using corporate money for your own personal expenses and then attempting to camouflage this fact so you do not have to pay taxes on it.

5. Keeping off-the-book accounts.

If you own all the stock of a corporation, you can do almost anything you want with the money. There is no law against having the corporation pay for your mortgage or automobile payments, or for that matter even the food on your table. On the other hand, those kinds of things are taxable income to you, and you have to report them as such. It is just as if the corporation paid you a salary and you used it for those purposes. If instead you try to camouflage this by fictitious accounting so that the corporation pays the expense and you do not report the income, the Internal Revenue Service is going to get very mad.

The IRS is currently concerned about tax shelters. They feel that some of these border on fraudulent activities. In the majority of situations, the IRS will bring any criminal action against the lawyers, accountants, and principals involved in the tax-shelter scheme itself. If they feel the program is not legitimate and the investors have taken deductions to which they are not properly entitled, they will only assess deficiencies against the individual investor. On the other hand, this assumes that the investor does not deliberately participate in organizing or structuring the fraudulent tax shelter. The best protection here is simply to avoid tax shelters which look too good to be true or which are not sponsored by reputable people.

ANTITRUST

Antitrust is a vast and complex body of law, but the portions that give rise to criminal liability are simple and straightforward. Criminal liability under the antitrust laws will arise when *competitors* get together and agree, or attempt to agree, on prices, territories, or customers. The portions of the antitrust laws which deal with price discrimination, distributorship arrangements, termination of distributors, unfair competition, deceptive advertising, mergers, and the myriad of other things that you read about in the newspapers all give rise to civil, not criminal liability. Further, these kinds of matters usually come up in normal business operations and there is time to discuss them with your lawyer. On the other hand, when you are meeting with competitors at business or social arrangements, your lawyer is not going to be around, and you are going to have to keep the antitrust principles firmly in mind.

Under no circumstances should you discuss prices, territories, or customers with any competitor in any setting—business or social. This includes trade associations. In fact, if there is a single common denominator to criminal price-fixing conspiracies, it is that those arrangements were either initiated or furthered at some trade association meeting. Government enforcement officials are highly suspicious of trade association meetings and will subpoena trade association records and the records of the people who attended trade association meetings in the course of any criminal investigation. In short, price fixing is a criminal no-no, and if you engage in it you are being foolish.

For antitrust purposes, prices are considered to be any aspect of the deal. They include, for example, whether or not you give credit, whether you give trading stamps, or what kind of formula you use to base freight charges.

Resale price maintenance is also a criminal violation, and the Department of Justice has brought some cases based on this. Resale price maintenance is an arrangement between you and your customer to fix the price at which your customer sells the product. A few years ago, this was legal. It was an exception to the antitrust laws and was referred to as "fair trade" in states which authorized such resale price agreements. However, the federal law has been amended to remove this exception, and what used to be "fair trade" is now "illegal resale price maintenance." You must remember that your customer—even if it is a distributor of yours—is an independent businessperson, and you cannot tell your customer at what price "your" products have to be sold. That is his or her judgment.

There is an unfortunate misconception in the minds of some business people about exactly what an agreement or conspiracy is. They feel that there must be some kind of *express* agreement. This is definitely not true.

ANTITRUST IS THE ONLY AREA OF LAW I KNOW ABOUT WHERE IT IS VERY POSSIBLE TO BLUNDER YOUR WAY INTO A CRIMINAL PROBLEM WITHOUT ACTUALLY KNOWING WHAT YOU ARE DOING.

EXAMPLE: You are at a trade association meeting, and a group of competitors consisting of six people from your city go out to dinner. During the dinner discussion, one of the people at the table says that he is no longer going to give trading stamps (or give discounts for cash, or whatever). Everyone else at the table says nothing. Later that month, the person who spoke stops giving trading stamps, and during the second month the other five people stop also.

That is enough to give rise to a criminal indictment. There would be enough evidence for the government to ask a jury to determine whether the six people at that table agreed—admittedly implicitly—to stop giving trading stamps. Of course, once you get a case this far most of the damage is already done. You have been indicted for a criminal violation, there has been much anxiety, attorneys' fees, etc., and the decision of the jury is completely subjective and impossible to predict. If this would be your first offense—and assuming you were not the one who suggested the elimination of trading stamps—you would very likely be placed on probation if convicted. If you were the one who instigated the scheme, and you took steps to talk to all the people involved to convince them to stop giving the trading stamps, you might face an actual jail sentence of a few days to a few months. If the facts involved a larger conspiracy with more money involved, the stakes would be higher. The fines themselves are also nothing to take lightly. They can be up to $100,000 for an individual and $1 million for a corporation. This is a felony—not a misdemeanor.

THE SECURITIES LAWS

Federal and state securities laws can give rise to criminal liability, but the possibility is fairly remote. The only time you will run into criminal problems under the securities laws is if you engage in some kind of deliberate fraud. For example, if you were to create a fictitious balance sheet and sell securities in a company representing that company to be financially solvent when in fact it was not, it is likely that you would violate the securities laws during this kind of scheme. If it was deliberate, the violation could be criminal. We are talking about some fairly deliberate con games here. I am not speaking about selling securities in a company when, in retrospect, it turns out that you forgot to disclose something which the court feels is material. Those are very serious problems because they could give rise to extremely large civil lawsuits. On the other hand, criminal prosecutions under the securities laws are reserved for deliberate fraud, the bogus balance sheet, the empty salad oil drums, the land which turns out to be under water, etc.

POLITICAL CONTRIBUTIONS

Federal law *absolutely* prohibits *any* political contribution from *any* corporation in connection with a federal election. This is true no matter how small the corporation and no matter how few shareholders. If you incorporate your one-person business operation, you cannot use corporate funds to make a political contribution. To do so is a criminal violation, and there is a separate federal agency—the Federal Election Commission—which is charged with the responsibility for ferreting out such illegal contributions and causing them to be prosecuted. At this time, this is a highly sensitive area, and it is extremely unlikely that you can get away with making any political contribution out of your corporate till.

The only way that a corporation can become involved directly in the political process is through a "political action committee," which is a separate, segregated fund consisting of voluntary contributions from the employees of the corporation. These funds are legal and highly desirable. Most large companies have them. Most small companies do not because it is easier for the shareholders to simply make whatever political contributions they desire directly.

State law on the use of corporate funds for political contributions varies. In some states, it is illegal; in others, it is not. Consequently, if you are thinking about making a political contribution to a state candidate—as opposed to a federal one—I recommend you specifically ask the question and get a letter from the candidate or the candidate's political committee (or counsel) stating that a corporate contribution would be legal. You can, of course, check with your own lawyer also. On the other hand, political candidates are certainly aware of the election laws—both state and federal—and it seems senseless to me for you to spend your own money on legal fees to separate out all these complex rules. Place the burden on the political candidate, his or her campaign committee, and his or her own lawyer. If you receive a letter from any of these people on their stationery stating that corporate contributions are legal under the laws of that state, it does not seem to me that you have anything to worry about.

ENVIRONMENTAL LAWS

Environmental laws are giving rise to increased criminal prosecution. Virtually all of the federal environmental laws—and most state environmental laws—contain provisions which impose criminal sanctions. Thus, if your business operation discharges harmful materials into the air or water or disposes of them by a landfill, it is incumbent upon you to understand at least the basic environmental rules which are applicable and to make sure that you do not engage in deliberate violations. Again, this is a politically sensitive area. Environmental protection agencies—at both the state and the federal level—are literally looking for targets for criminal enforcement actions. The biggest risk under environmental laws comes about through falsifying information or submitting false information to the government. This is discussed below.

OCCUPATIONAL SAFETY AND HEALTH

The Occupational Safety and Health Act contains a criminal provision which says that if there is a willful violation of the act which results in a death, the responsible corporate people can be criminally indicted. There have only been a few such indictments, but again, this is a politically sensitive area, and it is growing. The key here is "willful" violation which results in a death. For this purpose, the government would probably have to show that you knew about a hazardous situation and refused to correct it.

In a large company, the issue of who goes to jail if there is a criminal violation of environmental or OSHA laws is important. The enforcement officials want to prosecute the highest possible corporate officials—but they have to show something that the corporate official did in order to get a conviction. In most situations, this revolves around the question "What did the corporate official know?" If he or she knew of the environmental or OSHA violation and did nothing—thereby condoning the acts of the subordinates which actually constituted the violation—the government will likely prosecute the corporate official rather than the employees lower down the ladder.

However, in a small company this problem factors out. You as the owner are going to be the one the government prosecutes unless there are clear and convincing arguments showing that someone else in the company took the actions without your knowledge or consent. In a small company, that is unlikely. Many of the criminal prosecutions under environmental and OSHA laws are against the owners of small businesses for this reason. There is no bureaucracy for the government to cut through to find out who in the corporation was responsible.

BRIBERY

Bribing foreign government officials was made a crime under the Foreign Corrupt Practices Act. This is a controversial area because the bribery provisions of the act deal only with foreign government officials, and there are a host of problems in terms of United States laws imposing their own standards of ethics and morals on other countries where historically the practices have been different. The Foreign Corrupt Practices Act is essentially a compromise. It says that grease payments are not prohibited, but bribes are. The line between a grease payment and a bribe is hard to draw. This is a difficult and sensitive area. If you do business in foreign countries (particularly the less developed ones, and most particularly the middle east) you need legal counsel on the possible implications of this law.

Commercial bribery is this country may be and probably is subject to criminal prosecution under one or more of the ancillary criminal laws which are mentioned below. Some states have direct laws making it a crime. Of course, bribery of any government official—state or federal—is a criminal offense. There are many ways to handle government investigations or audits, but bribing the government representative is definitely not one of them. That is the quickest way I know to make a small problem into a big one.

ANCILLARY CRIMINAL LAWS

A large portion of criminal prosecutions are brought under what I call ancillary criminal laws rather than for a specific offense. The most important ancillary criminal laws cover the following areas:

1. Conspiracy

2. Making false statements to the government

3. Aiding and abetting

4. Obstruction of justice

5. The currency laws

For example, before the Foreign Corrupt Practices Act was passed, almost all of the improper payment prosecutions were based not on the illegal bribe, but on the fact that someone took currency out of the United States without filing the appropriate customs forms. Similarly, in many environmental criminal prosecutions, the case is based not upon the technical violation of the environmental laws, but upon some report or false statement that the person submitted. The prosecution is based upon the statute which makes it a criminal act to make any false statement to the government rather than upon the discharge of the harmful matter into the air or water.

Federal laws make it a criminal offense to conspire with another person to commit a crime. There is no requirement that the crime actually be committed. Prosecutions under the conspiracy statute are, therefore, much easier for the government to bring than prosecutions under the substantive laws. Similarly, federal criminal laws prohibit aiding and abetting someone else in a commission of a crime or obstruction of justice. The obstruction of justice statute is used in conjunction with the prohibition against making false statements to the government when people try to cover up some activity which in itself probably would not be too bad. For example, if your plant discharges material into the water in violation of your permit under the Clean Water Act, that is extremely unlikely to give rise to a criminal prosecution. On the other hand, if after this violation is discovered, you attempt to cover it up by means of falsifying documents, lying to environmental protection agency inspectors, or submitting false reports to the government, that can cause what would normally be a serious but civil matter to change into a criminal matter.

Similarly, if, during the course of a tax audit, the government finds items of income which you failed to report, that will usually give rise only to the assessment of more tax. On the other hand, if after the government finds these things, you continue to hamper their efforts to collect the tax by lying to them or submitting documents or letters which are at best misleading and possibly false, there is ample authority under these ancillary laws for the government to prosecute you—and they do not have to use the tax law which requires them to prove that you received income which you did not report. All they have to do is prove that you submitted a false statement to them.

Perjury is another of the ancillary criminal laws which can arise if you are called before a grand jury or if you testify in a case. Any testimony under oath which is false is a violation of the perjury laws, and you can rest assured that the government will give serious consideration to bringing a criminal prosecution.

The bottom line of this whole discussion is that, unless you deliberately engage in conduct which any reasonably intelligent businessperson would know to be criminal, you are probably not going to be subject to criminal prosecution for any of the substantive laws mentioned above. The one exception is antitrust—you must keep on your toes there. On the other hand, *it is rather easy to get trapped into a violation of the ancillary criminal laws.* It is only human nature to try to "defend" yourself or your company if you get into trouble on the basis of the antitrust, securities, environmental, or other laws. This is where most of the white-collar problems have arisen. The prosecution results not because the person violated the substantive law but because he or she violated one of these ancillary laws during the course of the government's investigation. Ever since Watergate, our society condemns any form of cover-up. This is reflected in an extremely high desire on the part of federal enforcement agencies to bring these kinds of white-collar cases.

CONCLUSION

The logical conclusion is that *any* government investigation should be discussed with counsel at the very earliest stages. If you go it alone, you are running what I believe to be an unacceptably high risk of criminal prosecution. Once the government begins any investigation in which you become involved, you have two exposures. One of them is the matter that the government is investigating, but the other, which I believe is the more serious, are these ancillary federal criminal laws which can trap even sophisticated corporate lawyers.

If you think that the government enforcement officials are there to help you, to learn the truth, and to prosecute only those people who are guilty of serious violations of the law, I am afraid that you are naive. The government prosecutors are there to prosecute. In my judgment, they start an investigation only when they feel there is a legitimate reason to do so. Further, I believe that they usually exercise an extremely high degree of discretion in favor of the public, and in fact refrain from prosecuting a lot of cases where they might be able to secure convictions. *On the other hand, once they do decide to start an investigation, they sweep with an extremely broad brush.* They do not limit themselves to the basic violations of the substantive laws.

If you get a subpoena to appear before a grand jury, you need a good criminal lawyer fast. Do nothing at all until you have spoken with your own lawyer. Further, make sure you have gotten a good criminal lawyer. Your corporate counsel is not the right person. Corporate lawyers may be able to suggest criminal lawyers who will help you, but the overwhelming majority of corporate counsel representing small companies do not know any more about criminal laws—let alone the federal criminal laws—than you do. In fact, if you have studied this chapter carefully, you may be ahead of some of them. Most corporate counsel do, however, have competent partners, associates, or friends to whom they refer criminal cases.

On the other hand, you should not conclude that any time any government official knocks at the door and asks for your records, that signifies an "investigation" which necessarily means you should start running up legal fees. This has to be a matter of judgment. I would not, however, endorse the feeling that if you have not done anything wrong, you do not need a lawyer. I am afraid that is way too naive.

16
ANOTHER VIEW

As I pointed out in the preface to this book, I was in private practice of law for the first few years of my career, practiced law with a major corporation for the next 10 years, and am presently operating a small legal publishing business. Therefore, I am technically in the position of the client rather than the attorney. For you, the reader, I believe this is a beneficial situation, because you can be assured that I have no axes to grind. On the other hand, I would also like to provide you with the views of lawyers who do currently engage in the private practice of law and who specialize in representing privately held corporations. I have, therefore, devoted this chapter to an interview with Mr. Robert J. Crump of the Cleveland law firm of Burke, Haber & Berick. This is a medium-sized, full-service law firm which has a wide variety of clientele and approximately 45 lawyers. Mr. Crump is a partner who represents many small privately held companies. As with most attorneys who practice with large firms, Mr. Crump's billing practices, the fees he charges, and his general philosophy on representing businesses are his own. Thus, even within a single firm, approaches may differ. I believe, however, that you will find the following interview to be useful, and I see no reason why you should not ask the same questions of your prospective attorney as I asked Mr. Crump.

BILL: Bob, I would like to start our interview on a subject which is perhaps most difficult but also of the highest level of concern with our readers—fees. I would appreciate it if you could tell me and our readers about your approach to fees, whether you quote them in advance, how you compute them, and what things clients should know when they discuss fees with their attorney.

BOB: Bill, you are absolutely right on the level of concern with fees.

239

All of my clients want to know how much money I am going to charge them and what I am going to do for that sum. I believe they are entitled to this information. It is most important in the case of new clients. I always try to provide an estimate of fees even if the client does not ask for it. However, they usually ask. I charge on the basis of an hourly rate—as do all of the other attorneys in our firm who work on matters relating to my clients. However, our hourly rates vary, and I usually do not quote my personal hourly rate to the client during the first interview because it may scare the client and it may be misleading. Many things that the new client will need can be accomplished by the use of junior lawyers under my supervision, and their hourly rates are lower than mine. Conversely, there may be some client problems which are super-technical and I may have to go to our most senior specialist and incur hourly charges greater than my own. However, my view is that one of the services that I provide clients is the judgment of which lawyer in our firm can most efficiently and economically provide the needed service. Therefore, I quote the client an "average" hourly fee which represents a reasonable composite of the hourly rates of our various attorneys based upon past experience.

BILL: Let's get into some specific numbers. We both know the standard kinds of services that corporate lawyers provide privately held businesses. Do you give your clients, and will you give me, rough ballpark estimates of the current fees that one might expect for these kinds of services?

BOB: I believe I can give ballpark estimates on the matters which come up with considerable frequency. Incorporating either a new business or a very small business can be done fairly inexpensively. I have done many for $350 to $400. Incorporating a rather substantial business which may have been conducted for a few years either as a partnership or a sole proprietorship and where there is more involved than simply drafting routine documents, the fee is going to be higher. If you add cross-purchase or redemption agreements and perhaps an employment contract to a standard incorporation, you would increase the fees to a total of approximately $1,500. Drafting an adequate partnership agreement would cost between $1,200 and $1,500.

BILL: Let me make sure I understand this correctly. If two people want to go into business as a corporation, you can form the corporation for about $350, but if they want to do it in a partnership form, it will cost them about $1,200 in legal fees.

BOB: That is right, but I should mention that if two people form a corporation, they will likely want a cross-purchase or redemption agreement at least, which would increase the cost.

BILL: Bob, I know that it is difficult to know in advance exactly how long it is going to take to do some of these things. How accurate have your estimates been, and what do you do if it turns out that your first estimate is too low?

BOB: I think that, in general, my original estimates of the fees I would charge for certain matters have tended to be a little on the low side when compared with the fee which would have been charged if our normal hourly rates had been used. This is an interesting factor that your readers should keep in mind. A new client talking with a lawyer will have a couple of advantages in discussing fees. First, the lawyer will want to create a favorable first impression and will want to charge the minimum reasonable fee for the first services. Lawyers, like all business people, are looking for repeat business. They want that client to come back, and they do not want to scare him or her off with the first bill. Second, the natural tendency is to underestimate the total time projects will take. Therefore, I strongly recommend your readers ask the lawyer for estimates of legal fees.

Whenever it is humanly possible, I stick exactly with the estimate I have given. I never charge a client more than the estimate unless there are unusual circumstances. Of course, if something completely unforeseen comes up or if it turns out that I have just grossly underestimated the amount of time required, I may have to call the client and discuss the matter again. However, I would never simply submit a bill which was more than the original estimate without a conference with the client. I think almost all lawyers who give estimates of their fees follow essentially the same practice.

BILL: What is your view on retainer arrangements?

BOB: I am against them. In fact, I have gotten quite a bit of business because clients have been unhappy with the retainer arrangement they had with another lawyer and wanted to switch. I do not use retainers. I know some lawyers do. It is clear in my mind, however, that the hourly arrangement is much better. Sometimes attorneys who advocate the use of retainers will say that it helps the client budget legal fees. I do not believe this is accurate because the retainer usually only covers certain basic minimal services, and the only way a client can budget legal fees is to have a history of experience with a lawyer. Sometimes in discussing fees with my clients, I point out that their legal fees over the past few years have averaged a certain amount per year, although they vary widely from month to month. Thus, the client should look at legal fees as an annual amount and should budget them that way. That does not mean, however, that they should be paid to the lawyer whether the lawyer earns them or not.

BILL: What is your philosophy on billing? Do you send long, itemized statements detailing exactly what you and the other lawyers in your firm did for your client that month, or do you send a one-line statement of services rendered and simply a total?

BOB: I see what you are getting at, but the question is really much more complex than might at first appear. First of all, the conclusion, at least in my judgment, is very simple. The clients should get whatever kind of bill they desire. If the client wants a detailed, itemized statement of every piece of work that was done, who did it, and what the hourly rates were, I provide it. However, as I am sure you know, the tax consequences of attorneys' fees are subject to considerable interpretation and planning. Some of them are capital expenses, some of them are currently deductible, and other expenses may be personal to the management of the company and should be paid personally by them. When you actually get down to talking about specifics, the issue is sometimes arguable. Thus, the client may prefer a simple one-line statement of the total due with a backup memorandum from me explaining exactly what we did. The client and his or her accountant can then make the determination as to how to treat these costs for income tax purposes.

My own preference is to send out bills which are between these two extremes. I like to send out a bill which fairly describes the services we performed for our clients but which does not go into the nitty-gritty detail of exactly which lawyer, at which hourly rate, did what. As I mentioned before, I think the client should trust me to make the judgment as to which lawyers in our firm to use. If a client has a complex tax problem, it may be much more economical for me to consult one of our most senior tax experts at $125 an hour and get an answer in one hour than to use a junior associate at one-third this rate and get an answer in

10 hours. Further, the senior person may see some tax planning possibilities that the junior person may not. When I send out bills which disclose that I have used members of our firm who do charge a higher hourly rate or that I have not personally been involved in matters to a considerable extent, the clients sometimes get concerned. I continue to believe, however, that this is in their best interest. After all, I joined this firm because we do have experts in various areas where I do not practice extensively, and my personal involvement in some matters would be wasteful for the client.

BILL: Bob, when you have an existing relationship with a client, how do you counsel that client to obtain legal services from you? Do you have periodic meetings, do you conduct audits, or do you just wait for the client to call you with a specific problem?

BOB: The answer is everything except the last. That is definitely bad. I say that not because of the small amount of fees which are generated by early consultations and meetings but because of the large, unproductive legal fees in litigation. If the client waits to call me until there is a severe problem, oftentimes the only option available is litigation. This is extremely costly. I have two standing suggestions for all my clients. The first is that I am a firm believer in meetings and having lawyers present at meetings. For example, if you have your lawyer present at a 2-hour directors' meeting, the lawyer's fees for that 2-hour meeting— even at $100 an hour—are $200. I think you have gotten an excellent bargain. This is particularly true if you have structured the meeting and planned it so that you have a good agenda and you know what kinds of questions you want to raise and where you want your lawyer to give you some helpful guidance.

The second standing suggestion is for the clients to call me whenever they think they *might possibly* have a situation where I can be of some benefit. The way we charge for telephone calls is on a *strict* time basis using *tenths* of an hour. Furthermore, an extremely short conversation where I simply tell the client that I really cannot make any contribution is not billed at all. Thus, if clients call me in advance with previously thought-out problems, we can have a telephone conversation which is almost always less than 30 minutes and sometimes under a quarter of an hour in which I tell the client whether he or she really does have a legal problem, and if so, approximately what would be involved in my assistance. Sometimes the matter can be handled right over the phone without any additional work. Other times,

I may have to check some files and do a little research and get back to the client. The key thing to remember on these telephone conversations is to end the conversation with a precise agreement between the lawyer and the client as to what is going to happen. Where you get into problems is if the client feels that the telephone conversation ended the matter and the attorney feels that the telephone conversation was only the beginning. The client is entitled to know, and indeed decide, whether the attorney is going to do anything to generate additional fees after that first conversation.

BILL: Bob, you mentioned directors' meetings and that leads me to another question. Do you like to serve on the boards of directors of the companies which you represent?

BOB: I am always very flattered to be asked to serve on the boards of directors of client companies. Sometimes, however, I decline the invitation. While I always like to be present at significant meetings of the board of directors, there are some cases where I do not really think I can add very much as a member of the board. This is largely a personal decision and has to be made on a case-by-case basis. The client is asking me to join the board because of business and judgmental contributions rather than simply legal advice, and I have to make the determination as to whether I can make this contribution on an individual basis depending in part upon the type of business involved. I also serve as a minor officer of many of my client companies. Usually, this is a matter of mechanical convenience. Many legal documents require multiple signatures and some legal documents are extremely routine, and we can save some time if I am authorized to sign them myself. Prime examples are certified copies of corporate resolutions. If I am the secretary or assistant secretary of a corporation, I can take care of some of these routine matters for my clients without the necessity of going to them for additional signatures.

BILL: What are the biggest problem areas in terms of clients coming to you too late?

BOB: Contracts, product liability, warranties, and inviting other people into the business. Let me explain what I mean by each of these because they are common occurrences.

In the contract situation, I often have been consulted by clients after they have signed a contract. I do not really know why otherwise reasonably intelligent people would come to their lawyer for legal advice on a contract after they have already signed it, but I have seen it happen so many times that I must list it as the first problem. A variation on the theme is where the client will sign a contract, put it away in the file, and then bring it to me only after a dispute has arisen. Obviously, this is not the way to get full measure of value from your attorney.

Let me deal with product liability and warranties together, because they usually involve essentially the same set of facts. Clients will fail to draft appropriate terms and conditions or warranty disclaimers to safeguard themselves from product liability claims. A product they make or sell will then cause an injury, they will be sued, and I will be consulted at a point where my only course of action is to defend the lawsuit. If, on the other hand, I had the opportunity to help the client draft the warranty, limit the warranty exposure, and draft the terms and conditions of sale, I could have either avoided the problem all together or at least increased the client's bargaining posture when it came to settling the case. As we all know, almost all product liability cases are settled, but the amount of the settlement is dependent upon the legal position of the parties. If my client has an extremely weak case because the client has not done a good job in limiting the warranty exposure, I will be unable to settle that case as favorably as if we had a stronger legal position.

The third item I mentioned is bringing other people into the business. I find with too much frequency that one of my clients will come to me and say that he or she has made a deal with someone to bring that other party into the business. Then, the client tells me what that deal is and asks me to reduce it to writing. Further, most of my clients feel that their word is law. When they make a promise to someone, there is simply no changing it. The client may have told the other party something which is rather disadvantageous to the client and may be unable to back off from it because of having already made a commitment. If you want to bring someone else into your business in a meaningful way, of course, you must have conversations with the other party before you discuss it fully with your lawyer. There is no point in generating legal fees before you even find out if the person is interested in coming with your company. On the other hand, this is a very complex area, and I would urge all your readers to refrain from making any commitments to another party until after they have had a chance to discuss the various alternatives and the advantages and disadvantages of these alternatives with their counsel. For example, I know you are going to put a chapter in your book about the problems involved in giving someone a minority stock interest in a company. This is a real problem and should be discussed with counsel before the businessperson promises the other party a certain number of shares of stock of the company. While there may be much better ways for both parties to accomplish the desired objective, if the businessperson has already made a promise, my experience has been that, at least in the case of my clients, he or she will not want to back off from it.

BILL: I have noticed that many firms have started to do a lot of things which you might refer to as "client education," including such things as client seminars, newsletters, and personal letters about recent developments. What is your philosophy about these kinds of things, what do you and your firm do, and do you have any basis for judging the client's reaction?

BOB: In one form or another, these things are almost essential in today's world. I think the clients appreciate them, and they are desirable from a legal standpoint because the client becomes more knowledgeable about the problem and can discuss the problem better. On a pragmatic level, they are an excellent marketing tool for legal services because clients appreciate this advice, and when and if they do have a problem, they will come back to you for specific help. Let me give you some examples of what our firm does and what I do personally.

When there is a new major piece of legislation, such as a tax reform act or a major change in corporate law, we have the matter thoroughly analyzed by the firm and then we usually send out a firm memorandum or have a seminar on the subject. For example, Ohio recently enacted a statute which spelled out with more clarity than before exactly what duties and responsibilities a director has. We had a summer associate completely research this area and analyze the statute and write a memorandum on what it meant for our clients. The individual lawyers then sent that memorandum to those clients that would be affected. There was no charge for this. Of course, these kinds of things do add to overhead. On the other hand, as professional attorneys, we are going to have to know about these kinds of developments. We would have to do substantially all the work anyway, and the added costs and expenses of sending out the client communication are relatively minor. The benefits to the client, on the other hand, can be substantial. The client knows about the problem and, perhaps most importantly, knows that you have expertise which has already been developed at no cost to him or her and which he can tap into at a low cost. A client can call me up on this matter, which might have generated thousands of dollars' worth of legal time in the form of the summer associate's salary, and get the necessary advice from me in 15 minutes or a half an hour. That is a good deal for both of us. The client gets top-quality, economical advice. We get business we probably would not have gotten otherwise. Perhaps most importantly, we have further cemented this attorney-client relationship that both of us are trying to build.

To give another example, a bar association publication recently included an excellent four-page summary of product liability law. I have discussed product liability law with many of my clients, and I simply copied this excellent four-page summary and sent it to them along with a covering letter that I thought it was accurate and was worth their reading. I am sure the clients appreciated it, and it did not cost them anything. We do not have any formal newsletters as some firms do. We may in the future—it is an open question at this time. On the question of client seminars, I think they are useful if the subject affects a number of clients in substantially the same way. Major tax-reform legislation is a prime example.

In summary, I would say that a good corporate lawyer simply must engage in some of this kind of activity. I am not saying that client seminars or elaborate newsletters are necessary. On the other hand, I believe it is very important to have a lawyer who takes the initiative to send clients these kinds of communications. I also believe there should not be any direct charge for them.

BILL: How do you approach a client who comes to you with a specific set of business-related questions but who obviously needs additional personal advice, probably in the form of estate planning?

BOB: I handle that directly and do not beat around the bush. I simply ask the client if he or she has a will, and, if not, I make a strong recommendation that he or she have one. Further, I set up a special meeting where we discuss the client's personal affairs. I believe it is better to do this than try to mix it in with corporate business. Also, this has tax implications. Attorneys should counsel clients that their personal matters should be paid for personally rather than having them billed through the corporation. Having a separate meeting helps this. This advice is sometimes not well received by the clients, but you can soften the blow a little by pointing out that estate planning advice is deductible for federal income tax purposes. Most of the things we are talking about here would fall into the general category of estate planning. For example, a reasonable charge for drafting two wills for a husband and wife would be $75 to $90. A more sophisticated estate planning job can run $500 or more. Everything except the first $75 or $90 would be geared to be deductible.

Further, I have a specific set of questions which the client should answer before we get to that second meeting. Most lawyers have similar questionnaires that ask for the pertinent information the lawyer needs in order to recommend a proper estate plan for the client. If the client takes the time to do a good job filling in these forms, the attorney's time, and therefore the fees, can be reduced. It is also a good exercise for the client. Many times the clients do not have a proper inventory of their property, stocks, insurance policies, etc., and my questionnaire helps them get this inventory. I find that my advice to have a separate estate planning meeting is almost always enthusiastically endorsed when the spouse is present at our meetings. I strongly recommend that the spouse thoroughly participate in and understand all decisions relating to estate planning.

BILL: Have you ever had clients object to this because they did not want to spend the money?

BOB: No. In fact, the opposite is the case. Clients appreciate this effort. They know estate planning is important, but they know it is a difficult thing to get around to. It always seems like something that can be postponed, and if the lawyer takes the initiative to set up a meeting and a schedule as to how the matter is going to be dealt with, the clients appreciate that. As in all matters, I think the client is entitled to an estimate of how much it is going to cost. On the other hand, automation has really reduced fees. The days when lawyers had to have a secretary type lengthy wills and trust agreements are gone. They are all on automatic typewriters, and it does not take a great deal of time for the lawyer to custom-tailor these to a particular client's needs. Many estate planning jobs can be handled completely for $400 or $500, and even if the matter gets a little complicated, it usually will not run over $800.

BILL: Some of the books I have read advocate that clients use a different lawyer for estate planning purposes than for their corporate work. What do you think of this?

BOB: I think it is a very bad idea. Clients have a lot of time and energy invested in their corporate lawyer. Any estate planning desires and objectives are going to be very much interwoven with corporate desires and objectives. This is almost certainly going to be the case for the owner of a small business whose major asset may be the stock in that business. I see no reason whatever to get separate lawyers involved in this. It is bound to increase fees. I have had a few clients ask me if we should split the corporate and personal work. When I explained how closely the two are interwoven, I have never had a single client actually make the determination to do that. I handle both subjects for virtually all of my clients except in extremely unusual situations. Obviously, previous personal commitments can be a factor. This is particularly true if you represent only one of the principals in a business and the business has historically used another law firm. Except for those unusual situations, however, I believe that business and personal matters, at least relating to estate planning, should be handled by the same lawyer.

BILL: Do many of your clients use your services as an arbitrator or negotiator rather than as simply a lawyer?

BOB: Yes. In fact, in some cases the major contribution I make to a problem is the ability to negotiate or arbitrate an amicable result. Obviously, it is a personal matter and depends upon the personal dispositions and abilities of the attorneys and their clients. Further, if you do get into an arbitration situation, where for example you are trying to settle a dispute between two partners, it is very important to make sure that both parties understand exactly what your role is. You do not want to get into a conflict of interest, and you must be careful to avoid violations of the canons of ethics.

BILL: Has the Pension Reform Law scared many of your clients away from pension plans?

BOB: No. In fact, it has not really been a factor. The area of qualified pension and profit sharing plans is still a booming business, and it is still one of the best tax shelters available. Also, for many it is one of the major reasons for forming a corporation. Further, the development of master or prototype plans has become so widespread that legal fees can be very reasonable. For example, it is now possible to tailor a defined benefit pension plan for a client with a few participants for approximately $800. We work with insurance companies, banks, and other financial institutions who already have prototype plans which clients can use free. The only charge is the specific tailoring necessary for their particular situation, and that usually amounts to only $400 or $500 in legal fees.

I know that the new vesting requirements and the antidiscrimination rules which prohibit you from establishing a plan which discriminates in favor of directors, officers, or highly compensated people are a factor. Nevertheless, it is still possible to slant qualified pension plans in favor of the owners or managers. Of course, you cannot completely exclude the other employees. On the other hand, a good lawyer can show you how to integrate a plan with social security, how to structure the vesting schedule in a way which will maximize the benefits of the plan for top management, and how to administer the plan in a way which is very efficient. Qualified pension and profit sharing plans are one of my favorite subjects. There is a substantial benefit for everybody. For a relatively small amount of legal fees, the client gets an extremely large benefit. Of course, you must have the right situation here. You need to have a company that makes money. If the business is very small or if losses are involved, the whole thing loses a lot of its appeal.

BILL: There has been quite a bit of talk about books like this. Some of it has been favorable because it will help business people get good legal advice, but some of it has been unfavorable because it may tend to cause business people to be their own lawyers, and we all know that is bad. What do you think?

BOB: I am all for it. I think the book is an excellent idea—*but it is a tool.* Just as with any other tool, if readers or clients use it improperly, they can hurt themselves. I do not know how to tell you to make your readers use the tool properly rather than improperly, but this is certainly very important. I would much rather have a client who has considered a problem and perhaps even prepared a draft of the documents he or she thinks are important. For example, when a client comes to me for a contract on a certain subject, I tell the client to write down exactly what he or she thinks should be included. I can go from there. Basically, that is the same kind of advice you are putting in this book.

On the other hand, if the client writes down what he needs and does not come to see me and get a formal contract, that is bad.

As all lawyers, I have seen some situations where this has happened. It is particularly troublesome in the area of wills and estate planning. I have seen cases where people have drafted wills improperly and the court had to refuse to probate the will. I have seen people use "canned" form wills which simply did not do the job. I had one case where a client drafted a form will which was perfectly adequate except that it did not have the executor of the will specifically authorized to sell real estate. At that time in Ohio, unless that power was contained in the will, the executor had no such power, and we had to go through an elaborate land sale procedure which cost this client an additional $1,000 or more in legal fees.

* * *

I think you can see from this interview that good small business lawyers are more than willing to have a candid discussion with you about how they run their practice, how much they charge, how they compute their fees, and what they can do for you. They are happy to do it. They are business people and they are selling legal services. Good and reputable business counselors will view a discussion like this with you as an opportunity—they will probably even pick up the lunch tab! They will not pressure you into entering into any agreements at that time. You may be asked what you think of their presentation, but they will not ask you for a decision or commitment. If they do, that is a bad sign.

However, you must take the initiative. Legal ethics as well as the sense of propriety of almost all business counselors prevents them from making the first call. It is not like selling insurance. You won't get many unsolicited calls from business lawyers asking to come over and meet you. Furthermore, you must be open and candid about your situation. If you already have a lawyer who is not performing satisfactorily for you, you must tell the new prospective lawyer this and be prepared to explain why you wish to make a change. The new lawyer will want to know why you are dissatisfied so that he or she doesn't meet the same fate as your old one. You must also be honest and realistic about what you want, or might want, the lawyer to do, and how you want the relationship to work. It is a two-sided involvement and you have to be certain how you want it to work in order to explain it to the lawyer. Would you like the lawyer to give you unsolicited advice about matters which might be of interest to you, even if he or she makes a modest charge for it? Or would you be annoyed at having to pay fees for something you did not ask for and which you decide against? Can your lawyer talk to your accountant directly, or would you get angry if you got a bill for a consultation with your accountant that you had not authorized?

Are you going to interview more than one lawyer? If so, there is no reason to hide this fact from any of them. You don't want to make the mistake of putting your legal work "out for bids." Nevertheless, there is a certain amount of "shopping" which might be useful because chemistry is an important part of the relationship. Don't be bashful! Good lawyers know it anyway —the chemistry factor functions both ways.

You should not have to pay for an inquiry interview which should not take more than an hour and doesn't involve specific legal advice. Sometimes it helps to have the interview over lunch or cocktails.

When you talk about fees, remember that the interview with Bob Crump occurred during the summer of 1980. Bob revised the figures when we got the page proofs in June of 1981, and the increases were substantial. Inflation affects lawyers just like everybody else.

The key point to keep in mind is that you should not be intimidated when searching for lawyers suitable for your requirements. The relationship between you and your lawyer ought to be a commonsense, open, and honest one, where you can discuss your problems freely. If you do not sense this kind of rapport, I would recommend looking for another lawyer better suited to your needs.

INDEX

Abatement periods in OSHA inspections, 179
Administrative employees, exemptions of, 107
Advertising, legal, 3
Affirmative action plan, 116
Age discrimination, 123–124
Age Discrimination in Employment Act, 123
Aiding and abetting, 235
Ancillary criminal laws, 235–236
  aiding and abetting, 235
  conspiracy, 235
  currency laws, 235
  making false statements, 235–236
  obstruction of justice, 235–236
Antitrust, 230–232
  price fixing and, 230–231
Apprentices and minimum wage exemptions, 101
Articles of incorporation, 37–39
Attorneys (see Lawyers)
Automobile insurance, 223–224

Battle of the forms, 148–153, 188
  legalistics, 150–151
  terms: for buyer's documents, 152
  for seller's documents, 152
Bonuses, 54
Boycotts, 231
Bribery, 234
  commercial, 234
Bulk Sales Act, 68
Business:
  buying (see Buying a business)

Business (Cont.):
  starting (see Starting your business)
Business advice, 12
Buying a business, 65–71
  compliance with Bulk Sales Act, 68
  employees, contracts and, 70
  help from seller, 69–70
  legal audit, 68
  legal fees, 70–71
  options, 65–68
    buying assets, 66–67
    buying stock, 66–67

Capital structure of corporations, 32–33
  and debt, 32, 33
  thinning, 32
Child labor laws, 110
Civil Rights Act of 1964, Title VII, 115, 125
Client seminars and law firms, 9
Commercial bribery, 234
Common stock, 29–31
  classes of, 30, 46, 47
Confidential information and inventions, 57–58
  employee agreement form, 214–217
Confidentiality agreements, 52
  form, 217
Conspiracy, 235
Consultation program, on-site (OSHA), 180–181
Consumer products and warranties, 154–155
Consumer Product Safety Act, 191–193
Convertible preferred stock, 30–31

Copyrights, 195, 203–208
 fair use concept, 205–208
 obtaining, mechanics of, 204–205
 life of, 205
Corporate tax rates, 19–20
Corporate taxation (*see* Starting your
 business, corporate taxation)
Corporation:
 buying an existing one (*see* Buying a
  business)
 forming (*see* Starting your business,
  forming a corporation)
 ownership of, 42
 shareholders and (*see* Shareholders,
  corporations and)
 valuation of, 50
 (*See also* Starting your business)
Coverage tests, 88–89
Credit laws, fair, 171–172
Crime, white collar (*see* White collar crime)
Criminal laws, ancillary (*see* Ancillary
 criminal laws)
Cross purchase agreements, 48
Currency laws, 235

Dangerous work, OSHA and, 173–174
Davis-Bacon Act, 102
Debt, capital structure and, 32, 33
Defined benefit pension plan, 85
Defined benefit plan, 85
Directors, board of, and company
 management, 45
Directors' and officers' liability insurance, 226
Disability, determination of, 50, 51
Discharges and EEO, 121–123
Discipline and discrimination, 122
Disclaiming warranties, UCC provision for,
 156
Discrimination in employment (*see*
 Employment discrimination and EEO
 laws)

EEO (Equal Employment Opportunity) (*see*
 Employment discrimination and EEO
 laws)
EEOC (*see* Equal Employment Opportunity
 Commission)
Employee discipline, OSHA and, 173–174
Employee invention and confidential
 information agreement forms, 214–221

Employee Retirement Income Security Act
 (ERISA) (*see* Pension plans, ERISA and)
Employee selection and EEO laws, 116–117
Employees, exempt, under Fair Labor
 Standards Act, 107–109
Employment agreement form, sample, 60–63
Employment application form, 120–121
Employment contracts, 51–63
 drafting, important considerations in,
  53–60
 confidential information and inventions,
  57–58
 essentials, 53–55
 restrictive covenant, 55–57
 sales representative, 59
 sample employment agreement form,
  60–63
Employment discrimination and EEO laws,
 115–129
 age discrimination in, 123–124
 compliance aspects of law, government
  help on, 128–129
 discharges and, 121–123
 employment application form, 120–121
 equal pay for equal work in, 118–119
 health considerations in, 119–120
 handicapped persons, 119–120
 job criteria and, 117–118
 litigation, Title VII, 125–127
 pregnant females, treatment of, 119
 promotions and, 121
 selection process and, 116–117
 sex discrimination in, 118–119
 state agencies settling disputes,
  127–128
 guides, 127–128
 statistics in cases of, 124–125
 tests of ability, 117–118
Environmental laws, 233
Environmental liability insurance, 226
Equal Credit Opportunity Act, 172
Equal Employment Opportunity (EEO) (*see*
 Employment discrimination and EEO
 laws)
Equal Employment Opportunity Commission
 (EEOC), 118–120, 123, 125–127, 129
Equal pay for equal work, 118–119
ERISA (Employee Retirement Income
 Security Act) (*see* Pension plans, ERISA
 and)
Executive employee, Fair Labor Standards Act
 exemptions of, 107

Exempt employees under Fair Labor
Standards Act, 107–109
Express warranties, 155, 189, 191

Fair Credit Billing Act, 172
Fair credit laws, 171–172
Fair Credit Reporting Act, 172
Fair Debt Collection Practices Act, 171, 172
Fair Labor Standards Act, 99–100, 103,
105–108, 110–112
Fair use, concept of, and copyrights, 205–210
False statements, making, to government,
235–236
Federal Election Commission and political
contributions, 232
Federal income tax, 94–96
minimizing, 95
pitfalls and, 94
Federal Trade Commission (FTC), 73, 172
and franchising, 73–74
Fees, legal:
approach to (interview), 239–242
for buying a business, 70–71
time recording and, 7
Finding a lawyer, 1–5
(*See also* Lawyers, using)
Fitness for particular purpose, implied
warranty of, 156
Foreign Corrupt Practices Act, 234–235
Forming a corporation (*see* Starting your
business, forming a corporation)
Franchise (*see* Franchising)
Franchising, 73–80
danger points, 77–80
definition of, 74
example of, 75–77
FTC rule and, 73–74
legal help and, 74–75
Fraud, tax, 229–230
FTC (Federal Trade Commission), 73, 172
and franchising, 73–74
Full warranty, 154
sample, 170

Garnishments, wages and, 111–112
General partnership, 42
Government publications:
OSHA, 182–184
payroll taxes, 93
wage and hour laws, 112–113

Handicapped persons:
and health considerations, 119–120
and minimum wages, 101

Implied warranties, 154–156
of fitness for particular purpose, 156
of merchantability, 155–156
Improving lawyer-client relationships, 11–12
Incorporation (*see* Corporation; Starting your
business)
Incorporation documents, sample, 36–39
Individual retirement accounts (IRAs), 91–92
Infringement, 199
Inspections, OSHA, 175–180
ground rules, 178–180
on-site consultation program, 180–181
rights during, 177–178
abatement periods in, 179
search warrants and, 175–177
suggestions, 176–177
Insurance:
directors' and officers' liability, 226
and lawyers (*see* Lawyers, and insurance)
and product liability, 186, 189, 191, 226
Intellectual property, 195–221
copyrights, 195, 203–208
fair use, concept of, 205–208
obtaining, 204–205
employee invention and confidential
information agreement forms,
214–221
patents (*see* Patents)
trade secrets, 56, 195, 211–213
trademarks and trade names, 208–211
registration of, 208–210
search, 210–211
Invention and confidential agreement forms,
employee, 214–221

Labor law, 131–146
checklists, 139–145
fault and need analysis, 135–136
location, importance of, 136
reasons for employee organization,
132–134
remaining nonunion, 134–135
union organization drive, 136–139
unions and, 131–132
Lanham Act (Trademark Act), 208
Lawyer-client relationships, improving, 11–12

Lawyers:
  advertising by, 3
  business advice from, 12–13
    personal services and, 13–14
  determining quality of, 8–10
  dissatisfaction with services of, 10–12
  finding, 1–5
  and insurance, 50, 223–227
    automobiles, 223–224
    vs. insurance agents, 225–227
    vs. tax advisor, 225, 226
  using, 5–8
    arrangements, 6
    fees, 6–8
Learners, minimum wage exemptions and, 101
Legal advertising, 3
Legal advice:
  and insurance (see Lawyers, and insurance)
  quality of, 8
Legal audit, importance of, 68
Legal bills (interview), 242–243
Legal clinics, 3
Legal ethics, 251
Legal fees (see Fees, legal)
Legal referral services, 3
Liability:
  limited, 27–28
  and partners, 42–43
Life insurance, 50
Limited liability, 27–28
Limited partnership, 42–44
Limited warranty, 154, 156
  example, 171
Litigation, Title VII, economics of, 125–127

Magnuson Moss Warranty Act, 154
Martindale-Hubbell Law Directory, 4–5
Merchantability, implied warranty of, 155–156
Minimum wage requirements, 99–109
  exempt employees (Fair Labor Standards Act), 107–109
  exemptions, 100–102
    apprentices, 101
    full-time students, 101–102
    handicapped persons, 101
    learners, 101
    presumptions about, 108
  overtime and, 103–107

Minors, employment of, 100
  and child labor laws, 110
Money purchase plan, 84

Negotiation advice and lawyers, 12–13
Noncompetition agreement, 55–56
Notification of product hazard, 192–193

Obstruction of justice, 235
Occupational safety and health, OSHA and, 233–234
Occupational Safety and Health Act (see OSHA)
Off-the-book accounts and tax fraud, 230
Officers' and directors' liability insurance, 226
On-site consultation program (OSHA), 180–181
Organization of employees, reasons for, 132–134
OSHA (Occupational Safety and Health Act), 173–184
  carcinogens and, 181–182
  criminal provisions, 233–234
  and dangerous work, 173–174
  and employee discipline, 173–174
  inspections (see Inspections, OSHA)
  noise and, 181–182
  publications, 182–184
  records and reports, 174–175
  small business rules, 182
Overtime, 99–100, 103–107
  exempt employees, 107

Partnership, 15, 42–44
  general, 42
  liability and, 42–43
  limited, 42–44
  terms of (Uniform Partnership Act), 43–44
Patents, 195–203
  employee form, 198
  infringement, 199
  laws governing, 195–199
  licensing, 200
  1-year rule, 203
  quality of, 200–201
  suggestions, 201–202
Payroll, 93–114
  and child labor laws, 110
  garnishments, 111–112

Payroll (*Cont.*):
  government help, 112–113
  Portal to Portal Act, 110–111
  record keeping, 112
  taxes and, 93
    federal income, 94–96
  unemployment compensation, 99
  wage and hour laws (*see* Minimum wage
    requirements)
  workers' compensation, 96–99
Pension plans, 81, 83–92, 249–250
  coverage tests, 88–89
  ERISA and, 86–90, 249–250
    requirements, 86–90
      management, 89
      personal liability, 89–90
      vesting (*see* Vesting requirements,
        ERISA)
  prototype, 85–86
  simplified, 90–91
  social security and, 83
  types, 84–85
    defined benefit, 85
    money purchase, 84–85
Pension reform law (ERISA) (*see* Pension
  plans, ERISA and)
Political action committee, corporations and,
  233
Political contributions and corporate funds,
  232–233
  Federal Election Commission and, 232
Portal to Portal Act, 110–111
Preferred stock, 29–31
Pregnant females, treatment of, and EEO
  laws, 119
Price fixing and antitrust laws, 230–231
Product liability, 185–193, 245
  examples, 187–188
  suggestions for minimizing, 188–191
    forms, 188
    insurance, 186, 189, 191, 226
    legal counsel, 190
    prevention, 190–191
    price, 190
    records, 189
    warranties, 189
Professional employee, Fair Labor Standards
  Act and, 108
Profit sharing plans, 81–84
  description, 84
Promotions and EEO laws, 121
Prototype plans, 85–86

Publications, government (*see* Government
  publications)
Purchase order and sales forms, 147–169
  samples, 157–169
    purchase order, 157–162
    sales, 163–169
Pyramid schemes, 79–80

Qualified plans, coverage test and, 88–89
Quality of legal advice, 8

Records:
  OSHA and, 174–175
  payroll, Fair Labor Standards Act and, 112
  product liability, 189
Redemption agreements, 48–51
Redemptions, stock, 31
Referral services, legal, 2–3
Regular rate and overtime wages, 103
Representation elections, union, 137
Restrictive covenant in employment
  contracts, 55–57
Retainer arrangements, 6
Retainers (interview), 241–242

Sales forms (*see* Purchase order and sales
  forms)
Search warrants, OSHA inspections and,
  175–177
Securities laws, 232
Service Contract Act, 102
Sex discrimination and EEO rules, 118–119
  equal pay for equal work, 118–119
  pregnant females, treatment of, 119
Shareholders, corporations and, 44–51
  buying out, 48–49
  minority, 45
Simplified employee pension plans, 90–91
Small business and subchapter "S"
  corporation, 21–22
Social security and pension plans, 83
Sole proprietorship, 15, 16
Starting your business, 15–39
  choices, 15–16
  corporate taxation, 19–27
    disadvantages, 25–27
      unreasonable-accumulation penalty,
        27
      unreasonable compensation, 25–26
    dividends received deduction, 20

Starting your business (*Cont.*):
    forming a corporation, 16–19, 28–36
        capital structure of, 32–33
        reasons for, 17–19
        stock selection, 29–31
        tax reality, 33–35
    limited liability of, 27–28
    sample documents, 36–39
State employment discrimination agencies,
    127
Statistics in employment discrimination,
    124–125
Stock:
    choice of, 29–31, 46, 47
    common, 29–31
        classes of, 30, 46, 47
    convertible preferred, 30–31
    preferred, 29–31
    redemptions of, 31
Subchapter "S" corporation, small business
    and, 21–22
Substantial product hazard, Consumer
    Product Safety Act and, 192–193

Tax fraud, 229–230
Tax rates, corporate, 19–20
Taxation, corporate (*see* Starting your
    business, corporate taxation)
Tests:
    coverage, 88–89
    for employee selection, EEO laws and,
        117–118
Time recording and legal fees, 7
Trade associations and antitrust laws, 231
Trade names, trademarks and, 208–211
Trade secrets, 56, 195, 211–213
Trademark Act (Lanham Act), 208
Trademarks, trade names and, 208–211
Trap lines and fair use concept, 207
Truth in Lending Act, 172

Unemployment compensation, 99
Uniform Commercial Code (UCC), 149, 150,
    154, 155
Uniform Employee Selection Guidelines, 129
Union organization, 132–134

Union organization drive, 136–145
    checklists, 139–145
    representation elections, 137
Unionization:
    remaining nonunion, 134–135
    selected readings on, 145–146
Unions (*see* Union organization; Union
    organization drive; Unionization)
Unreasonable-accumulation penalty, 27
Unreasonable compensation, 25–26
Unsolicited idea letter, sample, 216–217

Vesting requirements, ERISA, 86–88
    class year, 87
    5- to 15-year, 86–87
    rule of 45, 87
    10-year, 86

Wage and hour laws (*see* Minimum wage
    requirements)
Wages and garnishments, 111–112
Walsh-Healey Act, 100, 102, 103, 106
Warranties, 147, 153–171, 189, 244–245
    consumer products and, 154–155
    disclaimers, UCC provision for, 156
    express, 155, 189, 191
    full, 154, 170
    implied, 154–156
        of fitness for particular purpose,
            156
        of merchantability, 155–156
    limited, 154, 156, 171
    patent, 155
    samples, 169–171
Washington representation of law firm, 10
White collar crime, 229–237
    ancillary criminal laws (*see* Ancillary
        criminal laws)
    antitrust, 230–232
    bribery, 234
    environmental laws, 233
    occupational safety and health, 233–234
    political contributions, 232–233
    securities law, 232
    tax fraud, 229–230
Workers' compensation, 96–99